Along the Tracks

Tamar Bergman

Translated from the Hebrew by Michael Swirsky

Houghton Mifflin Company
Boston

Cover art © 1991 by Robert Wisnewski
Copyright © 1988 by Tamar Bergman
First American edition 1991
Originally published in Israel in 1988 by Schocken Publishing House Ltd.
Translation copyright © 1991 by Houghton Mifflin Company

Library of Congress Cataloging-in-Publication Data

Bergman, Tamar.
  [Le-orekh ha-mesilah. English]
  Along the tracks / by Tamar Bergman ; translated from the Hebrew by
Michael Swirsky.
    p.   cm.
  Translation of: Le-orekh ha-mesilah.
  Summary: Recounts the adventures of a young Jewish boy who is
driven from his home by the German invasion, becomes a refugee in
the Soviet Union, is separated from his family, and undergoes many
hardships before enjoying a normal home again.
  HC ISBN 0-395-55328-8   PA ISBN 0-395-74513-6
  1. World War, 1939–1945 — Jews — Poland — Juvenile literature.
2. Refugees, Jewish — Soviet Union — Juvenile literature.   3. Jewish
children — Poland — Juvenile literature.   4. Jewish children — Soviet
Union — Juvenile literature. [1. World War, 1939–1945 — Jews.
2. Refugees.]   I. Title.
DS135.P6B3914   1991   90-27521
940.53'159'092 — dc20   CIP
[B]   AC

Printed in the United States of America
QUM 10 9 8 7 6

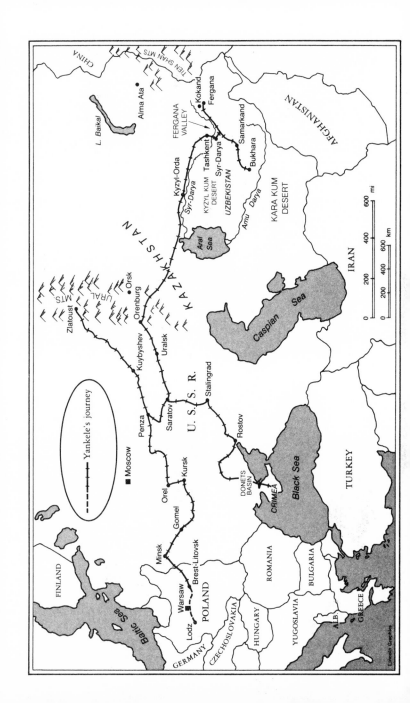

Along the Tracks

PART ONE
Yankele

One

"No!" Mama said. "I'm staying!"

"All right then," Papa said, getting up, "you'll stay here by yourself. I'm leaving tomorrow with the children. Get the bags ready."

Yankele turned away and looked at the window. An autumn rain pelted the glass. How long had his parents been arguing with each other? The war had broken out when he first started school. Kadya, the teacher, went on teaching the ABCs as if nothing had happened. Her face was radiant, and the dimples in her cheeks captured the boy's heart and made him forget the world outside. But one day, during recess, Moshik said to him, "Today I saw a German soldier, a real one!"

Shlomo sneered. "So what? I've seen lots of them . . . maybe ten! Right near my house, I swear!"

Was it that day that his parents had started to argue? Poland had been conquered; the German army had entered Lodz. The Jews were ordered to wear the yellow patch on their chests, the Star of David that distinguished them from the rest of the population, and Papa stopped doing carpentry; the orders dried up, people no longer had money for a new chair or table. As a matter of fact, very few people even had enough for bread. But the rundown Balut district, whose grayish stone houses were encrusted with tin and wooden additions, made the most wonderful playground: where else could you find such fine hiding places — stairways; outhouses; dark, gloomy basements? True,

3

the basements had lately been filled up by families fleeing or driven from the countryside, but there were still stalls in the market and the fat lady vendors whose backsides were broad enough for a little six-year-old to hide behind.

"You'll never guess what a treasure I've got!" Yankele said when they tired of playing hide-and-seek.

"A marble, I bet!" said Shlomo. "I've got one too!"

"No!" said Yankele, fingering the "treasure" in his pocket.

"An American stamp!" said Moshik. "My uncle went to America and sent a letter with a stamp, and what a stamp!"

Yankele gripped his "treasure."

"Never mind stamps. This is worth much more. Besides, you don't keep a stamp in your pocket!"

"So tell us!" Shlomo urged.

"Only if you promise not to tell anyone!" Yankele said, lowering his voice. "This is a real secret!"

"I promise!" whispered Shlomo, his eyes flashing, and Moshik followed suit: "I promise too!"

Yankele drew his hand from his pocket, turned over his clenched fist, and slowly opened his fingers. In his palm there lay . . . a pocketknife! A real pocketknife! A grown-up's pocketknife!

The three of them gazed at length at the knife, as though it were an apparition that could vanish at any moment.

"Where did you find it?" Shlomo asked, as soon as he had recovered his speech.

"At the end of the street, where they're building the new wall!"

"Are you serious?"

"Dead serious!"

"When?"

"Yesterday. I was on my way to Grandma's and stopped to see what they were doing there. Then all of a sudden I stepped on it . . ."

"Just like that?" Shlomo asked, amazed. "You mean it was just lying there in the street?"

"No, there was a pile of trash: wood and paper and all kinds of stuff. Then I stepped on it and saw the tip of something and picked the thing up, and then the German soldier started to yell at me — and I ran away. I didn't even notice what I had taken until I got to Grandma's and looked."

"Have you opened it up yet?" Moshik asked, reaching for the marvelous object.

Yankele took the knife in his left hand.

"Sure!" he said, opening it expertly. "See, it even has two blades, a big one and a little one."

The three of them bent over the treasure in amazement.

"It sure isn't one of ours!" Shlomo said at last. "No one around here has a pocketknife like that . . ."

"No one around here has a pocketknife, period!" Moshik decreed, running his fingers along the larger blade. "It's got to be German!"

"Maybe it fell out of one of the soldier's pockets," Shlomo said. "Aren't you scared to keep it? Maybe you should give it back. They must be looking for it!"

"Are you crazy?" said Yankele. "It's mine now, and that's that!"

He brushed a reddish-brown curl from his forehead. Mother would say, "So young, and already stubborn as a mule. He's a redhead all right, a real redhead!"

A shiver suddenly swept through Yankele's little body. It seemed to start at the yellow patch on his chest. *If I return the knife they'll say I stole it. They'll shoot me, the way they did Avreimele's father when he tripped on a stone and fell on the German soldier.*

He put the pocketknife back in his pocket and stood up. "You won't tell anyone, will you? You promised!"

"No one!" said the other two solemnly, getting up as well. They spit three times. "God help us, we'll never mention it to a living soul!"

But Yankele still felt a chill.

5

"I've got to get home," he blurted and ran off without saying goodbye. He had to see Papa, right away! To hug Mama, to be protected by the four walls of their room. Home!

He jumped down the four steps leading from the street to the basement, flung open the door, and burst into the room. Grandpa was sitting at the head of the table, looking more severe than ever. Papa sat across from him, his head in his hands, while Mama tried to comfort little Sarele, who was wailing in her arms.

"Shut the door!" Papa snapped.

Yankele closed the door behind him and came over to the table. Papa put his arm around him and drew him close. Yankele clung to Papa and buried his face in his shoulder. He wanted to cry but held himself back with all his might. Grandpa never visited them. What had happened? What was going on?

"I tell you again," Grandpa said, measuring his words, "tomorrow or the next day, within a week at the most, they're going to finish putting up the wall, and then you won't be *able* to get out. Take Rosa and the children and leave! Fishel left yesterday already!"

"With his family?" Mama asked.

"No," said Grandpa, rubbing his tangled brows. "Unfortunately I couldn't talk him into it. He said he would cross over into Russia and see what was going on there and then come back and take the family. But I'm afraid he won't be able to come back. They're putting up a barbed-wire fence all around and a wooden barricade as well. It's still possible to get in and out, but soon . . ."

Papa held his peace. He knew his father was right. In Balut, the poor part of Lodz, awful rumors were circulating: the Jews who were coming on foot and by wagon from all the little towns and villages roundabout had hair-raising stories to tell. Some of them said the neighborhood would soon be turned into a closed ghetto, that all its working people would be sent to do forced labor. Some even said the Germans were planning to kill them all, but most people refused to believe that: would it be so simple to wipe them all out — men, women, and children? Would they kill Itzel the tailor, with his nine hungry children at home? Or Shaye the teamster, who was no longer allowed to transport people outside the ghetto? Or Zissel's mother, or little Zissel herself, with her tiny braids, or her baby brother, who laughed at her in his crib? Or Grandpa and Grandma, or me, or you? All of us? . . . My God, it couldn't be! It simply couldn't be!

Mama looked at Papa questioningly.

"To get up and leave everything, just like that? Where will we stay? What will we live on? How will we get to the Russian border? The little one isn't even three yet!"

But Papa knew Grandpa was right. Since he had been forced to give up his carpentry, he had been wandering around the marketplaces, the railway station, nearby villages, and more distant ones. He would bake cookies from flour and sugar he had gotten somewhere and sell them to travelers and passers-by. At home, in the basement room, he would repair galoshes and boots with rubber glue. And when people stopped coming he would take his cookies and his glue pot out into the country. The country folk had no use for cookies — no one who had a cow, chickens, and a plot of land went hungry in those days — but occasionally a child would ask his mother for a cookie or two, or a peasant would have a pair of torn boots for the cobbler with the glue pot to repair. Papa would come back from the country with a loaf of bread, a few apples, a handful of potatoes, and sometimes even fresh eggs. Not many, not always. Whatever food he brought he would unload onto the kitchen table, but the sights he had seen he would keep to himself: convoys of Jews being driven to the ghetto while the peasants looked on in silence; the body of the owner of the tavern in Wolodenka, hanging from the rafters in the entranceway and being stoned by local teenage boys amidst taunts of *"Yid! Yid!"* It would not be long before the adults joined in . . .

"All right!" Papa said suddenly, rousing himself from his reverie. "Let's go!"

7

"Tomorrow!" Grandpa urged him. "Do it tomorrow, before it's too late!"

"We'll leave tomorrow," Papa agreed. He had been considering making a run for the Russian border for some time, and now his mind was made up. "And what about you?" he asked, looking his father in the eye.

"I'm staying here," Grandpa said, gazing down at his hands. They rested on the table, thin and sinewy, with bluish veins protruding from their backs like the branches of a dried-up tree and brown age-spots scattered among the veins like autumn leaves. "You know how hard it is for me to walk. You'll have to carry the little one, help Rosa, tote the baggage . . . No, I'm too old. I'll stay here, and whatever happens will happen."

Yankele went back to stand next to his father. He was a bit afraid of Grandpa, of his old hands, his limp, the strange odor in his room. It was the odor of leather-tanning, which had been Grandpa's source of livelihood until his vision dimmed and his hands began to tremble. The walls were saturated with this peculiar smell and with the smell of old age. Grandpa was not a strictly observant Jew, but after his late-born son died, he grew the beard of the Orthodox, and when he lost his wife he withdrew into silence and hardly ever left his room. No, Yankele was not sorry that Grandpa would not be joining them.

Once, Papa had taken Yankele along to the country. The sweet aroma of spring had hung in the air. The wind stirred up waves in the green wheat fields, and at the edge of the forest a hearty chorus of chirping broke from within the verdant foliage. Drunk with freedom, with light, with the clear sweetness in the air, Yankele had run and skipped and shouted with joy, and his father had watched him, smiling.

Now he said, "Papa, are we going to the country again?" The warmth of the light and freedom he remembered began to spread through his body. "Papa, are we going to the country again?"

"No," Papa said. "We're going far away. We've never gone so far."

8

"And there won't be any Germans where we go?"

"No!" said Papa. "We'll go to a place where there are no Germans!"

Yankele stroked the knife in his pocket. There, where there are no Germans, he would be able to take it out whenever he wanted to and do whatever you do with a pocketknife. What *do* you do with one? He didn't know yet, but he was sure to find out by trying, there where the German soldier could no longer catch him.

"Good!" said Yankele. "So we're really leaving tomorrow?"

Mama set Sarele down on the wooden floor and stood up. Papa looked at her inquiringly. He had not heard Yankele's question.

"I'm going to my mother's," Mama said. "Yankele, do you want to come with me to Grandma's?"

"Are we going to say goodbye before we leave for Russia? Mama, do you think she'll have a piece of candy for me?"

Mama smiled sadly. "I'm afraid not," she said, "but she might have a sugar cube. Let's go."

Grandma didn't have any candy, or any sugar cubes either. She kissed Yankele on both cheeks. "Well, how's school?" she asked. "Have you learned to read 'Papa' and 'Mama' yet? And have you started to write?"

"I do know how to read 'Papa,' and 'Mama' too. But I can't always write so well."

Grandma beamed. "Don't worry," she said, "you've got lots of time. By the end of the year you'll be reading and writing both Yiddish and Polish, and when you get bigger and finish school you'll be a great sage!"

Yankele laughed.

"Aha!" Grandma cried, joining in the laughter. "I see the mouse has made off with another one of your teeth!"

Yankele felt around with the tip of his tongue for the space left by the tooth he had lost.

9

"Yes, but the one next to it has already started to grow. See, Grandma? You can already see it!"

Mama set a few slices of bread and two potatoes on the table. Grandma's room was small. There were two chairs, a bed, a little table, a coal-burning stove for cooking. It was a good thing that Yankele and Grandma were small, because otherwise the place might have been cramped for the three of them; but Yankele was growing, whereas Grandma was getting smaller day by day. At one time she had barely managed to support herself by taking in sewing: she would hem a dress, sew on buttons, replace stitches that had come undone. A meager stream of work would flow her way, bringing with it a bit of food, sugar cubes, sometimes a sweet for her grandchildren. Now the stream had dried up, and for want of anything else to do Grandma would clean and polish her little room again and again. What actually needed cleaning? Sometimes there wasn't even a crumb of bread to dirty it up . . .

"What does she live off of?" Papa would ask.

"Nothing."

Nothing — Yankele thought this meant the bit of food Mama would bring Grandma. Now the "nothing" was on the table, and Grandma looked over at Mama.

"Well, what are you going to do? What have you decided?"

"David says we have to leave right away, that soon it will be too late. Yitzhak wants to get going tomorrow!"

"My God!" Grandma said, spreading her trembling hands in fear. "Go where? The Germans are everywhere!"

"Yitzhak wants to go to Russia!"

"But how will you live?"

"He says he will find work in Russia: they need carpenters there. He's ready to do any kind of work, and so am I — as long as we don't have to stay here!" Mama said.

She took Grandma's hands. "Mother," she asked, pleading, "Mother, will you come with us?"

10

"God forbid!" Grandma said. "I'm not budging. I'm not going to Russia!"

"But why? They say whoever stays here . . . that the Germans will take everyone."

Grandma pulled her hands away. She straightened the shawl around her shoulders and tucked her hands inside. In her clothes, which had become too big for her, she was like a little bird that wraps itself up in the mantle of its feathers trying to keep warm.

"I'm not going to Russia!" she repeated. "Russia is dirty! I'll die of the dirt there!"

"But here the Germans . . . ." Mama pleaded. "Come with us!"

"No!" Grandma said, looking up at Mama. "I'll die here, in my own room. Don't cry, Rosa, hush! I'm already an old woman. I'll die soon anyway. You go to Russia. You must go, for the children's sake! Don't worry about me."

Yankele looked out the little window above the stove. It had started to rain. Grayness spread through the street, and a slight chill crept inside. Evening came early in Grandma's room.

"Go!" Grandma repeated. "Now go home, Rosa. The little one is waiting for you, and Yitzhak. Don't cry, Rosa. They're waiting for you."

It was warm and pleasant at home. The cooking stove heated the big basement room. Papa had fixed up a wooden partition to separate the one bedroom from the kitchen and work area. Once there had been a smell of sawdust and wood chips there, but now the woodworking tools stood orphaned. The glue pot for repairing galoshes had been set in the corner, tightly covered. Only Papa's boots stood next to it. There were no more repairs to be done for pay.

Papa paced back and forth across the room, from the window to the partition and back. Yankele sat down on the windowsill and wiped the fog from the glass. *In the country there are birds,* he thought, *and animals.*

11

"But I can't leave Mother here," Mama said. "I'm all she has."

"I know," Papa answered, coming to a halt in front of her. "But she can't walk anyway. Don't fool yourself, Rosa. It's autumn, it's raining, and after that there will be frost and snow. She won't be up to it. Rosa, I have no idea how we're going to get to the border, but we've got to go! Say goodbye to her and start packing."

Mama looked at the window and fell silent. For some time she watched the tears streaming down the glass. Then suddenly she stirred, turned to Papa, and said, "No, I'm staying!"

"All right then," Papa said, getting up, "you'll stay here by yourself! I'm leaving tomorrow with the children. Get the bags ready!"

Two

They had been traveling the highways and byways for two weeks — Mama, Papa, Yankele, and little Sarele.

Poland was like an anthill that had been trampled by a cruel boot. The nest had been destroyed, and its inhabitants were in a state of utter confusion. In the deep bunkers, in the dark rooms, there were those who tried to rebuild, to gather food, to hold on until the storm passed; but many were simply scattered to the four winds. Before long, the dispersed population began clustering into little groups, columns, and convoys, all headed in the same direction: east.

Along all the roads of Poland wandered refugees with yellow stars on their chests and darkness in their hearts. It was the beginning of the war. German soldiers were everywhere, but the

SS had not yet spread its net over the land, and no one stopped the refugees from fleeing. Yet.

Individuals, families, whole caravans made their way toward the Russian border. It would not be long before the boot would come crashing down again, and it would continue to do so until it had crushed everyone.

Mama, Papa, Yankele, and little Sarele marched along the dirt road. Mama had a small pack on her back. In one hand she clutched an old suitcase, the other she gave to Yankele. Papa had two bundles on his back, one on each side. Everything they owned was there: blankets, warm clothing, winter coats. Nothing had been left in the house except bare beds, a table, and three chairs.

The two biggest bundles were on Papa's back, and he carried Sarele on his shoulders. She sat astride his neck, her hands in his hair.

"Papa," the little one said, "you've got straw in your head!"

"Not in his head," Yankele corrected her, "in his hair."

"You've got straw in your hair," said Sarele, running her little fingers through it. "Are we going to sleep in the straw again tonight?"

"I hope so!" Papa answered brusquely.

"I don't like straw!" Sarele declared. "It scratches!"

"Well, I do like to sleep in a barn!" said Yankele, trying to keep pace with Mama, "and even more in a cowshed! You can see how the cows eat. At night you can hear them. They're always eating. Don't they ever stop?"

No one answered. Papa plodded on stubbornly at an even pace.

"I wanna eat!" said the little one from her perch high on Papa's shoulders. "When are we gonna eat?"

"Soon, sweetheart, soon. First we have to get to the river."

In the distance wheels creaked. Yankele looked up: a horse-drawn cart was making its way along a side road. From a distance it looked like a bulky, shapeless, gray creature with humps and bumps all over it. Far ahead, near a big wooden cross, the two roads intersected and continued on their separate ways.

Yankele followed the cart with his eyes as it approached the cross. The humps could be seen more clearly now, and they turned out to be bundles and packages upon which sat dwarfs wrapped in gray coats.

Yankele marveled, "Grandma told me dwarfs wore all different colors of clothes — red, green, yellow — so why are these so gray?"

A man who could now be seen walking alongside the cart called out, "Whoa!" but the horse went right on dragging its hooves along with the indifference of one who has had plenty of experience with long journeys. Several feet could be seen walking under the cart.

It's a monster, Yankele thought, *a monster with wheels and feet, harnessed to a horse. Any minute now, the horse will begin to spit fire, like the airplane we saw the night we slept in the field . . .*

The cart drew closer and closer. The feet trudging underneath it lagged a bit, and out from behind the heap of bundles and gray dwarfs there appeared two women, walking. One of them limped a little.

Now the dwarfs could be seen more clearly, and they turned out to be children, five all together. An old woman was wrapped up on top of one of the bundles, and a man was stretched out full length, the yellow patch over his heart turned toward the sky. None of them said a word. Only the cartwheels squeaked, cried out again and again, wept bitterly.

Near the wooden cross the cart turned right onto the main road. The man who had been walking alongside the cart holding the reins turned to Yankele's father and said in Yiddish, "Is there a doctor here?" No greeting, no introduction. His face sagged like an empty sack, and his dark eyes were sunk in deep shadows.

"I have no idea," Yitzhak said, stopping short. "I don't know

14

these people." He turned around and called out, "Is there a doctor here? We need a doctor!"

Like a gust of wind the question passed among the groups of people along the road, passed and disappeared somewhere without a reply. The old woman sitting on the cart wrapped the blanket more tightly around the sick man and sank back into her thoughts. Her gray face was deeply wrinkled, like mud that had dried and cracked.

"I can pay!" said the man, looking at the people walking along the road. "He's had a fever for three days!" he added, nodding toward the sick man on the cart. Yitzhak wiped his forehead and gazed into the man's desperate eyes.

"I see," he said, "but there's no doctor here. It's not a question of money; there just isn't one! Better try in town."

"In town?" The man trembled. "If we go into town they'll never let us out! Either that or they'll send us to the ghetto."

"We're not far from the river. They say there's a small town on the other side of the bridge. Maybe there you'll find a doctor."

"What's the town called?"

"I have no idea," Yitzhak replied, wondering whether to put Sarele down and unload the bundles. His shoulders ached, and his arms were stiff. He looked at Rosa, who had sat down by the side of the road and was rubbing her swollen ankles.

"I don't know what the town is called," he said again, "but it's in the right direction, east. On the way to the Russian border. Come, Rosa," he added, "get up. We have to go on."

Pushing with one hand, Rosa struggled to get up, but she didn't have the strength. She was used to the streets of Lodz. There, her world had been the size of Balut and the adjoining neighborhoods. Now she was on an endless journey, marching on and on along an ill-defined route. The soles of her feet were swollen, her city shoes were tight, and now the tongue of her right shoe was torn. *My God, how much walking can one do?*

15

Yankele held out his hand to Mama. "Come on, I'll help you get up. I'm strong!"

Mama smiled through her tears. "Of course you're strong, my little chick, as strong as a seven-year-old!"

She was light, thin. Grasping the tiny hand that was stretched out to her, she pulled herself up. She picked up the suitcase and staggered with the weight of it.

"Let me have the suitcase!" said the man near the cart. "We're going together as far as the bridge anyway. And you can put the little one in the cart."

"No!" said Sarele, shaking her curls. "I don't wanna! I want Papa!"

"Then at least put the bundles on the cart."

"Nahman!" said one of the women who stood leaning against the back of the cart. "Look at the horse! He's having a hard enough time pulling what we've got already, and you want to add to his burden? Think about us! Pretty soon we'll have to make do without a horse altogether!"

"He's pulled everything this far; he can pull a little more!" said the man, trying to clear a bit of space on the cart.

"Thanks, it's really not necessary," said Papa, shifting the bundles on his shoulders. "I've managed up till now; I imagine I can carry on."

"You're a man, not an animal," the man said, adjusting his cap. "How long do you think you can carry a load like that?"

Papa lowered his right shoulder, and the bundle fell to the ground. Then he slid the other bundle off his left shoulder and heaved it onto the back of the cart. Sarele clutched his hair tightly. She wasn't ready to give up her perch. The children on the cart huddled together quietly and made some space. The man with the cap picked up the other bundle and immediately set it down, surprised at how heavy it was.

"What have you got in here," he exclaimed, "rocks? How can you carry such a load?"

"It's clothing," Papa answered, "and tools. I'm a carpenter."

He threw the heavy bundle onto the cart. The man pulled the reins and cried, "Giddyap!" The horse lowered its head, strained its chest forward — as if to say, "Oh well, what's the difference?" — and lifted its feet. The cart began to move.

Yankele gave Papa his hand. Papa's hand was big and thick and rough. He had strong arms, Yitzhak did. He had been apprenticed to carpenters since he was *bar-mitzvah** — hauling boards, sweeping up sawdust, taking care of the master's children — and finally he himself took up carpentry work. His shoulders were broad. Yitzhak was of medium height, but to Yankele he seemed like a giant. He put his little hand in Papa's and looked up at the cart.

The children eyed him with curiosity from their perch on top of the bundles. One of them, a small child with shining eyes, stuck his tongue out at him. Yankele, too, stuck out his tongue and the child smiled. Now the child wrinkled up his mouth and nose, bared his teeth, and made his upper lip quiver like a rabbit. Yankele responded with a "witch's face," the most terrible one he knew how to make. The little boy burst out laughing and tried to stand up. "Sit down!" his grandmother said firmly, pressing down on his shoulder until he fell backwards. "Sit down, you rascal! You're going to fall!"

The man who was stretched out on the cart suddenly heaved a sigh, turned his head this way and that and fell silent again. There were great beads of sweat on his forehead. The old woman wiped his face with a big handkerchief and sighed herself. Yankele turned to look at the passing landscape.

All gray, the fields stretched out to the horizon. The rye had long since been harvested, and with the coming of the autumn rains the stubble had begun to rot. The potatoes too had been picked, leaving nothing in the ground to greet the winter snows. Where were all the flowers he had seen in the spring? And the sun? And the birds? The colt in the pasture?

*The age of legal majority, which is thirteen in Jewish law.

They were crossing a gray, desolate plain, dotted here and there with isolated poplar trees.

What is Grandma doing now? Yankele thought, stealing a glance at the old woman on the cart. *Who is bringing her her "nothing" to eat?*

All at once he was flooded with the memory of the warm little room, the sound of the teapot hissing on the stove, the smell of Grandma, her clothes, the linens on her bed — a strange smell of old age and cleanliness, Grandma's smell. No, Papa was right: she could not have made it to the border with them. They had left Lodz on a wagon together with two other refugee families, but two days later the driver had to head back, and they were left on the road with their bundles in their arms. It was impossible to travel by train: some of the lines had been blown up, and those trains that still operated had been commandeered by the German army. The family headed eastward on foot. Occasionally, when a wagon came their way, they would go with it some distance, then shoulder their burdens once again as they plodded along the highways and dirt paths.

No, Grandma could never have made it, Yankele thought. *It was even hard for Mama. (I'm a good walker, though. Papa said I acted much bigger than my age!) Besides, wherever we went Grandma would have complained about how dirty it was. You can't polish the field you're sleeping in the way Grandma polishes her room. And when you sleep in a barn with a lot of other families, it's crowded and not at all clean. And what would Grandma have said if she had been with us when the farmer offered to let us sleep in the pigsty? It was raining cats and dogs, and we wanted a roof over our heads for the night, and Papa had no more money, so Mama took off her sweater and gave it to the farmer, and he went in the house and probably showed it to his fat wife, and then he came out and said, "All right, go to the barn." And how it smelled there. Fine, Mama says, when we get to Russia and settle down in one place, we can wash and dry our clothes; but for now we just have to keep going with*

18

what we have, because whenever we meet people on the road they talk about more Jews being driven into the ghetto and shot and hanged.

Once when they were still in Lodz — it seemed like such a long time ago — he had seen three big dummies hanging on posts in the square in the distance. The dummies were as big as people, as grown-ups, with Jewish beards and sidelocks, and they were hanging by their necks from ropes. Yankele was frightened. He ran home and hid his head in Mama's bosom. That night he cried in his sleep. In school the next day, they said they were real people, not dummies, and they had died, just as Avreimele's father had when the German soldier shot him.

"I'm hungry!" Sarele said from high up on Papa's shoulders. "Mama, I'm hungry!"

"Soon, little one," Papa said, patting her knee, "as soon as we get to the river."

The man in the cap turned around and called out to one of the women. "Leale, can you give the little one something? She's hungry."

The round-faced woman who was walking behind the cart pulled her kerchief tight, came up to the slow-moving cart, and began to rummage through a bundle that lay next to the packages. She pulled out a big loaf of dark bread and a well-worn knife. Then she paused for a moment, held the bread against her big, full bosom, and, with practiced movements, cut a thick slice.

"Here," she said, handing the slice to the little girl. Yankele followed the movements of her hand. His mouth watered.

"You want some too?" the woman asked with a motherly smile. "Here's some for you too."

Yankele watched as the woman again pressed the loaf of bread against her heart.

She slices it just the way Mama and Grandma do! he thought, and out loud he said, "Thanks!"

"Thank you very much!" said Papa. "Really, thank you! These days not everyone would give . . ."

"When you have, you have to give!" the man said, smiling sadly. "We still have. One must help."

The other woman, the thin one, muttered something from the back, but Yankele didn't hear. The bread was dark — heavy, full-grain country bread. He hadn't eaten a bite since that morning. He tried to eat slowly, so that it would last for a while, but his hunger took one chunk after another out of the bread.

"We still have," the man said again. "My brother is a furrier, and I went into partnership with him last year. We had everything. Before we left we wanted to sell the business, but the Poles laughed in our faces. 'It's all going to be ours anyway!' they said, 'So why buy it?' We took all our money and as many furs as we could carry and left the rest behind."

"And the cart?" Papa asked.

"The cart belonged to the business," the man explained.

"And it wasn't confiscated?"

"No, you see before they confiscated the wagons we entrusted it to one of our workers, who lived in the country. We took our families and our mother, and we've been on the road ever since."

The woman with the sallow face who had been walking along behind the cart muttering now suddenly said aloud, "You'll never learn, Nahman. Why do you have to go telling everyone what we have and don't have? In the end, we'll be robbed and left in the fields without a stitch on our backs!"

The man pursed his lips and urged the horse on with a crack of the reins on its back. "My God, Beile," he said, "can't you see what sort of people these are? To you everyone is a robber and a thief."

They were silent for a few minutes, and then the man added, "They want us to become animals like them. But human beings were created in the image of God. Jews must help one another, otherwise we'll lose our humanity and turn into beasts, just like them."

"Words, words," said the woman. "You can't live off of

words. Noah would not have acted the way you do!" she went on, as if talking to herself, drawing closer to the sick man, who was mumbling feverishly. "God Almighty, he's burning up! Where are we going to get a doctor?"

"We'll get to the river soon."

"The river is full of water, not doctors!"

"They say there's a town on the other side. Maybe there we'll find a doctor."

"I wish!" the woman muttered, touching the sick man's limp arm. The man was murmuring. She stroked his hand, wiping the corners of her eyes with a handkerchief. The cartwheels squealed desperately.

Now the cart was making its way over the top of the hill. One of those riding on it, a girl about four, was hugging a doll with a muslin dress. She took out a small comb and combed the doll's hair. Sarele gaped.

"Look, Papa, the doll has hair!"

"Yes, I see," said Papa.

"Where's the doll Grandma made me?" the little one asked.

Papa stroked her knee again. "The doll's in the bag. I'll take it out for you in a minute."

"I want my doll! Now!"

"In a minute," Papa said wearily, "as soon as we get to the river."

The little boy on the cart now picked up an imaginary gun and began shooting at Yankele. "Ta, ta, ta, ta, ta!" The "bullets" hissed by. Yankele picked up a "pistol" in his free hand and shot it. "Boom!" The child fell backward and played dead. Then he got up and was about to let loose a new barrage when he suddenly froze: from high up on the cart he saw something the others had not yet noticed.

"The river!" he shouted. "There's the river!"

Three

The river flowed placidly, wide and full. In the distance, at the base of the hill, where the fields of stubble ended and the grassy banks began, tall poplar trees stood like guards at attention. They were almost bare of leaves. Green willows dipped their branches in the water. The river at last!

A bridge could be seen in the distance. A winding road that ran along the riverbank turned toward the bridge and continued across it, directly into the tangle of streets of a small town.

The horse raised its head. Its nostrils quivered as if it had caught the scent of a faraway stable, and it gave a long whinny. The gentle slope relieved some of the horse's burden, and it quickened its pace. The cartwheels began to squeal with joy. The children sitting on top of the pile of bundles and the people walking alongside the cart all set their gaze on the river and the bridge, and only the old woman sat bent over as before, her eyes fixed on the sick man who lay beside her.

Suddenly Yitzhak said, "The bridge! Something's happened to the bridge!"

The women at the back were frightened. "Oh no! What happened?"

"What happened to the bridge? It's there, isn't it?"

Yitzhak squinted, trying to make out the situation from a distance. "I think," he said hesitantly, "I think the bridge has been blown up! It's damaged at one point . . . no, at three!"

"But people are crossing it!" said the woman with the round face. "I see people crossing it!"

"Yes," Yitzhak said, "the question is whether we'll be able to cross with the cart. I see only people."

A truck rattled down the road and stopped near the bridge with a screech of its brakes. It was an army truck. As they approached they could see the German soldiers jumping out of it. Other soldiers, who had been huddled around a little fire, got up to greet them, their rifles in their hands.

Yankele held Papa's hand tightly and snuggled up against him. The knife! The knife in his pocket suddenly began to burn, the pocketknife he had found in the ghetto, near the wall, that a German soldier must have lost! They were waiting for him! They would search him and find the knife! They would shoot him with their big rifles, the way they shot Avreimele's father, or they would hang him on a tree like the dummies.

He put his hand in his pocket and clutched the knife. He could throw it away now or just drop it, and no one would notice. But he held onto the knife with his little fist. No! The pocketknife was his! He had found it, and no one was going to take it away from him!

Papa squeezed his little hand. He didn't know about the knife.

"Don't be afraid, Yankele, they're soldiers, not police or SS, just soldiers. They won't do anything to us."

They were close to the river now. The long bridge stretched from one side to the other, supported by mighty stone piers. It had been damaged in several places, as if by tremendous blows. The stones of the railing were gone, like pulled teeth.

A thin stream of refugees moved across it. Eastward, only eastward. A few German soldiers came toward them, their bayonets sticking up above their helmets. The driver of the army truck started his motor, and some of the soldiers climbed on and sat on the floor. The truck turned around and went back up the crooked road that ran along the riverbank. Those who stayed behind gathered round the fire, rubbing their hands over it, their weapons hanging from their shoulders.

"This is the bridge guardpost," Yitzhak said. "Don't be afraid, Yankele. You see? They're letting everyone go by."

In his pocket, the boy's fingernails dug into the palm of his hand. As if in a seizure, his fist was clenched around the pocketknife. A soldier left the fire and called out to them in an unfamiliar language.

"What is he saying?" Yitzhak asked, tense as an animal ready to pounce.

The man with the cap turned pale. "Halt. He says to halt."

He pulled in the reins, leaning back with all his might. "Whoa!" he cried to the horse. "Whoa!"

The horse came slowly to a halt. The squeak of the wheels died out. Everyone was silent.

The soldier sauntered over to them and said something very long in German. The owner of the cart went up to greet him and doffed his cap.

"*Ja!*" he said. "*Ja!*"

He turned around and gestured toward the cart, then turned back to the soldier and asked something. Yankele put his arms around Papa's leg. Mama came over and stood near them. Her face was pale. Even little Sarele, up on Papa's shoulders, tightened her grip on his hair and looked at the soldier with big, frightened eyes.

"*Nein!*" the soldier said, shaking his head. Yankele tried to catch the words. They were oddly like Yiddish, but different. He didn't understand a thing.

"*Danke schön!*" the owner of the cart said, bowing his head a bit, "*Danke schön!*" The soldier turned on his heel and went back to the fire.

"Nahman, what did he say?" Leah asked, her hands pleading, trembling. "My God, are they taking the cart?"

"No, they're not taking anything, Leale. He said we can't get across the bridge with the cart. The bridge has been bombed. Only pedestrians can cross."

"And what about a doctor?" his sister-in-law asked. "Did you ask him where we could find a doctor?"

"I did, but he doesn't know. There might be one in the town on the other side. He says there's sure to be one in the city."

"City? Where is there a city?"

"Not far. He says to go north along this side of the river. There's a fairly large city there."

"What's it called?" Leah asked.

"I didn't catch it. In German, names sound different. He says it's about a two-, two-and-a-half-hour trip."

"So what are we going to do?" asked the thin woman, her face scrunched up with fear. "We've got to find a doctor!" She nearly burst out weeping. "He'll die on us along the way, before we ever get there."

"If we go to the city, they'll catch us. The SS. They'll catch us, and who knows what will happen then."

The woman began to cry. "Maybe we should try to get him over to the other side. Maybe there's a doctor there, in the town."

Yitzhak stirred. "Listen," he said, "why don't the two of us try to take him across, find a doctor, and leave him in his care?"

Mama clutched his arm. "And what about us, Yitzhak? What will become of us?"

"You just wait here," Yitzhak said softly. He knew very well that he shouldn't do this, shouldn't leave his family alone even for a short time.

"And what about us? What will happen to my husband without us?" the thin woman pleaded. "How will we get to him once you leave him there?"

"You go on with the cart and find another bridge. Cross over and come back to fetch him. In the meantime he's sure to recover."

"This is crazy!" the man with the cap blurted. "Completely crazy! We can't leave our families here alone!" With his chin he motioned toward the soldiers around the fire. One of them pointed at the cart and said something, and they all burst out laughing. "It's dangerous!"

"Then what will you do? What have you decided?"

The man looked at the cart. His whole life was on it: his mother; his children; his brother's children, who looked at him in silence; his unconscious brother; his wife and sister-in-law, who stood near him; what remained of his property. He had to decide quickly, immediately, right on the spot. All of them hung on his words.

"We have no choice," he said at last. "We'll go to the city. We'll go our separate ways."

Yitzhak lifted Sarele and took her off his shoulders. The little one tottered over to her mother and put her arms around her legs.

"The doll," she said, "Grandma's doll!"

Mama took the bag off her shoulders and pulled out of it a cloth doll, one that Grandma had sewn and filled with rags, whose hair was made of wool and whose eyes were buttons and nose was embroidered. Sarele took the doll and embraced it tightly in her little round arms. She laughed. "Dolly! Grandma's dolly!"

Papa trudged over to the cart and unloaded his bundles. Lifting one up, he passed its tied end over his head. This one had been on the right side of his back, hanging from his left shoulder. Then he took the second bundle and shifted it to the other side. His shoulders ached. The heavy bundles had cut into them during the many days of walking. He stooped, and Mama lifted Sarele onto his shoulders. The owner of the cart looked wordlessly at Mama and handed her the suitcase.

"Thank you very much!" Papa said. "Thanks for everything. It's hard nowadays to find people who are willing to help out."

"That's all right, that's all right," the man mumbled, turning away.

"Good luck to you!" Mama said, taking Yankele's hand. "I hope you find a doctor and everything goes well."

"Amen!" the old woman said suddenly, as if awakening from a deep sleep. "Amen!" she repeated and then let out a deep sigh, lowering her head to her left shoulder, like a bird in a cold wind. She went back to gazing at the sick man.

"Goodbye, Grandma!" Yankele whispered. Papa started

walking. Mama pulled Yankele by the hand. He turned toward the cart. "So long!"

Sitting on Papa's shoulders, Sarele hugged the rag doll. The cartwheels groaned and began to squeal as the cart pulled away. The little girl on the cart went back to combing her doll's hair. Her brother put his thumbs in his ears, waved his fingers at Yankele, and stuck out his tongue.

Yankele stuck his tongue out too: *Naa, here's to you!*

They had already gotten past the first obstacle on the bridge, where three huge bombs had hit and destroyed large sections of it. Long boards had been placed over the gaps, through which the water of the river could be seen, and the refugees, heavy-laden and weary, made their way across them with care.

Now Papa stood facing the last obstacle. The people in front of him had already gone across, and the boards had stopped shaking. Far below, the water surged in a mighty stream. Papa hesitated. The bundles felt heavier than ever. Sarele held on tightly to his hair, sensing Papa's fear. He hesitated for a moment and looked back. Two German officers were coming toward them. He looked at Mama. Yankele was holding onto her dress, trying to hide from the eyes of the officers.

"You go first," Papa said to her. "At least you will make it across!"

Mama hesitated.

"Go ahead, get across fast!" Papa said. "Get across right now! Don't look down at the water. Look straight ahead!"

Mama and Yankele began to make their way along the boards. A tremor arose from under their feet and spread through their bodies. Yankele stole a glance downward. The powerful current made his head spin.

"Straight ahead! Look only straight ahead!" Mama said, almost shouting.

With the bag on her back, the suitcase in one hand and Yankele's hand in the other, Mama balanced carefully on the boards. Now they were almost to the other side, to the strong part of the bridge.

Papa breathed a sigh of relief. Now it was his turn. He took a step and put his foot on the board. Suddenly he stopped short: someone was lifting Sarele off his shoulders! He turned. His blood froze. The German officer was standing there with the child in his arms.

"No!" Papa cried. "No! Don't throw her off!" He tried to snatch the little one from the officer's arms. "No!"

"*Nein!*" the officer said. "*Nein!*"

There was no threat in his voice. Papa stood still. Then the officer smiled and said something at length in German. Papa stood there helpless. He didn't understand a word. Another officer pointed to the boards and the other side of the bridge. He smiled at Sarele and pinched her cheeks gently. Sarele turned her head away shyly, then looked at him, smiled, and held out her doll to him.

"Doll!" she said. "Grandma's doll!"

"*Gut!*" the man said, laughing. He looked at the boards and began to walk across them confidently, like someone who is on his own home ground. His comrade came along after him, the child in his arms.

Papa watched them from behind. They moved away with Sarele. The little one chattered in the officer's arms. Mama stood on the other side, eyes wide open. At last, the boards stopped shaking. The officers reached the permanent part of the bridge. One lowered the child straight into Mama's arms, while the other patted Yankele's head, and the two of them went on.

Papa's body, too, stopped shaking. His feet came back to life. He began to walk across the boards. The heavy bundles helped him keep his balance, but now he hardly felt their weight. He walked on and reached his family, reached Sarele, who was looking at him and laughing, waving her doll at him, Grandma's doll.

Four

At night, in the dark, the big barn door opened. The rain that had begun falling early in the evening blew in with the squeak of the hinges. The cold wind sprayed Yankele's face. In front of the open door loomed three shapeless shadows.

"Come in, come in quickly and close the door!" growled a voice deep inside the barn.

The door closed with a long squeak. Someone took a step and slipped, falling over someone else, who cried, "Watch out! There are people sleeping here!"

"Anybody got a match?" asked a voice near the door.

"No lighting fires here! It's dangerous!" someone called out from the darkness.

Somewhere a woman sighed. "And today is Friday . . . We can't light candles . . ."

"Is that all?" a man said, scolding. "If that's all you have to complain about, you're doing fine! Go back to sleep. You're certainly not going to get your Sabbath rest tomorrow."

Yankele was next to Papa. He lay on the straw fully dressed near Sarele, with Mama and Papa on either side of them. It was warm under the blankets, and he hardly felt the cold wind that came through the cracks in the walls.

The newcomers groped about in the dark. Those lying on the floor grumbled and squeezed closer together, and Yankele closed his eyes once more. A strange odor hung in the air of the barn, a smell of straw and many people and clothes that had not been laundered for a long time and, above all, heavy dampness and the breath that goes with an empty stomach. Yankele too was hungry. He put his thumb in his mouth and started to suck it, as did his little sister who lay next to him. He had long since stopped sucking his thumb, but on the road and during the nights spent outdoors under the stars, in granaries and isolated barns,

29

his thumb had come to console him once again. Hunger and fear were somehow diminished when he had it in his mouth. Now he also felt the warmth of Papa's body. Tranquility spread over him. The rain drummed in a steady rhythm on the wooden walls of the barn. Yankele fell asleep.

Papa woke him at the first light of morning. The farmers were afraid the Germans would discover they were hiding Jewish refugees, and if the Jews didn't get under way at the crack of dawn of their own accord, the farmers would throw them out bodily.

Papa had gathered up their things, buttoned Sarele's coat, and tied her shoes. Yankele was all ready to go. He bent over Mama and looked at her face. Mama was breathing heavily, and her eyes were closed.

"Get up, Mama!" he said. "I'll help you!"

He brought her coat and boots.

"Here, see, I'm big already!"

A weak smile crossed Mama's face. She opened her eyes and turned over. Papa carefully pulled back her blanket and held his hand out to her.

"Come, sit up. I'll take care of everything. Just put on your coat and we'll go. It's late."

Mama sat up on the straw. Her clothes were wrinkled and gave off a sour smell of sweat. She coughed and put her hand to her throat. "It hurts. Yitzhak, could I have something hot to drink?"

"No, not here," Papa said, "when we get away from the village. Now just put on your coat and let's go. Everyone else is already gone. We've got to get going!"

Yankele kneeled down and tried to wedge one of Mama's feet into a boot, as he did with his little sister. Mama's feet were swollen. Along the way she had developed big blisters that had swelled up and burst, and she had bandaged them with whatever was at hand. Her city shoes pinched and bruised so badly that she had had to use a pair of big old boots, found on the outskirts of the marketplace, instead.

Mama could hardly get her bandaged feet into the boots. She leaned on one side and slowly got up. A muffled cough filled her throat.

The coughing did not cease even when they stopped en route and heated a little water over a fire. By noon Mama could go no further. She sank to the ground at the side of the road. A deep cough seized her. Yankele stood next to her, not knowing what to do.

"Papa," he cried, "Papa! Mama's sitting down!"

Papa stopped and turned around.

"Come, Rosa," he said, "we've got to go on! We can't stay here!"

Mama did not respond. She rested her elbows on her knees and her head in her hands and sat silently.

"Rosa, if you don't get up, I'm going on alone!" said Papa without turning back. With the bundles on his shoulders and Sarele on his neck he could continue to move eastward. Anything to move eastward.

Yankele got scared.

"Mama, get up!" He nearly burst into tears. "Get up!"

He pulled her by the hand, but she began coughing again. When it stopped she was still sitting there. Her head drooped between her knees, as though she were folding up.

Papa trudged over to her and picked up the suitcase.

"I'm going on with the children," he said. "If you don't get up I'm leaving you here! I'm going on with the children!"

Mama said nothing.

Papa took Yankele by his other hand and began walking.

"Mama!" Yankele cried. "Mama, come!"

Mama didn't move.

Sarele, on Papa's shoulders, began to cry, "Mama, come! Mama!"

31

But Papa did not stop. He pulled Yankele after him, and Yankele kept turning to look back. "Mama!!!" Papa kept walking.

Then Mama got up. From a distance Yankele saw her rise to her feet, stagger a bit, and then begin walking.

"Mama's coming!"

Even now Papa did not stop. He only slowed down to let Mama catch up, and then they went on together, the four of them.

It was then that they saw the dead man.

They had seen many bodies along the way. People died by the roadside from hunger, sickness, soldiers' rifle shots. Yankele would go by the swollen bodies as if they were merely big rag dolls.

Once in Lodz a man had gone through their street pulling a big trunk on wheels. The man called out, "Theater! Puppet theater!" Yankele saw him later in the city square, standing behind his trunk and making marionettes dance on it. One, a witch with wild hair and a hook nose, took in her hand a broom on which she had been riding and beat a fat man made of rags and with a face like a potato. The man collapsed to the ground with arms and legs splayed out and lay there like a pile of discarded rags. All the dead people Yankele had seen up until now had seemed like him, like that marionette all spread out on the lid of the trunk.

But this one was different.

"Don't look!" Papa said. "Just look straight ahead!"

Yankele stole a glance at the corpse lying in the ditch. It was partly hidden in the tall grass, but its face, which was visible, was frozen into a horrible mask of pain and terror.

"Papa," Yankele whispered, choking with fear, "Papa, what happened to him?"

"I have no idea," Papa replied, "but we're already pretty close to the border. When we get to Russia everything will be different. Everything! Remember? Flowers in the spring, and cows, and calves . . ."

"And colts?"

"Yes, colts too!"

"And can I pet them? And play with them?"

"Yes, son, you can play with them all day long."

Five

"Papa, where's the border?"

"There, in the forest."

"Is it far?"

"No, they say it's just a short way into the forest."

"And then we'll be in Russia?"

"Yes," Papa answered curtly.

They had been waiting near the border for a week now. The long drawn-out journey across Poland had finally come to an end. Now they found themselves in a field among hordes of refugees who had gathered there, and soon they would have nothing left to exchange for a crust of dry bread. Thousands of refugees had collected all along the Russian border; they arrived as individuals, families, and whole groups, pursued by horror stories about the sealing up of ghettos, about relatives who were taken away for forced labor but never came back, about detention camps and executions. An invisible dam stopped the human flood at this point: the border. It was still closed. The guards at the crossing points didn't let anyone across. Those who tried to break through were shot to death by the German soldiers, and the few who managed to steal to the other side were caught by Soviet soldiers and sent back, delivered up to the Germans. But waves of refugees continued to arrive. The water in front of the dam was rising.

"But I don't see anything different! It's just like here in Poland. Are you sure this is the border?"

"That's what they all say. On the highways, on the main roads, the border is clearly marked. There are guards and barbed-wire fences there. But not every point along the border can be marked and sealed."

"All right, but why does it look just like Poland?" Yankele asked again.

"A border is something people decide to make. They could have decided to have the border run through the middle of this field, say, between you and the place where Mama is sitting; then the border would be here, but it would still look the same on both sides, wouldn't it?"

"As a matter of fact," Mama said, "it's Poland over there too. In the forest. And behind us."

"I don't get it," said Yankele, looking at her. "Isn't that Russia?"

Mama tucked her hands into the sleeves of her coat. It was chilly; a freezing-cold wind whirled isolated snowflakes. The big snows were evidently not far off.

"Now the Russians are there," she said, "but it was Poland. Until the war."

"The Russians and the Germans divided Poland between them," Papa explained. "They just decided where the new border should be, and that was that!"

"So the Russians and the Germans are friends?"

"No, not exactly. But before the war their foreign ministers signed a nonaggression pact."

"A nonag . . . what's that?" Yankele asked.

"They decided that there wouldn't be . . . that the Soviet Union wouldn't fight Germany, and Germany wouldn't attack the Soviet Union. Then, when the Germans went into Poland from the West, the Russians came and took the eastern part of the country. They simply moved the border."

"And who's on the other side of the border?"

"I think there are Poles there, just as there were before. But the soldiers are Russian."

"Then if the Russians and the Germans are friends, how come we're going to Russia? We'll have to wear yellow badges there too, won't we?"

Papa smiled, but it was a sad smile.

"No, son, there we'll be like everybody else. The Russians don't want to kill the Jews the way the Germans do. There we'll be like everybody else, without yellow badges."

"Then why don't they let us cross?"

Papa hugged Yankele and didn't answer.

"Papa, really, why won't they let us go across?" Yankele insisted. "And if the Russians and the Germans are friends, why go to Russia?"

Papa was silent. There are questions even Papa can't answer. Yankele got up.

"Can I go play with the kids who came yesterday? There's a boy there who's seven and already knows how to whistle! He promised to teach me. Yes, he did! He said that now that my front teeth have grown in I can even whistle between my teeth. So can I go?"

"Yes," Papa said, "but don't go too far away. I want to be able to see you all the time. And don't get lost among all those people."

"I wanna go too!" said little Sarele. "I wanna go with Yankele!"

"No!" said Mama. "You stay here. See, your doll is tired. Come and put her to bed."

Grandma's rag doll had withstood the hardships of the journey. True, she had lost an eye-button, and almost all her woolen hair had fallen out, but Mama promised to repair her once they got to Russia; and anyway, this was the doll Grandma had made! Sarele, too, had changed. When they first set out she had been pudgy, like a baby. Now her round face had grown thin and the soft cushions of fat on the backs of her hands had disappeared.

"Come, let's put your doll to bed," Mama said to her.

The little one protested. "No! I want Yankele!" She was close to tears.

Two strangers wrapped in shabby coats came over to Papa. The little one fled into the secure refuge of Mama's arms. Mama unbuttoned her coat and hugged Sarele tightly inside it. The child peered out at the strangers with curiosity.

"They say the other side is very lightly guarded," one said. "And over here the German soldiers hardly ever come by. They're busy with other things."

"I hear they're fighting in France," the other stranger said.

"You hear a lot of things," Papa said, "but they're everywhere. There are enough Germans to drive the Jews into the ghettos, to put them to death . . ."

"There aren't many German soldiers here," the other stranger said again, "and there are lots of us! What would happen if we all just got up and went across, all at once?"

"There are hundreds of people here," said the first stranger, "maybe thousands! Even if the Germans started shooting, most of us would get across!"

"And on the other side, in Russia?" asked the other.

"They could never catch so many people. Most of us would get away!"

"Looks like a snowstorm is on the way. We can't just stay here in this field."

Papa held his peace. Yes, he knew they couldn't stay there much longer. They had almost nothing left to exchange for food, and even if they found something they'd have to go a long way to get a potato or a few slices of bread. In fact, all they had left was a single blanket. It was cold in the field, very cold. Papa and Yankele would spend hours foraging for branches for a fire, to heat up a little water for their hungry stomachs, to thaw their

36

frozen bodies and their fingertips that had turned blue. Hundreds of other refugees were doing the same. At night the grass would freeze, and the four of them would huddle together on an old raincoat, under the one blanket they had left, praying that it would not rain and that the snow would take its time in coming. But now it looked as though praying wouldn't help. The big snowfall was on its way; the harsh winter was beginning.

Leibele puckered his lips, drew them tight like a reed, and let out a long whistle. Yankele watched him excitedly.

"Like this?" he asked, pressing his lips together. He blew and blew, but the hoped-for whistle never came. "How do you do that?"

"What will you give me if I teach you?"

Leibele had grown up in the country. He was dark-haired and quick. Along the way to the border, his face had lost the pleasant roundness of a child of seven, but he had meanwhile become more and more adept at something of inestimable value: he knew how to take advantage of everything that came his way. There wasn't a thing he couldn't turn to profit.

"What will you give me if I teach you to whistle?"

"I'll let you see my pocketknife!" said Yankele in a low voice. He looked around warily. Even here among the hundreds of refugees he was scared of the owner of the knife, the German officer who had dropped it way back in Lodz.

"Pocketknife? You don't have any such thing! Nobody here has a real pocketknife!"

"But I do!" said Yankele, fingering the treasure in his pocket.

"First let me see it!" Leibele insisted.

"Okay, but then will you teach me to whistle between my teeth?"

"All right," said Leibele, his eyes shining with curiosity.

"On your honor?"

"On my honor!"

Yankele took his hand out of his pocket and briefly opened

37

his fist. In his palm lay the pocketknife, a real pocketknife, a grown-up's pocketknife! Leibele let out a long whistle of enthusiasm.

"Wow!" he said at last, "what a great knife! Can I touch it?"

"Only after you teach me to whistle! Between my teeth too! And don't tell anyone I've got this knife! I don't want anyone else to know about it!" he whispered. "It belongs to a German!"

At last Papa found Yankele, standing next to a dark-haired boy and trying to whistle. "Come on!" he said to Yankele, taking his hand. "Now you're going to stay with us and not budge!"

"But Papa, I haven't learned to whistle between my teeth yet. Leibele taught me to whistle like this" — he pursed his lips and let out a long whistle — "but I still can't whistle between my teeth!"

"There's no time for games now!" Papa said firmly. "Something's happening. We've got to stay together now. The whole family!"

"But he promised me!"

"When we get across the border he'll keep his promise. Tomorrow you'll learn how to whistle between your teeth too."

"Tomorrow? Papa, you mean we're crossing the border? They're letting us?"

Papa said nothing. They made their way among the people scattered about in the field. In families, in groups, they sat there as before, but something had changed. Their meager belongings were tied up in bundles; mothers were holding their babies, fathers were holding their children's hands, and everyone was looking toward the forest expectantly. The sky was a solid, leaden gray, a sky that promised snow. A cold north wind blew in heavy gusts, bearing a few snowflakes, a taste of what was to come. There was something strange in the air, something tense and taut, something that had been ripening for a long time and was now ready to burst.

A man with a white beard sat nearby. Wrapped in a prayer

shawl, doubled up like a question mark, he sat mumbling something that might have been a lament or a prayer, swaying like a *lulav*.* Suddenly his voice welled up loud and clear: " 'Before thee shalt thou see the Land, but thou shalt not enter it!' "

The wind grew stronger, its powerful gusts scattering handfuls of snow. People started to get up. Now it was snowing heavily, the large flakes driven onward by the freezing, whistling wind. The whole crowd was on its feet. Clumps of whiteness spotted their coats, fell on their heads, blew like stars through their hair, covered their hats, their kerchiefs, their scarves.

Then it happened. It wasn't clear who took the first step, who broke out and ran for the east, the forest, the border. A few young people began running, and others began to stir from their places. A father with his children, a mother with an infant in her arms. Suddenly they were all running, running heavily, wearily, but running nevertheless, not stopping, running toward the border. The waters had risen and the dam had burst: a human gale was storming the invisible wall. To get across! To get across to freedom!

Yankele ran alongside Papa, holding Mama's hand. Papa held Sarele in his arms, a small bundle on his back — the last blanket.

"Hold on! Hold on to my coat!" Papa grunted. "Don't get lost!"

Darkness descended over the field. The wind shifted, plastering their faces with huge snowflakes, an avalanche of white fragments. Yankele closed his eyes for a moment. Holding on to Mama with one hand and clutching Papa's coattails with the other, he ran blindly.

"Ow! Mama!" Someone slipped and fell nearby. Yankele opened his eyes. The forest was not far off; solitary trees stood here and there, with the darkness of the forest behind them. All around, people were running with heavy steps. Whoever fell

*The cluster of palm, willow, and myrtle branches carried and waved by worshipers as part of the ritual of the feast of Tabernacles.

would get up again and go on running. An infant started to wail. A little girl cried out in fear, "Mom! Mommy!"

A mighty human wave, hundreds of men, women, and children, reached the forest. The wind that had been pounding at their faces was broken by the thick, tall trees. The snow caught in the treetops and piled up on the upper branches and long fingers of the evergreens, and only a few flakes reached the faces of the runners.

"Stop!" Mama said, panting. "Stop, Yitzhak! Not so fast! I can't go on!"

Papa slowed down. Night was falling. Darkness was settling over the trees.

"We can't run any more anyway. Soon we won't be able to see a thing."

"But you mustn't stop, Rosa! Keep going!"

So they went on. Half the night they kept walking. Where to? It seemed to them they had lost their way. Could they be going in circles? From time to time they would hear the crack of a branch under the feet of someone walking in the darkness, or a woman's distant, desperate cry — "Esther! Estherel!" And there was fear in her cry, a terrible dread — "Estherel, where are you?" Finally they slumped to the ground and fell asleep right where they were, the little ones bundled together like two puppies and Mama and Papa on either side, under their one blanket, exhausted from the cold, with the snow falling endlessly.

He was soaring above the pasture like a bird, light as a feather, with Leibele flying at his side, flying and whistling. They were both whistling the same cheerful song that Kadya, the teacher, had taught that first day of school, whistling and trilling like birds. Leibele's father stood below, a dark spot on the pad of green grass. He stood calling skyward: "Leibele! Lei–bele!"

Yankele opened his eyes. A pale bluish light filtered through from somewhere, the first light of morning. He closed his eyes again. Someone called out in the distance, "Leibele! Leibele dear!"

The voice was hoarse and gruff. Again Yankele opened his eyes. Leibele's father was hunting about among the trees for his son. During the night Leibele had gotten lost somewhere in the darkness, in the forest. His father's voice sounded farther and farther away: "Leibele! Lei–be–le!"

Now he heard the other voices. The forest echoed with the voices of the searchers. People had lost their way during the night, gone round and round in circles, gotten separated from their families. A young woman was coming toward them like a sleepwalker, her black hair disheveled, her eyes wide. As she walked, she slipped in the white snow. It had fallen heavily during the night, slid between the branches, and plummeted softly to the ground. Here the trees were sparse, and a thick white mantle covered the carpet of pine needles. The woman slipped and went on walking, her lips working soundlessly. She went by them like a ghost. Yankele slid out of the blanket, sat up, and followed her with his eyes. Papa woke up.

The four of them were there: Papa, Mama, Yankele, and little Sarele. Yankele felt in his pocket. Yes, the pocketknife was still there. He hadn't lost it; nothing was missing. Papa got up. He was stiff.

"Leibele got lost!" Yankele said to him.

"Leibele? Who's Leibele?"

"The boy who was teaching me how to whistle. He didn't finish teaching me. Do you think they'll find him?"

"I hope so," Papa said.

"He promised to teach me to whistle between my teeth! If you make a promise, you have to keep it, don't you?"

"If they find him, he'll keep his promise!" said Papa, leaning over to wake up Mama. A layer of soft snow covered the blanket — a blanket on top of a blanket. Carefully, Papa rear-ranged it. Sarele was wrapped in Mama's arms, deeply asleep.

"Are you cold, son?"

"A little. It's not so bad."

"You're lucky!" said Papa, rubbing his hands together to warm them up. "You're always the last one to feel the cold."

Yankele hesitated. A strange feeling gripped his heart, gripped it and didn't let go.

"Papa," he said at last, "if I ever get lost, what will happen?"

"If you get lost, we'll look for you, and you'll look for us, until we find each other!"

"Do you promise to look until you find me?"

Papa hugged Yankele and looked into his eyes — brown eyes, warm eyes, eyes filled with a sudden fright, a deep dread.

"What a question, son! I'll look till I find you! I promise!"

Then the eyes smiled, the little face relaxed, and the clot of fear in the boy's heart dissolved.

"I promise too!" said Yankele joyfully. "I promise I'll look for you. And when you make a promise," he added, looking at Papa . . .

"When you make a promise, you've got to keep it!" they both said at once, laughing.

The daylight lit up the soft snow. Clouds filled the sky, but the snow had stopped, and the wind had died down. They were wandering along the edge of the forest with other refugees who had emerged from among the trees and banded together, wondering whether this was the far side of the forest, the Russian side, or whether they had gone astray in the dark and retraced their steps to the Polish side. Off in the distance, on the white plain, smoke arose from several chimneys: a small village. Was it Russian or Polish? The snow had cast a spell over the world and transformed it. Might they have come back to that Polish village where, the day before yesterday, they had exchanged Papa's wedding ring for a little bread? They heard a sound in the distance, the sound of bells.

"Papa, someone's coming!"

"One of our people?"

"No, someone with a horse. A horse and cart."

Papa squinted at the white expanse that stretched out before him.

"It's not a cart, it's a sleigh!" he said. And as if the snow all around were not proof enough, he added in astonishment, "A sleigh! Winter is really here!"

"Yitzhak, let's hide!" said Mama, taking hold of his arm.

"Why? I don't think there are any soldiers there. If we're back in Poland, there's no problem. And if we're in Russia . . . it's best to find out, isn't it?"

The sleigh was coming close now. The horse was trotting — the snow was not deep — its hooves striking the hard ground that lay under the white covering. On the sleigh were logs for heating, and there was a man sitting on them, wrapped in a peasant coat. On his head was a fur hat, and under the hat he had tied a faded kerchief that covered his ears and half his face. When he noticed the people standing in anticipation, he reined in his horse. He looked them over from a distance, wondering if he should turn back to avoid the danger or dash by at a gallop.

The crowd stood there glumly. They were waiting for him. Now he saw that each of them had a yellow patch on his chest. And he knew. He had seen such people on the roads before, and he knew he had nothing to fear from them. He whipped the horse's back and went on his way.

"Hey!" one of them called out in Polish. "Hello there!"

"Hello!" the peasant answered curtly.

"Are you Polish?"

"Yes," called the peasant, "what did you expect?"

The people conferred with each other in their strange, foreign language.

"Don't run away, man!" the fellow in the gray coat called out after him. "Is this Russia — or Poland?"

"This is Poland!" the peasant shouted, spitting contemptuously in the snow. "It's just as much Poland as the other side of the border is! It just happens to be the part of Poland the Russians conquered!"

And then the peasant saw something he had never seen in his life: the fellow tore the yellow badge off his gray coat and threw it down, and then they all did the same, men, women, and then children — all threw the yellow badge on the ground and stamped on it, stamped on it again and again. One woman pulled the badge off the clothes of a child in its father's arms. Near them stood a little boy of about six with chestnut curls sticking out from under his cap, who stared in wonderment at his palm, a big, happy smile on his face. The peasant squinted in order to see better: in the boy's open hand there lay a pocketknife, a grown-up's pocketknife.

Six

The smoke rose from the chimneys straight up into the gray sky. The air was motionless; no wind blew. Somewhere way up high the smoke slowly dispersed and mingled with the gloomy blanket of clouds.

The chimneys protruded from the snow, which covered the roofs of the little cottages. Some of the chimneys drew their smoke up out of the snowy slopes, as if some form of life were hidden deep in the ground, under the white winter blanket. Someone who lived there, some subterranean creature, was sending signals of his presence to the outside world.

The caravan approached the settlement to the tinkling of bells and the whinnying of horses. Dozens of sleighs glided across the unsullied snow. Upon them sat masses of people, refugees, bundled up in all kinds of gear, huddled together against the bitter cold and the unrelenting fear.

Yankele sat between Papa's knees watching the thin columns of smoke that seemed to hold up the sky. "Are we here?" he asked hoarsely.

"So it seems," Papa answered. His voice, too, appeared to have frozen during the course of the long journey. It had begun in Brest-Litovsk, in a temporary camp where the refugees who had crossed the border had gathered. How long ago had that been? A week? Ten days? The trip to the mountains seemed to have erased the days in the camp from Yankele's memory. All he remembered were the inoculations, Sarele's wailing, the needle piercing his arm, how he managed to hold back and not cry, not at all, just like a grown-up.

Then began the long trip to the mountains, the Urals. The steam engine sounded its whistle long and loud across the white expanses, and from the silent void snow fell ceaselessly on the pine forests and sleepy little villages. Yankele stood for hours at the window, his nose glued to the glass, while great lumps of snow struck it from the other side, adhered for a moment, and then scattered like fine grains of sugar. The white stripe at the bottom of the pane rose higher and higher.

And when the train ride ended they continued on by sleigh. A long column of horse-drawn sleds made its way up into the mountains. The Urals: twenty degrees below zero. Everything was frozen, and all that could be heard among the snow-covered trees were the bells and the neighing of the horses.

Suddenly, out of nowhere, came the sound of an explosion. Yankele was frightened.

"Papa!" he whispered. "Papa, are they shooting here too? Is there a war here too?"

Papa looked ahead at the columns of smoke that were coming closer.

"No," he answered, "there are mines here. They must be dynamiting in the mines."

"And are you going to work there?"

"I suppose."

Again, a muffled bang that seemed to come from the bowels of the earth. Far off to the left, on the round shoulder of a mountain, people could be seen crawling about like ants on an anthill. Railway cars went by in a row like a toy train. The mine!

The horses quickened their pace, as if they knew that the end of the trip was in sight. "Giddyap!" the driver shouted, cracking his whip to loosen his muscles. "Hurray! Wake up, everybody! We're here! We're here!"

The column of sleighs slowed to a stop. The drivers clambered down. One patted a horse's back affectionately. Another clapped his hands and stamped his feet to warm up. Several turned away from the sleighs, spread their legs, and peed in the snow.

The refugees remained sitting on the sleighs, huddled together, silent.

Along a path that had been dug in the snow to one of the cottages came a short, husky man in a long military tunic and fur hat. He waved his arms and said something in flowing Russian, as if making a speech.

"What did he say?" Papa asked the woman behind him.

" 'Welcome!' " she translated. " 'Mother Russia greets you and bids you welcome!' "

The man waved his arms and raised his voice so as to be heard by the whole column of sleighs.

"He says we should get off," the woman said. "He says we should come down off the sleighs. He says they're going to arrange a place for us right away."

Yankele tried to get up, but he couldn't straighten his legs. They were frozen. Papa tried to get up too but fell back down.

"Not so fast!" Papa said, rubbing his legs. "Do as I do."

Yankele was hesitant. His hands were tucked inside the sleeves of his coat for protection against the bitter cold. At last he pulled them out and began rubbing. The frostbite sores on his hands turned blue. He had no mittens.

46

Slowly, people started to climb down from the sleighs, their limbs stiff from the cold. They gathered around the man, who looked them over with beady eyes. They stamped their feet and smacked their hands against their bodies again and again.

"*Tavarishchi!*" the man said. Yankele understood and felt happy: that was the first Russian word he had learned, "comrades." But then the words began to gush again, round and strange.

"What now?" asked Papa. "What is he saying?"

"He says he's going to show us our living quarters right away. He says someone will come to get the children and take them to school, and the adults will already start work today."

"And what about food?" Papa asked. "Tell him we're hungry. We haven't eaten for two days! And there are small children here!"

The woman translated. The man opened his hands, indicating he had nothing. His mittens were thick, like his coat. Then he said something very firmly and deliberately, spitting out each word.

"He says we have to work first! We get bread only if we work. We have to go to work right away."

"Here are some more twigs," Srulik said. "Yankele, give me the knife. I'll cut them off."

"No!" Yankele said, turning the branch over. "I'll do the cutting!"

He opened the big blade and began scraping the whole length of the branch. His eyes focused in intense concentration, his lips pressed together, Yankele wielded the pocketknife like an expert.

"Don't be like that," Srulik protested. "You never let me play with your knife!"

"A knife is no game. You can cut yourself!"

"You can cut your finger, too. Besides, I'm almost half a year older than you. Papa says that's a lot for little kids."

Yankele kept working.

"But I'm taller," he said, "and stronger too!"

"Strong people can get cuts too."

"But I'm an expert already! I've never gotten cut."

Yankele really was an expert — was he ever! Back in the transit camp, in Brest-Litovsk, he had carved little wooden dolls for Sarele, secretly engraved pictures on the walls of the barracks, and some days later, when the worst of the hunger was over, he had cut bread into little cubes before putting it in his mouth. Here in the Urals he no longer played with his bread. The adults who worked in the mine got a pound a day, but children only got half a pound, and not always that. Some days, for some reason, no bread was given out at all, and sometimes none was given for two or three days running. Once, a whole week went by without it, a whole week! Under the deep snow the ground was frozen solid. Only during the brief summer could small amounts of potatoes be grown, but now it was the middle of winter, and whatever little bread there was was brought from far away. People were dying of hunger, exhaustion, disease. No, here you didn't play with bread before eating it. Here you gathered up every crumb.

"You see?" Yankele said. "I've taken off the twigs. They won't scratch us anymore. Now we've got a lot of branches. We can tie them together."

"I've found some rope!" Srulik said, feeling very grown-up. "If I hadn't found it we could never make a sled! See? It's not just your pocketknife that counts!"

"And if I hadn't hauled all these branches here we wouldn't have anything!"

"Stop bragging!"

"You started it!" Yankele said, putting his knife in his pocket. "Now let's tie it up. Did you see the sled of the son of Volodya the foreman? Let's put the branches together the way he did, crisscrossed, and then tie them, okay?"

"Fine!" said Srulik. "Let's get started."

Srulik was short for his age and black-haired. He had big, dark eyes, innocent, wondering eyes, with curly lashes. As he tied the branches together he pushed his tongue into the space left behind by a baby tooth that had fallen out. Yankele tightened the knots, his lips compressed.

Winter evenings come early in the north. No sooner had they left the snow-covered schoolhouse than it began to get dark.

"Think we'll get in some sledding today?" Srulik asked hesitantly.

"Sure!" said Yankele. "We're almost done."

"But it's nearly dark. My mother will be worried."

"So we'll just have one go. We've got to check out the sled, don't we?"

They headed up the hill, pulling the sled after them like a reluctant puppy. The snow was dry and crunchy. They both sank in up to their knees. Yankele's face shone. Srulik's cheeks too grew ruddy.

"This is far enough," he said, "let's push off from here."

Yankele stopped and looked back. Far below lay the camp. The wooden huts were buried in snow, and the smoke rose from the chimneys straight up to the gray sky, just as it had on the day they arrived. The cold was biting, but since there was no wind it did not penetrate their patched coats.

"All right," said Yankele, "but I'm sitting in front!"

Srulik did not object. Below, when they were putting the sled together, he was a big hero, but now, high up in the mountain, he felt a twinge of fear.

Yankele sat on the front of the sled, his shoes planted in the snow as a brake. They were too big for him, but that was all to the good, because Mama put layers and layers of newspaper inside to protect his feet from the cold. Now the paper was sodden with snow that had gotten in and melted, but Yankele paid no attention. He was excited by the climb and looking forward to the adventure of riding back down.

49

"Well, what are you waiting for? Sit down!" he said.

Srulik climbed hesitantly on the back and wrapped his arms and legs around Yankele.

"Hurray!" Yankele cried, imitating the Russians, and dug his feet into the snow to push off. The sled moved and began sliding forward. Yankele lifted his feet, and suddenly, all at once, they were gliding rapidly down the slope, the wind whistling in their ears. Faster, faster. Off to one side, a lone tree whizzed by. Srulik clung to Yankele and shut his eyes.

"Ho-ho!" Yankele shouted excitedly. "We're flying!"

Down they flew. The slope was clear, and the sled bounded forward as if it had a life of its own. Srulik held on tight. Snow was blowing to either side. Cold air rushed past their burning cheeks.

Suddenly Yankele shouted, "Jump, Srulik, jump!"

Srulik opened his eyes. Directly ahead of them, a big fir tree was coming up fast. Yankele dragged his feet in the snow, but the sled flew straight on.

"Jump!!!"

Srulik hung on to his friend, paralyzed with fear. Yankele lifted one leg and threw himself off to one side. Clinging to each other, the two of them rolled away down the slope, getting whiter and whiter, until they hit a tree and came to a stop. And the sled, as though it were alive, made straight for the big fir, until — wham! — it crashed into the broad trunk. Then there was silence, and splinters of wood scattered all over the soft snow.

When they opened the door of the cabin, the two were almost bowled over by the thick, suffocating air. The cabin was a bee-hive of activity. Six families inhabited its four rooms, and the one kitchen had to suffice for them all. Bella, Srulik's mother, pushed her way out to greet them, wringing her hands with emotion.

"Dear God, where have you been? It's already dark out! What have you been doing all this time?"

"Sledding!" Yankele answered proudly. "We made our own sled, and we rode it down from the top of the hill! Just like Volodya!"

Bella wiped her hands on her heavy thighs. She was a big, broad-hipped woman, and even the hardships of the journey and the constant hunger had had no effect on her solid body. She was about to reprimand the latecomers, as she always did, but Srulik ran to her arms without saying a word. He was like a fledgling that had made its first daring foray out of the nest and was now coming back, frightened, to the comfort of its mother's wings. His little heart was pounding, the sight of the pieces of wood scattered in the snow still vivid before his tightly shut eyes. Bella's reprimand caught in her throat.

"Shhh," she said, stroking his head. "The main thing is, you're home now."

Yankele looked into the kitchen. "Where's Mama?"

"What happened to you?" asked a woman laboring over the sink. "Good God! Did someone hit you? Look at his forehead!"

"It's nothing," said Yankele, "just a bang. Where's my mother?"

"In your room," said the woman. "Come, I'll press it with a knife so it doesn't swell up."

"Mama will do it!" said Yankele, heading for their room.

"But she's in bed!"

"Again?"

Yes, Mama was back in bed, covered with a blanket and a coat. She opened weary eyes to look at Yankele. Her face was pale, her cheeks sunken.

"Mama, what happened? Are you sick?"

Mama tried to smile. "It will pass, son. It's nothing."

Sarele was playing in the corner with Srulik's little sister. They fed their dolls and put them to bed, absorbed in an endless game.

"Bella will make you some tea," Mama said, "and we got bread today too. Go and eat."

The light was dim. Mama didn't notice the bruise on his

forehead. He hurried off to the kitchen. Suddenly he felt hungry. The slice of bread he had had at school was long forgotten. The fresh air and the cold and the hike up the mountain that had distracted him from everything else were now replaced all at once by real hunger pangs. There was a bit of bread, and even the tail of a smoked fish that Bella had managed to get hold of in some secret way, and tea, hot tea that slides down your throat and warms your insides, and it didn't matter that there wasn't any sugar. The main thing was that the terrible emptiness of his stomach was gradually filling up, and warmth was spreading through his body. Soon Mama would get up, come into the kitchen, embrace Yankele, sit down next to him, and sip some tea the way she always did; and as always she would recover from her day's work, because she wasn't sick at all but only needed to rest a bit, to rest after finishing her shift; and when Papa came she would get up to greet him, and everything would be like always!

Papa came back from work that night, but Mama didn't get up to greet him. She slept exhaustedly, with Sarele in her arms.

The next day, after his shift, Papa took her to the doctor.

Dr. Goldman was the camp physician, a physician without medicine. His stock of drugs had been depleted during the long flight from Warsaw to the Russian border. The tide had brought him here, to this remote place in the Ural Mountains, and here he worked each day in the mine offices, bent over the account books. As a doctor, he was the only one of the refugees who was not swallowed up day after day in the belly of the mine.

Dr. Goldman examined Mama. He listened at length to her lungs and her heart. Then he took the stethoscope out of his ears, wiped his glasses with his shirttail, and said, "It's nothing serious. Just exhaustion."

"What should she do?"

"Stay in bed, rest, eat well."

Papa looked at him helplessly. "You know as well as I do that whoever doesn't work doesn't eat!"

Dr. Goldman flexed his hands. He was a short, thin man with a gaunt, prematurely wrinkled face. The corners of his mouth were deeply furrowed. At the upper end of one of the furrows grew a big, dark mole. Yankele watched him, spellbound.

"Why did you bring the boy along?" the doctor asked, his mole bobbing with each word.

"My little 'treasure' has taken quite a beating!" Papa said. "Here, look at this forehead. Quite a mess, isn't it?"

Dr. Goldman pushed his glasses up to his forehead and looked closely at the bruise. His fingers probed tenderly among the reddish curls.

"Does this hurt?"

"No."

"How about this?"

"Ow!"

"How did you get hit?"

"I was sledding," said Yankele. "I made a sled and went sledding with Srulik. We were coming down the hillside, and there was this tree in the way."

"A tree in the way, eh?" said Dr. Goldman, a soft smile flitting across his pale face. "I wonder what it was doing there."

Mama caught the doctor's glance. "Doctor, it's not serious, is it?" she pleaded.

"The boy, you mean? No, it's nothing. By the time he gets married it'll be gone."

"But I'm only seven and a half."

The faint smile passed once again over Dr. Goldman's face. The mole quivered as if it had a life of its own. "In that case I'm not worried! You've got plenty of time."

"Shouldn't we put a little iodine on the scratch?" Papa asked.

"I haven't got anything, not even iodine," said Dr. Goldman, gesturing at the bare room. "There's no medicine. I examine people, give names to their ailments — and that's it. People die here with God's help. But really, there's nothing to be done. The boy is healthy and strong. He has a good chance of surviving all the hardships. The strong endure, but the weak . . ." A cloud passed over his face, and he bit his lower lip. "No, you don't have to worry about the lad, but I would take good care of his mother!" he said, turning to Papa. "She's got to rest and eat proper food!"

Papa shrugged. "Proper food. You know as well as I do what kind of food we get around here. This week there was no bread for three straight days!" He lowered his voice. "I'm sure the local people are stealing it! The people in charge of the warehouse take for themselves."

Dr. Goldman sat down on the room's one chair. He squinted up at Papa. He too spoke in a whisper. "You've got to complain! Why don't you complain?"

"What good would it do? The thief is probably giving part of his take to the authorities. They'd just throw a complaint out, and we'd go on being hungry . . ."

Mama put on her coat and turned to Papa. "Let's go, Yitzhak. We've taken enough of the doctor's time."

She was unsteady on her feet, and Papa quickly got hold of her to keep her from falling back on the examining table.

"Why don't you ask for Soviet citizenship?" Dr. Goldman asked. "Give up your Polish citizenship, get Soviet ID cards, and you'll be all right. You can leave the Urals and go somewhere else. Any other place would be better! You can find easier work and eat every day; your wife can rest and get well. Here you're doing slave labor. People here are dying like flies of hunger and exhaustion!"

"I'm afraid," Papa answered.

"What are you afraid of?" Dr. Goldman asked.

"I'm afraid they won't let me go back to Poland!"

"When?"

"When the war is over."

54

"When the war is over," Dr. Goldman echoed, raising his eyebrows skeptically. "The war has only just begun; and besides . . . besides, there won't be anything to go back to. There won't be anyone to go back to."

There was a look of pain on Papa's face. "My father is there; he's an old man. And the whole family . . ."

"Your family is here!" said Dr. Goldman. "This is your family! You've got to think about your wife. Here, if she doesn't work, she won't get any bread!"

"I'll do her work for her!"

"But you're already working!"

"Then I'll work two shifts!" said Papa, pursing his lips.

"Two shifts? Loading rocks onto freight cars two shifts a day? On hardly any food? Who do you think you are — Samson?"

Yankele looked up at the doctor. "My papa's strong!" he said, smiling proudly. "He carried Sarele the whole way, and the bundles too! My papa's the strongest one around!"

Now the doctor smiled a real smile. "I can see that!" he said. "And you're going to be big and strong just like your papa!"

The mole quivered at the corner of his smile, but the doctor's eyes were still sad.

Seven

It was a clear day. The warm spring sun poured its light into the yard. The sounds of the carpentry shop filled the air with a happy chorus. Papa stood in the middle of the shop, a pencil stub above his right ear, measuring and checking boards he had prepared to build a table. Srulik's father was laboring over a long bench. He was sanding the bench, stopping occasionally to blow away the fine sawdust, his big cap flopping down over his forehead just like in the old days in Poland. Boris's father was hammering. A bunch of small nails stuck out of the corner of his mouth. You could tell he was an experienced carpenter, trained and competent like Yankele's father. From time to time he would take a nail from his mouth, give it two or three taps, and it was in, as if it had been there since the Creation. The other members of the cooperative were professionals too, experts in their craft. Only Srulik's father would often peer out from under the visor of his cap at the others working around him, and when Yitzhak, Yankele's father, caught his eye he would know that Srulik's father needed help.

Yitzhak was the one who had brought him here to this southern Garden of Eden; or to be exact, not Yitzhak but his illness. It had been the pneumonia he had gotten in the mine in the Urals that had made up their minds. When Rosa had become too weak to work, Yitzhak had taken her place, working two shifts. He would leave before sunrise, plunge out into the deep snow, and disappear into the darkness of the mine. All day long he would load the blasted rocks onto rail cars, either the little ones inside the mountain or the big ones that waited outside on the main line. At the end of a long day's work, sixteen hours of backbreaking labor, he would make his way back to the cabin in the darkness, collapse onto the bed and sleep like a log, exhausted. Yitzhak was stubborn, but the rocks and the bitter cold were more stubborn. He finally came down with pneumonia, and he had to give in: he gave up his Polish citizenship, got Soviet papers for himself and his family, and agreed to go wherever the authorities would send them. The illness, which had overcome him and forced his hand, then opened before him the best of all possibilities: he was sent to the southern part of the Soviet Union, to the Crimea. No sooner had he recovered his health than he found a place in a carpentry cooperative in a small town. Everyone immediately recognized that he was a fine craftsman, but he insisted on bringing along Mendel, Srulik's father, whom fate had also sent southward. Mendel's previous work experience as the owner of a small clothing shop had not prepared him for manual labor, but Yitzhak vouched for him, and so the manager of the cooperative agreed to bend the rules on Yitzhak's account. Yitzhak helped him from the very first moment, and whenever necessary he would finish his friend's work for him as if it were his own. Yitzhak was diligent and loved his work.

Srulik looked out over the second-story railing into the yard. The homes of the members of the cooperative were there, arranged around the yard, and in the middle was the carpentry shop.

"Hey, Yankele, has your mother finished milking the nanny goat yet?"

Yankele looked up. In the sunlight his hair turned a dusky gold. He squinted. Tiny wrinkles appeared at the bridge of his nose.

"Yes! Come on, Srulik. Come and watch the kids suckle!"

Srulik rushed down the stairs and knelt beside the goat, excited as always to see the kids. Yankele crouched down next to him and looked at the kids butting their heads against the udder and sucking hungrily.

Finally, Vanka, the kid, let go of the nipple and turned toward Yankele. "Is that it? Have you had enough, little one?" Yankele asked, getting up. He stroked the kid's white hair. "Come on, let's play a bit."

But the kid turned back to the bountiful udder, not yet satisfied. Boris's brother, a boy of seventeen who had already helped his father do carpentry, called to them from the corner of the yard, "Hey, how's your Vanka-Stanka?"

"All right," Yankele declared. "They're eating!"

The children already spoke fluent Russian, and after a few months in school they could read and write too. On the way home they would try to outdo each other reading aloud the street names and the signs in the marketplace, and they even tried to read the posters put up near the council office. Yankele had called the twin kids by the Russian name "Vanka-Stanka," because shortly after they were born, when the two kids had tried to stand, they would get up, wobble about on their little legs, fall, and then get up again. Just like the Russian dolls — Vanka-Stankas — that have lead in their round bottoms; if you knock them over, even if you lay them flat, as soon as you let go they stand up straight again, over and over.

"Vanka's all right, but what kind of name is Stanka?" Srulik said then.

"What do I care?" said Yankele. "They'll be Vanka and Stanka, and that's that!"

A small white chicken darted out of the storeroom and began to hop about and peck at the ground, coming closer and closer to the goat and her kids.

The families on the second floor kept goats and chickens in the storeroom below. Here in the cooperative no one went hungry; besides the ample bread and the vegetables that could be bought, they provided milk and eggs, and so nothing seemed to be lacking. Sarele's cheeks filled out again, Papa got well, Mama got stronger, and the color came back to the faces of young and old.

Stanka turned to look at the chicken that was pecking nearby: step, peck, step, peck. Suddenly he darted toward the chicken and tried to butt it with his head. The chicken fluttered away with a rush of its wings and a hysterical cackle. The kid began to run around the yard, with Yankele on his heels. Stanka turned and ran straight into Srulik's arms.

"Catch him!" Yankele cried, his cheeks red with excitement. But now Vanka leaped out and butted Srulik, who fell on his back. All at once the yard was filled with commotion: the cackling of the chickens, their feathers flying, the bleating of the kids, and the laughter of the children. Boris's brother put down his plane and began to run around the yard too: "Yo-ho-ho!"

Papa stopped working. "Hey! You there! You're bothering us!

Take that goat to the field across the way. Let it graze there and let us have some peace!"

Yankele stopped chasing around and untied the long rope. Immediately, the goat turned toward the gate, as if this were what she always did. Vanka and Stanka rushed to join their mother, and the whole gang made its way across the muddy lane to the field, which was turning green.

Soft, bright-green grass covered the ground. The first spring flowers had begun to blossom, and the white goat was already grazing, tearing off grass and flowers and chewing them together. In the spot where she had grazed the day before new blossoms had already appeared. Spring was burgeoning with full force.

Yankele tied the long rope to a post at the edge of the field and went to play with the kids. With the whole field before them, they now began to bleat, jump, and gambol about.

"I've got Vanka!" Yankele shouted and ran after the kid.

"Meh, meh, mehhh . . . !" Srulik bleated and ran after Stanka.

Mama stood at the entrance to the yard, leaning on the gate. The afternoon sun poured its golden light down onto the green field, on the goat and the kids, on the frolicking children. Mama folded her arms and smiled. For a moment she forgot that a war was raging. Even Grandma, who had been left far behind in the ghetto, in Lodz, was forgotten for a moment. A strong smell of wood, of sawdust, and carpenter's glue, rose from the yard. How she loved that smell! She felt as though she had everything she wanted in life. Yankele leaped and caught Vanka. He hugged the kid, and his laugh rang out like a clear-toned bell. *God, make this moment last forever!*

Papa stood at the counter picking out potatoes.

"Hey!" the peasant woman said, shoving him. "That's not gold, my friend! For all the feeling you're doing one could have thought you were choosing precious stones!"

"For all the money you're charging for these miserable potatoes one could indeed acquire a treasure!" said Papa, adding

59

one more to the scale. The loudspeaker in the entrance to the council building let out a squawk. Someone inside was fiddling with the radio dial.

"O Lenuchka, my love!" crooned a deep voice, and a roll of accordion notes surged after it in a cascade of sounds. Again the unseen hand turned the dial, and the big loudspeaker blared the tones signaling the start of a newscast. The marketplace suddenly fell silent. The vendors stopped hawking their wares, and people stood still in anticipation of the news. The old Tatar who sat off in a corner humming a monotonous tune that went on forever stopped too. Words streamed from the loudspeaker, rolled and scattered across the square:

"The General Secretary of the Soviet Union, Comrade Stalin, has awarded a medal of distinction to the workers of the Donets Basin coal mines. The workers won the prize on the basis of their great diligence and their loyalty to the Party and the Soviet people. A five-man delegation was received at the Kremlin . . .

"A new government has been formed in Britain headed by Winston Churchill. The British believe a unity government will be best equipped to fight the Germans . . . The German army has invaded Holland, Belgium, and Luxembourg. Hitler's generals have launched a blitzkrieg and conquered . . ."

Papa listened tensely. Yankele looked around. He wanted to ask a question, but Papa motioned to him to keep quiet. They had no radio at the cooperative, and the local council's loudspeaker was their only source of news. Yankele took out of his pocket a bag of raisins Mama had given him and began to pop them in his mouth one at a time. Mama worked at the information desk of the hospital in the neighboring town. The personnel manager there was a Jew, and he was glad to give the job to one of his own people, especially since she was good at languages, even managing to communicate right away with the local Tatars. Her salary didn't amount to much, not much at all, but many people came during hours when visiting wasn't permitted and, after depositing jars of honey, bags of raisins, and homemade cakes on her desk, they pleaded with her:

"Well, comrade, you'll let us in, won't you? We've only come for a minute, just a few minutes . . ."

No, here in the Crimea people had plenty of food.

Yankele thrust his hand into the bag and took another raisin. Suddenly he froze. A pair of big eyes was staring at him, staring at him without blinking. The boy was peering at him from behind an empty wagon. He might have been ten years old. He was shabbily dressed and barefoot, his thin face was black, either from the sun or from not having washed for days on end, and his dark eyes were riveted on the bag.

Yankele reached back down and folded up the bag in embarrassment. He looked up at Papa, wanting to say something, but Papa put his finger to his mouth. "Shhh!"

A skinny gray cat crept under the counter, its burning eyes fastened on some unseen objective. It was creeping stealthily now, crouching low, its body flattened and its head thrust forward, ready to pounce. Yankele bent over to see what the cat was after . . . when suddenly he felt someone snatch the bag from his hand, and there was the boy, running past the counter and disappearing into an alley just around the corner. Yankele looked dumbfounded at his empty hand. He could still feel the paper of the bag.

"Papa! He took them! He took my raisins!"

The newscast ended. A nostalgic song filled the square. Papa's eyes came into focus. There was a strange look in his face, but Yankele didn't notice it. There were tears in his eyes.

"Papa! He stole my raisins!"

"What? What happened?"

"The boy . . . the boy grabbed my raisins! He stole the bag!"

"What? What boy?"

"The boy who was standing over there . . . the barefoot one . . . he was standing there looking at me and then all of a sudden . . . all of a sudden he stole my . . ."

61

At last Papa's gaze came to rest on Yankele's face.

"The one who was standing in the corner?"

"Yes! Go after him, Papa! Catch him!"

"No," said Papa, stroking Yankele's head, "I'm not going after him. He must be hungry."

"But he stole from me! It's forbidden to steal!"

"True," said Papa, "it's forbidden, but when a person is hungry . . . when I'm hungry I work and earn my bread. When I couldn't work I sold everything we had. But this boy . . . maybe he has no parents. I'm sure he has nothing to sell, and he's hungry. No, Yankele, we have enough now. I'm not going after him. Let him eat in peace."

Boris came running into the yard, his cheeks red with excitement.

"I found them! I found them!"

Yankele jumped up. "Where are they?"

"Over at the house of that skinny Tatar who lives by the Communist Youth office, the one with the white mustache."

"Are you sure they're Vanka and Stanka? Did you see them?"

"Honest to God!" Boris swore. "I saw them with my very own eyes! Two white kids. In the whole world there isn't a pair of twin goats like them! I called them 'Vanka-Stanka,' and they answered with a long 'mehhhh,' as if they knew me. I swear, I'm sure they knew me!"

Yankele dashed out of the yard. Boris hurried after him. Srulik stayed behind, his big, dark eyelashes fluttering with excitement. He'd found them! Boris had found the kids! He went over to the gate. His two friends were already at the end of the street, and they would soon disappear behind the big building.

They had been looking for the kids for a week. Yankele's father had sold them. He had made no secret of what he planned to do: now that the kids were a little bigger and had begun to eat grass, Papa had decided to wean them and sell them.

"We have no choice, little man," said Papa. "The storeroom

is small, and we have to make room for another goat. Boris's father wants to buy a milk goat."

"But they'll grow up and give milk too!"

Papa laughed. "You know they're males, don't you, Yankele? What will we do with two grown-up billygoats?"

Yankele opened his mouth to answer, but he was at a loss for words. No, Papa had no choice. The carpenters in the cooperative needed the animals in the storeroom. There wasn't much room there, and they needed it for egg-laying hens and a milk goat. After trading everything they had for food on the long trek from Lodz, Papa was in a position to buy clothes for the family at last.

Then, one day Yankele had come home from school, and the kids were gone. Since then he had been looking for them. He had stopped doing his homework, and with or without Boris he had been spending all his time from after school until dark looking for the kids. Mama had gotten angry, reprimanded him, and finally just sighed and said to Papa, "Yitzhak, maybe we should get the kids back? Look what's come over the boy."

But Papa wouldn't give in. "You know I'd give him the shirt off my back, but what I've got on my back is precious little! We have no choice, Rosa. The boy must learn to give in."

But Yankele didn't give in. He ran to the Communist Youth office now as fast as he could. Even Boris, who was the fastest boy in the neighborhood, lagged behind.

In the green field behind the building, a small flock of goats was grazing, and a lanky figure stood among them. Now Yankele could see Vanka and Stanka. They were grazing quietly among the other goats. There was a rope around their necks, and the other end of it was in the hands of the goatherd. Apparently he was still worried that they might run back to their mother.

Yankele plunged into the flock and knelt down to embrace the two kids. He wanted to shout for joy, but he was out of breath. He buried his face in Vanka's white hair. The kid raised its head and bleated happily. Stanka stuck out its warm, rough tongue and began licking the boy's face. It seemed to like the taste of his tears. Then Boris arrived and hugged the kids as well.

"Hey!" the Tatar said. "You're keeping them from eating!"

Boris looked up at the goatherd. "None of your business!" he scowled. "They're not yours!"

The Tatar looked at him in amazement. "What are you talking about, you little runt? I bought them at full price!"

"They're not yours! They're his!" Boris said, pointing at Yankele.

"How the devil can they be? I bought these kids from the redheaded carpenter at the cooperative!"

Boris stood up and put his hands on his hips. That's what his mother would always do when she was bargaining in the market.

"That carpenter," said Boris, "is his father. But Vanka and Stanka are his!"

The Tatar paused for a moment. He stroked his thick, gray mustache, smoothing its ends, and swallowed several times. Boris watched his Adam's apple bob up and down in his scrawny neck like a bouncing ball.

"I'm sorry, boys," he said at last, "but these kids are mine. I bought them a week ago, and they're mine, all mine!"

Yankele did not answer. He hugged the kids and stroked their silky, white hair. No, Vanka and Stanka were his, forever!

The old goatherd looked at them, perplexed, hesitating. Finally he bent over and tried to pull the boy away from the kids; but Yankele held on and wouldn't let go. The Tatar slowly straightened up and turned to Boris.

"Go call his father," he said. "This is for him to deal with. Let him come and get the boy."

Mama always said nobody was as stubborn as Papa, but now Yitzhak would meet his match. Yankele compressed his lips and held on to the kids for dear life. He was deaf to explanations, pleas, scoldings, and warnings: he would never leave Vanka and

64

Stanka! In the end, Papa bought the kids back from the Tatar, paying even more than he had charged. Even someone who didn't know the first thing about bargaining could tell that the price had risen astonishingly.

By the time they got home, a procession had formed behind them. All the children in the neighborhood joined in, with Yankele in the lead and the two kids at his sides like faithful puppies. Excited and waving his hands, Boris told the story of what had happened over and over again, and his listeners would then repeat it to the other children who came running out of the yards and the houses to join the joyful throng. Here's to our Yasha! Hurray!

Mama was waiting for them at the gate, wiping her hands on her apron.

"Now you know who the real stubborn mule in the family is," Papa said. "If you had only seen how your little 'treasure' held on and wouldn't let go, Rosa! This child is going to get what he wants in life, no matter what!"

News of the invasion hit Yankele like a ton of bricks. Not that it came as a surprise, not at all. Although the Soviet Union and Germany had signed a nonaggression pact, they both knew that any pact with the Devil was bound to be short lived. For Hitler, the Devil meant the Communist regime in the Soviet Union, headed by Stalin, and he secretly planned a great attack on him; while in Russia there was no doubt that Hitler and his fascism were the embodiment of Satan, to be treated with extreme care. The war had been raging in Europe for a year and a half. Central and western Europe groaned under Nazi oppression, while the Soviet Union enjoyed a brief "time out." And it was not only a "time out"; the pact "awarded" her pieces of her neighbors' territory: eastern Poland at the start of the war, Estonia, Latvia, and Lithuania later on. But any sensible person, watching the hour glass, could see that the sand was quickly running out.

65

Papa would listen to the news stony faced. In the evenings, Yankele's parents would sit with Srulik's and talk in low voices. There had been no news from home, from Poland, but they had heard while making their run for the border that the Lodz ghetto had been sealed off, with no one allowed in or out. They knew, too, that all the Jews in Poland had been rounded up into ghettos. Rumors circulated that they were being taken from there to work camps, and there was talk of executions and terrible decrees, but no one could confirm anything. From Grandpa, Grandma, brothers, and sisters there was no sign of life.

Yes, Yankele knew all this. Mama had started lighting candles on Sabbath eve. Though Yankele had never before seen his mother pray, now she would stand before the candles a long time, her hands to her eyes, her lips moving. Then Yankele would remember Grandma, the special smell in her little room, her shining eyes.

But usually he was busy and didn't notice the growing tension, the storm clouds gathering in the west. The days grew longer, spring yielded to the onset of summer, and Yankele took his place at the center of an active, happy group of children. Since that day when he had brought the kids back home he had been treated like a king. Vanka and Stanka were with him whatever he did, whether it was running footraces, playing hide-and-seek, or skipping stones at the riverbank. The two of them were always there, and the gang of children around them.

The river flowed north out of the mountains in the southern part of the Crimea. By the time it reached the town, it was already flowing lazily through level fields of wheat and hay. When the first hot days came, the gang, including Yankele, skipped off to the river. There, he scampered and jumped about, taking care not to stray too far from the riverbank. At last, he flapped his arms and jumped in. He swam like a fish now, diving, coming up, and squirting water from his mouth like the whales in the picturebooks. The kids, tied to the white trunk of a poplar tree, fed on the soft grass on the bank.

66

One day, Srulik suddenly burst upon this scene of water, light, and laughter, shouting at the top of his voice, "War! War!"

Yankele let loose one more jet of water in a high arc. Not bad, almost as good as Boris! Srulik reached the riverbank.

"Yankele! Come! Come home!" he cried, panting from exertion. "There's war!"

"What are you talking about?" Yankele said. "There's always war, there, far away, in Poland."

"No!" Srulik said, beginning to cry. "You don't understand! War here, in the Soviet Union. They announced on the radio that Hitler has invaded Russia. Come home quick!"

No, Yankele didn't understand. The sky was still blue, Vanka and Stanka were still munching grass peacefully, and a pair of storks, on their way back from the south, were circling over the river, around the big nest on the cottage chimney. He climbed up on the bank, his cheeks puffed up with water, and gave one last squirt straight up at the sun. The drops sparkled in the grass at his feet.

"Wait a minute," he said. "Wait till I dry off!"

"No!" Srulik begged, bursting into tears. "Your dad says he's going off to fight. Mine, too! They're going to join the army!"

"What do you mean, Rosa? How can I stay home now?"

Mama wrung her hands. "But you have children, Yitzhak, and you're not so young anymore! Stay here. Men are needed on the home front too!"

But Papa had made up his mind. There was a new wrinkle between his eyebrows. "You simply don't understand, Rosa. This is my chance!"

"Chance for what?"

"To get back at the Germans! To get back at the Nazis for everything they've done there, in Poland. How do we know what's happened to my father, to my brothers who stayed behind, to your mother, Rosa? This is our chance to drive them out of Poland!"

67

"But what will happen to *us?* What will we live on?"

"I'll be paid," Papa said, "a soldier's wages. You'll get it all. What will I need there, at the front?"

Mama fell silent. She knew her Yitzhak. When he made up his mind to do something, he couldn't be budged.

Yankele looked at the wooden walls of the little kitchen. Above the hissing teakettle the big eye in the wood was staring at him like a dark whirlpool fixed there forever. During the day it was a benevolent eye that watched over him, but at night . . . well, at night it was a little scary. Only a little . . . Nothing had changed. Everything was the same as always. How do they know there's really a war? Only because the radio said so?

Bella, Srulik's mother, knocked at the door.

"You're both going?!" she said, standing in the doorway, her hands on her broad hips. "What's gotten into you? We've finally made a place for ourselves and already you're running off and leaving everything behind?"

"It won't be for long, Bella," Papa said, getting up. The kitchen seemed smaller than ever, as Bella's big body invaded it like a battleship entering a little fishing harbor.

"What are you talking about?" Bella scolded. "This isn't child's play! It's war!"

Papa patted her on the shoulder. "What are you worrying about, Bella? The Soviet Union is a big country. It has a strong army! This isn't the Polish army, it's the Red Army!"

Mama lowered her head. Tears began flowing noiselessly down the newly carved furrows in her face. Papa took her by the shoulders and tried to wipe her cheeks with his rough hand.

"Don't cry, Rosa. We'll be back soon. Hitler is nothing compared to the Red Army. In a few weeks it'll all be over. You don't believe me, Rosinka? We'll trample him, we'll pay him back for everything, we'll finish him off once and for all!"

"How many weeks?" Bella asked. "What are you saying, Yitzhak?"

68

"Well, all right," Papa said, "maybe two or three months. But don't you worry, Rosa. You'll see: we'll be back soon!"

Eight

Three months later there was nowhere to return to, no home left: the Crimean peninsula had been captured by the Germans. There was no one to go back to either: Mama had taken the children and fled, again, to the east. The German army had invaded the western provinces of the Soviet Union, and the Nazi boot was trampling those Jewish communities that remained there. The extermination machine roared on, this time on the soil of Russia.

Whoever could, fled eastward. It was not only the Jews who ran this time: Russians too, Communist Party activists, ran for their lives. The Germans were killing them as well.

A mighty wave of refugees poured across Russia. People used whatever means they could find to flee. Most motor vehicles and trains had been pressed into service in the war effort. Whoever managed to get on a railroad car, even a freight car, considered himself lucky.

Yankele sat in a freight car with Mama and Sarele. Srulik sat next to him on a little bundle of clothes. Having boarded in Rostov, they had been traveling for months, and the bundle, which had been large to start with, had gradually dwindled in the tried and true way: a sweater for a loaf of bread, a scarf for a salt fish . . . Only Bella, Srulik's mother, was still as fat as ever, and even now, as she sat leaning against the wall of the car, holding her little Feigele in her arms, she took up twice as much space as Mama. Wherever the wind blew them they would stay together. The train had stopped. It had been standing there for hours. Yankele couldn't sit still.

"Mama, can I go out for a little while?"

"No! God forbid! The train could start moving any minute!"

"But that's what you said this morning!"

"We've been told not to go out. The train could start up, and whoever couldn't get back on in time would be left behind in the snow."

Yes, there was snow on the ground again. Summer had passed. The Crimea was far behind them. The sunshine, the clear, blue skies, the abundance of fruits and vegetables, the clusters of grapes, and the figs that grew in the warm southern valleys — all this was behind them now, fading into the distance as if it had never existed.

"But Mama, why are we always standing still?"

"I have no idea, son. They say they need the tracks for trains going to the front. And maybe . . . maybe they've been bombed somewhere and they're fixing them. When they finish we'll get moving."

And as if to confirm what she had said, the car moved a bit. A slight lurch, then another. It seemed as if they were starting up. Through the half-open door trees could be seen moving backward and disappearing. A tree heavily laden with snow entered the picture frame, withdrew, and was gone, and a new tree intruded in its place. With wheels screeching, the train moved along the track like a giant snake that had awakened from its slumber.

"Great!" said Yankele. "We're finally moving! If only we could really get going!"

But the steam engine plodded slowly along as if dozing. A tired snake, almost asleep.

"Hey, you there by the door, would you mind closing it?" a woman called from the end of the car. "It's cold in here!"

A young man, who stood gazing out, called to her, "Not yet,

70

comrade. It's not even crawling yet. We'll have plenty of time to suffocate here together once it really gets going!"

He took a long drag on the remains of a cigarette and tossed it out into the soft snow. "If my leg can get along in the cold the way it's packed," he said, tapping on the cast on his right leg, "then you, in your rags, should be sitting pretty!"

The train continued to creep along. It was in no hurry to get anywhere. Srulik curled up in his coat and retied the earflaps of his hat under his chin.

"Mama, why don't we have a stove? It's awfully cold!"

"This isn't a passenger car," said Bella, "it's a freight car. Freight doesn't need heat."

"Or windows either!" declared the man near the door. "They take on people like animals, with a bucket for a toilet, no windows . . ."

An elderly man who was rolling himself a cigarette in the corner of the car looked up and said, "Be happy you got a ride! You could be out there in the snow, or doing hard labor for the Germans, curse them! You think they'd care a whit about your leg?"

"Any other complaints?" the woman yelled from the end of the car. "Things are provided for our soldiers, the Red Army, our boys — God bless them — and you stand there smoking and complaining!"

The young man fell silent. Yes, he knew: it was risky to complain here in the fatherland, even in wartime. One loose word could cost you dearly.

"When we had a stove, it didn't give any heat at all," Yankele said to Srulik. "It just made a lot of smoke, and we all got black from the soot. You could only get a little heat if you sat practically on top of it. I wouldn't mind sitting in this car if it would only get moving!"

But as if out of spite, the engine ground to a halt with a great sigh. The train was standing still again. They were just switching tracks. On the track that was now clear another train began to

71

move, its cars all sealed up. Its wheels clattered faster and faster — clackety-clack, clackety-clack, whoosh! — and it disappeared.

"You think there's snow in the Crimea now too?" Srulik asked.

Yankele shrugged. "Dunno. It was like summer when we left, so hot."

"If there's snow," Srulik went on, "what are Vanka and Stanka eating?"

"The Tatar must be taking care of them," Yankele declared. "He promised! He told me not to worry."

Yes, the same Tatar goatherd had bought the kids again, this time from Mama. Dirt cheap, of course. He had bought the nanny goat too, for practically nothing. When you're abandoning your home to pick up and run away somewhere you can't quibble about prices. Mama took the few rubles the goatherd was willing to give her, packed food and clothing, and set out once more — this time without Papa but with her friend Bella, Srulik, and little Feigele, who was Sarele's age. For months now they had been moving eastward.

"Do you think Boris is playing with them?" Srulik asked.

Yankele wiped his nose on his sleeve. "How should I know? Do you think the Germans let people play? Maybe they don't even allow non-Jewish children to play!"

Srulik said nothing. They both remembered what Boris had said, "We Russians have nothing to fear —" Suddenly he had seen them as *"yids,"* not as the two boys he had known. Why did things change so drastically as soon as Hitler arrived on the scene?

Yankele emerged from his reverie. "Even if they let Boris play with Vanka and Stanka, they're not as cute as they once were."

Srulik was surprised. "Why do you say that?"

"Papa said they'd grow up to be billy goats, and they must be grown up by now, so that's that. Anyway, when we get to the east we're sure to get new kids, even cuter ones," Yankele

72

said defiantly, his heart seized with longing for the twin kids they had left behind in the Crimea.

"You think they have kids in Bukhara and Tashkent?"

"Somebody told me they have everything there. Even camels. Do you remember the picture of the camel that we saw in the book?"

"Yes, but do you think they have . . . little ones, babies . . . tiny things that were just born, like our Vanka and Stanka?"

"Sure they do. All animals do! They must have tiny camels, cute little things. You'll see, it'll be nice there."

Suddenly the engine gave a long whistle. The people in the car looked up: Is it ours? Not ours? Ours! The train began to move. A tree white with snow appeared once again in the frame of the half-open door, withdrew, and left the picture, and a new tree took its place. Faster, faster. The long snake was stirring again from its slumber. A cold wind came through the doorway, blowing snowflakes into the car. Those standing nearby shut it quickly. The cars rattled along the track, the engine whistled again. Finally they were really moving. Onward! Eastward! On and on to the east!

Nine

At night Yankele mumbled in his sleep. Mama, worried, felt his forehead. No doubt about it, he had a fever.

Oh no! Mama thought. *Anything but this!*

An epidemic was raging aboard the train: diphtheria. Those affected were mainly infants and small children, but the disease struck adults too, especially the old and the weak. It would appear first in the form of a headache, a sore throat, and a low

73

fever; but then it would rip off its mild mask and reveal itself in its full virulence. The first child to have come down with it in their car was already buried somewhere in the deep snow, near an unknown station where they had made a brief stop. At first he had breathed with difficulty, then choked and turned blue. He gasped for breath and finally died of suffocation. Two infants and a little girl followed in his footsteps. The strange, repulsive odor of the disease still hung in the car. It rose from the choked-up throats of additional victims who lay helpless on the baggage.

Why him? He's such a strong boy. The doctor in the Urals said he could withstand anything.

Yankele mumbled again, pushing off the blanket Mama had wrapped around him. In the darkness, Mama caught sight of Sarele's face. The little girl was quiet, sleeping deeply to the rhythm of the wheels.

Why him? Sarele — may she be well! — is the weaker of the two, and Bella's Feigele and Srulik — may they too be well! — are much weaker than Yankele. So why him? Or maybe it's just a cold, and the fever will be gone by morning. O dear God, Mama pleaded, *let the fever be gone by morning!*

But in the morning the fever was still there. Yankele's head felt heavy. His throat started to hurt. Why was there no doctor on the train? Why was there no medicine?

The train stopped somewhere in the snowy vastness.

"This is going to be a long one!" said the old man, climbing back into the car. "Damn it, you can't even find a cigarette!" He had used up his tobacco some time before, and he had very few Majorca cigarette papers left either.

"How do you know it's going to be long?" Bella asked him.

"I walked all the way up to the engine. I spoke to the engineer, and he said —"

"What did he say?"

"He said they bombed the railway line near Uralsk. Evidently it's serious. We'll have to wait a long time until it's fixed."

74

"A whole day?"

"Maybe a day, maybe two days, who knows?"

"Here in the snow? There's no way to heat up water for the sick or to buy bread. If we were only at a station. But in the middle of nowhere . . ."

"Got a gripe, comrade?" the man asked, kicking the snow off his boots in the doorway. "If you don't like the accommodations, go somewhere else!" He gestured toward the expanse of white snow. Mama looked up. Somewhere off in the distance, smoke rose from a chimney, then another — the hint of a village. Maybe there would be a doctor there? Maybe there some medicine could be found? She decided on the spot.

"Bella," she said, already wrapping herself up in Papa's big coat, "I'm going to the village. Maybe there's a doctor there. Keep an eye on —"

"No need even to ask," Bella interrupted her. "Of course I'll look after them. What a question!"

Mama jumped heavily out of the doorway of the high freight car. The deep snow broke her fall. She shook the snow off her sleeves, tightened the kerchief on her head, and set out, a tiny moving dot in the vast desert of snow.

At noon she returned, the dot growing bigger, advancing with weighty determination across the white expanse. It was with great difficulty that she climbed back up into the car, sinking down exhausted next to Yankele and examining his face. His eyes were shut, he was breathing heavily, noisily. Yes, there could be no doubt: here were all the symptoms the doctor had asked about. Mama pulled off a glove and put her hand to his forehead. Right, the fever was not especially high. It was diphtheria without a doubt!

Bella helped her off with her coat. "Did you get any medicine?" she asked. Mama replied with difficulty. The effort of the long hike and the bitter cold had worn her out.

"She didn't have any left!" she said at last. "Only cough syrup."

"Did she give it to you?"

"Yes, she gives it to everyone. She said it might not do any good, but it wouldn't do any harm. I got bread too, a few boiled potatoes, and hot water in a jug."

Yankele opened his eyes, two dark spots on his pale face. A reddish-brown curl stuck to his white brow. "Mama!"

"Yes, Yankele, I'm here. I brought you medicine. Drink it up, and you'll get well."

She helped him sit up a bit.

"Here, I've filled the spoon."

Yankele opened his mouth. The sweet, sticky fluid slid into his throat. He made an effort and swallowed it. He had almost forgotten the taste of sweetness. It was sweet like Grandma's sugar cubes, like honey, like dried Crimean figs, sweet, so sweet.

Mama turned to fill the tin cup with the hot water she had brought. It had not yet lost all its heat, and even warm water is good for a sore throat. Suddenly Yankele grabbed the medicine bottle and put it to his lips. The liquid that slipped down his throat was sweet, so sweet! He drank it down to the last drop. It would drive away the pain and help him breathe, and he would get well, all well!

But by nightfall his breathing was labored and noisy. He lay with his eyes closed and wheezed, as if suffocating, thirsty for every breath. Mama watched him in despair. Unwittingly she breathed deeply with each breath the child took, as if trying to infuse the elixir of life into him through the tightening muscles of his throat. She took him in her arms to make it easier for him to breathe. She took one step and almost fell. People were lying about on the floor of the car. She knew she mustn't just let him lie there but that she had to walk with him, at least walk with him. She had to do something. She wasn't going to lose her Yankele!

"Put the blanket over him!" she said to Bella suddenly. "Help me get him out of the car!"

"Out of the car? What's the matter with you, Rosa? Have you gone mad? To take him outside? In the snow?"

"Not in the snow, Bella, to the engine!"

"The engine?"

"Yes. Help me, Bella, and don't ask any questions. Hurry!"

Grimacing with effort, Bella lowered the bundled-up boy into his mother's outstretched arms. She saw Rosa walk along the track and disappear in the darkness. She shook her head. *Crazy,* she thought. *Out of her mind with grief.*

A glimmer of light shone from the engine. The head of the silent train-dragon was glowing in the dark. The boilers were stoked and lit. If they were to let the fire go out the water would freeze in the pipes, and it would be impossible to start up again. In front of the boiler compartment there was a platform for the mechanic in charge of firing up the engine. It was hot as a bathhouse in there now; the steam that wafted into the cab filled it with heat. A woman emerged from the darkness and bitter cold and lumbered up the narrow ladder leading to the upper part of the engine.

"Hey, what do you think you're doing here, comrade?" a deep voice boomed. The woman looked up. A heavyset man loomed above her in the cab. He had a salt-and-pepper mustache and wore a big fur hat and a gray military tunic.

"Did you think this was open to the public, comrade?" the man asked. "This isn't the town square, you know! I think you've got the wrong address!"

The woman looked into his eyes. Though they were overshadowed by a prominent forehead and thick, dark eyebrows, they were blue and shiny. No, he wouldn't refuse her. He couldn't!

"Take the boy!" she said abruptly. "Put him in the doorway, near the boiler, near the steam engine. Let him breathe the hot air! Let him breathe the steam! The child is suffocating!"

The motorman gaped at her. She held the boy out to him,

urging, pressing. Unthinkingly, he reached out and took hold of the child. The woman climbed up into the cab.

"Here!" she said, pointing to the narrow platform. "This is the place!"

He put the boy on the floor, then straightened up with difficulty and turned to the woman. She was small and thin and wrapped in a man's coat that was too big for her, and she had a dark woolen scarf on her head. He could hardly see her face, but he saw her eyes, which had in them an irresistible determination and stubbornness.

"We won't get moving until morning, right?" the woman asked.

"Right," said the motorman. "This was a serious bombing, and they're fixing the track. But —"

"Then that's that!" the woman said, interrupting him. "The boy stays here. It's freezing in the car. How do you expect him to get well in such cold? He's staying here!"

Now the motorman noticed the boy's labored breathing. He was tossing restlessly from side to side. The woman took the blanket off him. It was hot in the narrow passageway. She sat down and squeezed in next to him, her back to the wall, her knees to her chest. She glanced up at the motorman standing over her and looked down again.

The man shrugged and turned back to his cabin in front of the engine. *Leonid,* he thought tenderly, *where are you, my dear son? Your mother was left behind in Stalingrad, in the siege. She guarded you like delicate china, and now you are fighting somewhere in the cold, in the snow, and who knows whether we will ever see you again?*

He took a handkerchief out of his pocket and blew his nose again and again. *"Goddam war!"*

In the morning the woman took her son back to their car. He was breathing easily, his throat clear. Once the train got under way he slept deeply, the sleep of recovery.

*   *   *

78

The train came to a halt somewhere in the heart of the white wilderness. There was nothing but snowy desolation round about, no city, no village, not even an isolated house. Now there was no reason to stop. No one had bombed the railway, the track was intact, and there was enough coal for another day's journey. But they had to stop. That night many infants and children, as well as an old woman and two old men, had died of diphtheria. The train stopped so that people could bury their dead. It only stopped briefly. They had to move on, so that they could get off the track at the next station to make way for another train.

Bella dug in the deep snow with her bare hands, her eyes blinded by tears. Srulik lay still before her. He had wheezed all night, choked in her arms the whole night long struggling for breath. The train kept on going, and the miracle could not be repeated. The train kept going even when he stopped breathing, when he lay still, when his body began to grow cold, began to freeze. It did not stop until morning, and then only briefly, and now Bella was digging and digging. The hole was already ample for the little body that lay before her, but Bella dug on, trying to reach the ground. Even if she had, she would have had neither the tools nor the time to dig a grave for her son.

Yankele watched her from inside the car. He was still weak, and it was only with difficulty that he was able to stand up and make his way to the open door. The thing that lay there near Bella could not possibly be his Srulik! A tiny, dark spot on the white snow. Only yesterday he had spoken to him, and the day before that they had chatted. Srulik had talked again of the camels in Tashkent. He had asked if they had wings too, like the horse in the storybook, and Bella had felt his forehead worriedly. Afterward, when he could no longer talk, Yankele had promised him he could have his pocketknife for a whole day.

"A whole day, Srulik, I swear! But you've got to get well! You can do whatever you want with it, use both blades if you like.

You can even have it for more than a day, even three or four days, only get well!"

But Srulik would never get well. Srulik lay in the white pit his mother had dug for him. Now she had to cover him up, cover him quickly, because the engine was already whistling. The train could not tarry, it had to move on, and in another minute it would start up.

The whistle blew again. Bella began to push the snow into the hole. The people who were outside hauled themselves up into the freight cars. The engine gave a third blast and started to inch forward. Bella stepped back as if awakening from a bad dream. She ran for the car. The snow was deep, and Bella's body was heavy. She was slipping back into her dream again. For her, it was reality. Her friend Rosa stood in the doorway with Feigele in her arms. Suddenly the little girl reached out and cried, "Ma—ma!!!"

"Hurry!" Yankele shouted. "Hurry!"

But Bella stumbled and fell in the snow.

"Try to catch up with us!" Rosa cried. "You'll find us on the way east, in Tashkent, in Bukhara, or somewhere else in the east! I'll take care of Feigele! Don't worry, Bella, I'll look after the child!"

The train picked up speed. One figure after another emerged from behind the snowdrifts. People were trying to catch up with the train, waving their arms — but in vain. The train didn't stop. Those who had had trouble parting with their dead were left behind.

Someone called out from within the dark car, "Hey, you there, close the door! We're moving!"

The old man slid the door shut and threw the latch. "God, it's cold," he grumbled, as though apologizing. He looked at Feigele, who was wailing. "It's all right, sweetheart," he added, wiping her wet cheek hesitantly with his finger. "Mama will catch up with us. She'll find us."

80

Rosa sank down onto the baggage. She hugged Feigele, who was four. Sarele snuggled up to her, and Yankele lay down at her feet again, exhausted. She had three children now.

"Mama will catch up with us," she said to the toddler in her arms, and as if trying to convince herself she said over and over again, "Feigele, my little bird, she'll find us yet. She'll find us . . ."

The morning began in the usual way, with bombing. There was never the slightest warning. The German Stuka planes would appear out of nowhere and swoop down over the train like a swarm of angry hornets. The motorman would stop; it was too dangerous to continue. The train, moving or standing still, was an easy target, but when it stopped, people could at least get off and run for cover. Everyone would jump off the cars and run and hide: under the snow-laden trees, behind hillocks, wherever they could. The Stukas would rain down their bombs, two or three with each sortie, and disappear into the gray sky. If the passengers were lucky and no damage was done, they would all get back on the train, which then continued on its eastward journey. But if luck was against them and the track or one of the cars was damaged, they would have to stay put and wait until someone came to make repairs.

The first time he had to jump out of the car, Yankele hung back. The doorway was high off the ground, and the track itself was on a raised embankment. A chasm yawned at his feet. Someone pushed him from behind and he jumped against his will, falling onto the slope of the embankment and rolling down through the snow into a ditch. He picked himself up and looked back. Mama stood in the doorway, Sarele in her arms. A young woman came out of the dark interior of the car and jumped down without hesitation, hugging Feigele.

"Jump!" she called to Mama from the ditch. Mama, too, jumped and then rolled down the slope. The snow was deep and soft, and no one was hurt.

"Run! Get away! Get away from the train!" someone cried, off in the distance.

The plane came back and dived. Yankele had the feeling it was coming after him, just him, and he ran with all his might, his hair standing on end. He ran, stumbled and fell, got up and ran some more, climbing the slope of the hill. Then he heard the whistle of the bomb dropping, coming toward him. He put his fingers in his ears, shut his eyes, and froze like a rabbit under hot pursuit. A flash and a terrific boom. Big clumps of snow fell from the trees. The bomb had fallen not far from the track. This time it had missed.

By now he was almost used to it. He was eight years old, a big boy, and children his age could take care of themselves. After all, Mama had to look after Sarah and Feigele! Now he would jump as far as he could, in order to get a head start. Once he jumped on a man's back, holding on to his neck, and they fell together, separated, rolled down the slope, and rushed for cover. When the danger was past and everyone was getting back on the train, he could no longer remember on whose back he had ridden.

Yes, this morning had begun the way they always did, with bombing.

A muffled explosion was heard in the distance. The engine braked, the train slowed down, and everyone prepared to flee. Mama held on to Sarele and looked at Yankele, pale. The young woman picked up Feigele and pushed her way to the door. Before the train even came to a halt, they pulled the latch and slid the door aside, and the big doorway opened wide. Yankele was pushed from behind and thrust forward. He saw people's backs and dark coats. He was squeezed from all sides. And suddenly he was at the edge. He jumped off into the clear, cold air, landed in the snow, and rolled down, bumping into one of the passengers from the car ahead. Then the approaching bomber was heard. It shot out of the gray skies behind them, turned, and came in low. Now it was coming toward them, diving straight for the track, straight for the train, straight for the fleeing passengers. Yankele tried to run, but he sank up to his knees in the deep snow. He heard the whistle of the bomb and threw himself into the soft whiteness. The sound of a blast came from the other side of the train, echoing among the white hills.

"He'll be back!" the other passenger called out. "What are you standing there for? Run, boy, run!"

Yankele began to climb the hill toward the forest. The white slope was dotted with dark spots moving away from the stricken train.

"Hurry!" the man shouted, holding out his hand. "He's coming!"

He pulled the boy toward the trees, where they could take cover under the bower of snow. But they were too late. The plane came back, appearing over the ridge of the hill. It dived even lower, lower than ever before. The man threw himself face down in the snow, pulling Yankele along with him. The roar of the motors came closer and closer, as if the bomber were going to land right on top of them. They waited for the whistle of the bomb, but then there was a different sound, a volley of gunshots. Someone up there was raking them with machine-gun fire.

Yankele saw the snow spatter: a hole and then another hole. A row of little holes was coming rapidly toward them, piercing the crunchy snow. A hole near the man's thigh, a hole in his back, a hole in his shoulder, a hole in the snow near his head, and then the spattering trailed off somewhere and disappeared. The man's body was convulsed by the first bullet and again by the second, but then it no longer moved. Blood began to ooze from his coat. The red liquid flowed out into the whiteness and was absorbed. The plane flew off and disappeared.

Yankele got up and began to run. He ran as fast as he could, ran to the forest, ran to the cover of the trees, ran until his strength was used up, until he collapsed and sat down under a big fir tree. He listened to the beating of his heart: ta–*dum*, ta–*dum*, ta–*dum!*

It was a long time before his heartbeat returned to normal. Little by little, it slowed down. Then he heard the silence, the silence of the forest, the silence of the world. A laden-down branch suddenly released its load of snow and sprang up, and the silence returned. He felt smaller than ever, alone, abandoned. He stood up and began to retrace his steps. His footprints in the snow were deep and clear. All at once he wanted to see Mama, immediately! He wanted to be in the crowded car, to hear the endless clatter of the wheels, to see Sarele and Feigele. He wanted to tell a boy who had just gotten on two days before how the man had shook and bled and how the blood had run out. And again he wanted to see Mama, and the terrible silence pursued him, pressed in on him from every side.

Sinking into the snow with each step, he climbed up the little rise. Beyond it were the valley and the track. The train, their car, and Mama. He reached the top and looked down. The valley was spread out at his feet. The dark track stretched off into the distance and disappeared behind the mountain. But the train was not there. The car was gone, and with it Mama and Sarele. Nothing was left. Not a soul remained behind.

PART TWO
Yasha

Ten

The track was empty, just the two rails extending off into the snowy hills and disappearing around the bend. I wished it were only a dream, a bad dream, and that in a moment I would awaken and see the train, the car, Mama, and Sarele. But I knew it was no dream and that I was wide awake.

On the other hand, I might simply have made a mistake and come to the wrong place. Maybe the train was hidden just ahead, behind the hill! I was about to run on when suddenly I saw the man. He lay face down in the snow, motionless. Near his shoulder I saw a blood stain, a patch of red on the white snow. It was the man who had been running alongside me, who had pulled me along when the bombing started. And we hadn't managed to get very far from the train. So I hadn't made a mistake after all. The train had stood right there!

"Hey, kid, did they leave you behind too?"

I froze with fear. Who was that — the dead man?

"Why so scared, little boy? They left me here too!"

Now I saw who it was. A tall, thin man was climbing up the other side of the embankment. He limped, dragging his right foot.

"What's your name, son?"

"Yankele," I gasped.

"What? What's that?"

Something caught in my throat, like tears that wanted to flow and couldn't. I tried to swallow them and raised my voice.

"Yasha! My name is Yasha!"*

"Yasha? I'm Sergei. Well, what are we going to do? I guess we're on our own here, eh? Who was with you on the train?"

"Mama," I said, choking on my tears. "Mama and Sarele and Feigele . . ."

The man looked at me and wrinkled his forehead. He had a tangle of scary-looking eyebrows. Like a magician I had seen once in the ghetto street, except that he had kindly eyes.

"Well, never mind, never mind," he said, patting my shoulder. "You'll find them all eventually. You'll find your mama. She didn't just disappear into thin air. She must have gone somewhere, don't you think?"

Maybe he really is a magician! I thought. *Maybe he's a magician, and if I tell him where Mama went he'll just clap his hands and pull the engine and the train out of his sleeve, drawing out one car after another until ours appears, and Mama will be there, and Sarele, and . . .* But I didn't know exactly where she had gone.

"She said we were going east, to Kazakhst . . . Kazakhst . . ." I couldn't remember the exact name.

"Kazakhstan!" Sergei said. "Kazakhstan isn't just a place, it's a huge country. Where in Kazakhstan? Maybe it was Uzbekistan?"

I nodded.

"That's better. Now what city were you going to? Didn't she say? Bukhara? Tashkent? Or could it have been Samarkand?"

"Yes! She mentioned all those names to Bella, but she wasn't sure which place the train would take us to."

"Well," said Sergei, "nowadays no one knows where the wind is going to blow him. So we'll stay together at least as far as the

---

*Yasha is the diminutive of the Russian Yakov; Yankele is the diminutive of the Yiddish Yankev; both are derived from the Hebrew Ya'akov (English: Jacob).

next station. I bet the train is standing there waiting for us. That train always stood still more than it moved anyway."

Too bad, I thought, *too bad he's not a magician. But he's right: our train sometimes pulled off onto sidetracks and often stood waiting for days while they repaired the tracks or until troop trains or army freight trains or trains with red crosses on them that carried the wounded went by.*

"Let's get a move on, Yasha!" Sergei said, turning to go. "We'd better be on our way."

I looked at the man lying in the snow. Sergei stopped and looked at him too. He squinted and rubbed his cheeks. "Hold on!" he said. "I'll be right back."

He limped up the slope to the man. He looked at him for a while, then bent down and turned him over on his back like a rag doll.

"Dead!" he shouted to me. "Dead as a doornail!"

He began pulling at the sleeve of the dead man's coat, tugging and cursing until he got the sleeve off. Then he turned the man over and pulled the other sleeve off. Like a rag doll in the snow.

"They did him in, the buggers!" Sergei said apologetically as he climbed back up the embankment. "There's nothing to be done. It'll rot in the snow anyway, so it might as well do us some good!"

I didn't know what he was talking about, the coat or the corpse. Actually, it didn't much matter. I was already used to seeing corpses. I knew that Sergei was right. In fact, I'd known it for a while. But something was welling up inside of me, and suddenly it burst out and I shouted, "Ma–ma!"

Sergei laid his hand on my shoulder. "Yasha," he said softly, "she can't hear you from here. You've got to go look for her."

I looked around: nothing but snow and more snow, and not a sign of Mama. A cold wind was blowing in the hills, howling through the trees and disappearing into the distance. "Ma–ma!"

"Come, Yasha," Sergei said again. "Let's go look for your mama. Maybe we'll find her at the next station!"

89

Eleven

We got to the station that evening. The square in front of it and the platform inside swarmed with people. It looked like all the other stations I had seen, full of people with bundles and suitcases who sat and waited days on end, sometimes weeks, for a train to take them away. But one little thing made this station different: Mama was there, on the train that stood inside.

It was hard to get through the crowd and the baggage. I reached out and took Sergei's hand.

"Let's ask, Yasha," said Sergei, squeezing my hand understandingly. "You're going to find your mother and I'm going to find my poor suitcase. When I find it I'll be off to Orsk, and you and your mother will head for warmer places."

Getting to the information window was no easy matter. People were sleeping, covered with coats and gray blankets, on the wooden floor of the station. On the far side a single lamp was lit. It was painted blue because of the blackout, so that enemy planes would not see it at night. Its light barely reached the closed information window.

"Wouldn't you know it!" Sergei grumbled. "Let's look outside."

Carefully, he climbed down to the empty tracks, then reached up and lowered me as well. I looked around. Way off in the darkness I saw a train parked. Sergei began limping across the tracks. Again I took his hand. I held on tight, the way I did with Papa. Suddenly I wanted Papa to be next to me, so badly did I want to feel his big, rough palm and to smell the smell of wood in his clothes, the smell of sawdust and carpenter's glue. There was that strange, suffocating lump in my throat again. I could hardly hold back my tears.

The train stood on a sidetrack. I squinted. *My God, that's it! That's our train!*

I let go of Sergei's hand and broke into a run. I crossed one set of tracks, then another. In another minute I would see Mama. Mama!

But before I got there I realized this was not our train. Its freight cars had no doors, no roofs. They were the kind of cars you loaded coal and timber and God knows what else onto from above. Everything but people. It wasn't our train!

Sergei caught up with me. He spit between the rails.

"Hell, from back there I was sure this was it!"

In the darkness, a man came out from among the cars and turned toward us. "Hey, you there, are you crazy? What do you think you're doing on the tracks? You're not allowed down here! Go right back!"

Dumbstruck, I clung to Sergei's leg and didn't say a word.

"We're looking for our train!" Sergei shouted.

"Are you crazy, man? On the tracks? A train could come through here any minute!"

Way off in the darkness, there was a change of signal lights.

"Just tell me, comrade," said Sergei, stepping backward, "did a freight train loaded with people come through here this morning?"

"A freight train? Lots of them came through here!"

"A train with people on board. It was coming from Uralsk, headed for Tashkent."

"We did have one bound for Tashkent. It stopped and then went on."

"Are you sure it's gone?" Sergei asked insistently. "It's not here on a sidetrack?"

The man raised his voice, almost shouting. "No! There's no train with people here! And you'd better get out of here, damn you! Now! If you don't, I'll call the police!"

The rails began to rumble. I recognized the sound: a train was coming.

"Run!" Sergei cried. "Get a move on!"

I could hardly see a thing. I tried to guess where the tracks were so I could jump over them. Anything not to trip on the tracks! I heard Sergei's footsteps. He was limping along behind me. At last! We made it! Here was the platform, but it was high, so high! How would I ever get up onto it? Now I heard the train coming. I reached up to the wooden platform, jumped, and hoisted myself up. There! Now Sergei!

The train whistled.

"Sergei!" I shouted as loud as I could. "Hurry! Hurry!"

Sergei tripped on the last rail and almost fell. His outstretched hands rested on the edge of the platform.

I heard the train approaching fast. There was a sudden gust of wind.

"Climb up!" I cried.

At the very last moment Sergei pulled himself up onto the platform.

With a tremendous roar and a screech of metal wheels the train went by, right by us. A fast, dark train, like a great monster, making earsplitting noises. One car, then another, then another.

Then it was over. The train went by, sped away, and vanished into the darkness. The terrible roar faded, and the wind died down.

Sergei cursed over and over. He was huffing and puffing. "Damn it! Damn it! I just about . . ."

I was shaking all over. "You just about got run over!" I said, snuggling up to him. "You just about got run over!"

Sergei too was trembling. "Damn! Damn!" he kept saying. "Damn! I just about . . ."

Twelve

That night we slept on the floor of the station, under the dead man's coat. It was cold. I snuggled up to Sergei's back and tried to fall asleep. Now and then I suppose I caught a few winks, but the trains kept roaring through, startling me in the darkness. I wanted to get up and run away, run to Mama, but Sergei turned over and held me.

"Go to sleep, Yasha, go to sleep. That's not Mama's train. She's not here. You'll find her tomorrow." He hugged me and stroked my head. "Sleep, child, sleep."

"Mama," I mumbled, "Mama." Hot tears gathered under my closed eyes. "Mama!" I whispered, but my sleepiness got the better of me, and I sank into oblivion.

Mama was smiling at me through the steam of the samovar.

"Come, Yankele," she said, "come and have some tea, hot tea."

"Me first!" Sarele declared, fluttering into the room. "I'm always first, because I'm the littlest!"

Mama gave me a slice of bread, but Sarele's doll opened its big mouth and swallowed it whole.

Mama said, "Get out of here, little girl! This is for Yankele!"

She reached out to me and said again, "This is for my Yankele."

"Mama!" I said, wanting to tell her everything. "Mama!"

But suddenly there was a sharp whistle, and Mama disappeared. The big loudspeaker began to make sounds, as if coming to life; the blanket slipped off, and I started to get cold. I opened my eyes and saw Sergei sitting next to me. He was holding the coat. No, it wasn't a blanket after all. Mama had the blanket, and Mama was far away. Sergei looked at the loudspeaker.

Now a woman's voice came out of the loudspeaker. I didn't understand a word she was saying. It was names, names of places. But not Tashkent. I didn't hear Tashkent. People were getting up and hurriedly packing up their belongings, closing their suitcases.

"It's to Orsk!" said Sergei, getting up. "The train to Orsk is coming!"

I looked around. It was daybreak, and a pale light shone across the ceiling of the station from the direction of the tracks. People were beginning to crowd toward the edge of the platform.

Now things happened quickly. The approaching train whistled. Sergei got up and began fumbling in his pockets.

"This is my train," he said. "I've got to go. But you mustn't take it. You're going to Tashkent. Remember, Tashkent! That's where you'll find your mother, there or somewhere around there. Maybe even on the way there!"

What was going on? Mama was nowhere to be seen, but the dream went on and on.

"Goodbye, Yasha!" Sergei said to me.

Now I was wide awake.

"But what about your suitcase?" I said. "It's on Mama's train!"

"To hell with the damned suitcase!" said Sergei. "I'll never find it anyway!"

He rummaged through his pockets some more, then turned the pockets of the dead man's coat inside out. They were empty. The train pulled into the station and ground to a halt. Sergei said loudly, "Too bad. I wanted to leave you something to eat. We polished everything off yesterday, didn't we?"

I didn't answer. I couldn't. The train had stopped. People had begun to swarm into the cars. Sergei patted my shoulder and cried, "So long, Yasha. Good luck! Say hello to your mother for me!"

Then he turned and disappeared into the crowd squeezing onto the train. It was then that I recovered my voice.

"Sergei!" I cried. "Sergei!"

I don't think he heard me. Everyone was shouting. Someone pushed me, and I nearly fell. I grabbed a pillar and clung to it

94

for dear life. Again the whistle blew, and the train began to move. In the open entranceways and on the steps, knots of people were still trying to push their way in. I thought I saw Sergei in the entrance to one of the cars. The train picked up speed. Someone tripped and fell onto the platform. Luckily he wasn't hurt and quickly got up. Car after car. Here was the last one. Now the train looked like a single car receding into the dim, bluish light. It had taken Sergei from me, and now I was left alone, completely alone.

Again I felt the lump rising in my throat, choking me, and suddenly I burst into tears and began to cry aloud, like a little child. I cried and cried, but no one came to comfort me. People came and went, but no one came over. No one.

Thirteen

What was I going to do? I knew the tickets were cheap, very cheap, but I didn't have a penny to my name. I had seen people sneak aboard the trains without tickets, but the conductors almost always caught them. If they had money they would buy their tickets on the spot and pay the fine. But if not the conductor would throw them off at the next stop, straight into the waiting arms of the police!

No, the police had never detained us. We always had everything in order. Mama would take care of everything: documents, tickets, food, a place to sleep. But now I was on my own. The main thing was to get to Mama as quickly as possible, to find her, so that I wouldn't have to worry about anything anymore.

I grew hungrier and hungrier. I started to wander around the station. In the square outside I heard a woman calling. She must have been selling something. I went to the gate.

"*Pirushkes!*" she announced. "Fresh dumplings!"

Dumplings! I was sure they would be potato dumplings, just like Mama made, or cheese dumplings or maybe even blackberry. My mouth watered: sweet blackberries, with lots of sugar. But no, this wasn't the season. They must be potato filled!

I went through the gate and looked around. On the other side of the square, near the wall of a house, sat a woman as fat as a barrel. She was wrapped in a gray wool coat and had a gray kerchief on her head. From a distance she looked like a big ball of faded wool. I made my way around the people sitting on their bags and went over to the peddler. She had a little pan of coals in front of her. She was warming her feet on the pan while keeping a sharp eye on the dumplings, which lay next to her on an old trunk.

"Dumplings!" she cried, over and over again. "Fresh dumplings!"

Now I could smell them. I swallowed again and again. I couldn't help wondering what was in them, potatoes or cheese. Too bad, I would never find out.

A blast of cold wind came out of the alley nearby. Well, at least I could warm up a little. I crouched down, took my hands out of my pockets, and held them, red and frozen, over the pan of coals. I had no mittens. I'd left them on the train.

The woman looked at me suspiciously. She had little beady eyes that seemed to have been squeezed in among the folds of fat. She suddenly waved her hand and began shrieking, "Get out of here, boy! Away with you!"

She was talking to me!

"Away with you, you rascal, or I'll call the police!"

Frightened, I got up and began to move back. I didn't understand: I hadn't done anything, not a thing!

A man with a gray beard butted in. "Why are you chasing

the boy away? It's freezing. At least let him warm up a bit. He's not bothering you!"

"Oh no?" the woman shouted. "I know these little gangsters! They stand around pretending to warm up, taking the place of customers, and when you turn away for a second they snatch your merchandise and run! And try catching them! It's easier to catch the wind!"

My eyes were filled with tears of humiliation: I hadn't touched a thing! I hadn't stolen!

I turned back toward the station. Suddenly, through the bars in the gate, I saw a train rolling into the station. A freight train! It hadn't whistled, there had been no announcement over the loudspeaker, and yet here it was. Maybe Mama had come back? Maybe they had been waiting on a side track after all and were now getting ready to move on? I began running toward the train, jumping over baggage and sidestepping people. I got stuck, ran on, then bumped into something and fell. The train was picking up speed again now, and the cars were going by faster and faster. I got up and looked at the last car as it was going by. I had run for nothing: the car was open to the sky; it was just another coal train.

There was nothing to be done; Mama was a long way off by now, and I was lost. *Lost!* The word kept flashing in my mind. *Lost!* Papa had told me once — when was it? What exactly had he said? — Yes, Papa had told me, "If you get lost we will look for you, and you will look for us, until we find each other." I couldn't remember when he had said it, but, yes, that was what he had said.

But Papa was far away too, at the front, and he couldn't look for me. He didn't even know that I was lost. Mama knew, but Mama couldn't look for me either. She had Sarele with her, and Bella's little Feigele too. She couldn't just go looking in all the stations. I knew that I would have to do the looking. If Papa had said so, we were sure to meet up. I would find Mama!

97

Fourteen

Hunger was gnawing at me now like a hole in my belly, like an open wound. I couldn't just sit there waiting for the train, so I wandered around the station.

I went back to the gate, but this time I didn't go out. I was afraid that the train to Tashkent would come, and I was also scared of the woman with the dumplings. Did she really think I was a thief?

A tall man, thin and bent over, came through the gate. He didn't have any bundles or suitcases, just an open carton under one arm. He held the carton close to his body as if it were something precious. As he made his way through the crowd he was mumbling softly. I wondered what was in the box.

I caught up with him and peeked in. Chocolate! A bunch of chocolate bars! Again my mouth began to water: sweet chocolate, the kind that melts in your mouth, the kind Papa used to buy in the Crimea, so sweet . . .

Mama never bought me chocolate. "No! No chocolate!" she would say. "You should eat real food: bread, potatoes, milk. What do you need chocolate for?"

Everyone there seemed to see it that way, because, although the chocolate was quite cheap, what they wanted was bread. In fact no one went up to the man. I would have bought from him if I had only had something to barter. I searched my pockets. What did I have? I had jumped off the train with my coat, hat, and boots — these I always had on; in the car I never took them off — but there was nothing in my coat. Hiking up my coattails I began to go through my pants pockets. Then, even before I came upon it, I thought of it: the pocketknife! In my left pocket I had the German officer's knife, the one I had found in the ghetto, in Lodz.

Gripping it in my pocket, I thought: this I'll never give up! I had hidden it all the way to the border; no German had ever discovered it. Later it had made a king of me. Even in the Urals all the children had wanted to touch it, or at least to look at it, and in the Crimea it had made me the most popular boy in the neighborhood even before I got Vanka and Stanka back. They would have given me anything to touch that knife, to use it for a few minutes. I got marbles, stamps, a bunch of grapes, a donkey ride, even money: three kopeks during the short recess, five during the long one. No, I would never barter that knife!

I stood there, my hand in my pocket, holding on to the knife tightly. The thin man moved away. He made his way around the bundles and the people toward the line at the information window, mumbling the whole while, "Chocolate! Real chocolate!" Now I knew what he had been saying before from a distance: "Real chocolate!"

Only one woman came over and bought a bar from him. That was all. No one else. He looked around, got a grip on his carton, and made for the gate. In a moment he would be gone, and the chocolate with him.

Then, suddenly, without thinking, I ran after him. I pulled the knife out of my pocket and held it out to him. The man stopped, looked at me, and reached for the knife. I pulled my hand back. "How much will you give me for it?" I asked.

"One!" the man answered.

I shook my head. I couldn't speak. Just one? That knife was worth at least three, maybe even ten. No, it was worth the whole carton of chocolate bars!

"Let me see it," said the man, looking me straight in the eye. "I might give you more . . ."

I hesitated for a moment. What if he kept the knife and didn't give me anything for it? I was only a boy, eight years old, without a father or a mother. If he took it and didn't give it back, who would even know the knife was mine? Who would believe me?

"I might give you more than one!" the man said again.

I gave him the knife. He looked it over, examining it from every angle and opening the small blade.

"The other one is bigger!" I said. I thought the big blade was worth a fortune. During all those months on board the train I had been carving with it, and it had never gotten dull. The man opened the big blade, ran it carefully across his thumbnail, then closed both blades.

"It's not worth much," he said. "Hardly even one bar!"

I almost burst out crying. I really had trouble holding it in. All I could do was shake my head vigorously. The man looked around. He must have noticed that no one came to my aid, that I was alone, and now he would never give the knife back. I held out my hand.

"Not interested? Then take your knife and let me be!" he said, putting the knife in my hand. "You're just wasting my time!"

At that he turned and walked away. He was already at the gate, almost through it. In another minute he would be out in the square. Then he would be gone, and the sweet chocolate with him. I felt a terrible hunger pang.

"All right!" I suddenly called out, as if against my will. "All right, just one. But make it a big one!"

The man stopped and turned toward me. He fumbled in the box and pulled out a chocolate bar. I handed him the knife and took it. Just one, but at least it was big!

Fifteen

I polished off the first row of squares straight away. I hardly chewed them, just wolfed them down. Finally I had something in my mouth and something sweet to boot! By the time I got to the

100

next row I was ready to ease up a bit. I ate one square at a time, trying to pause in between but not succeeding. I just couldn't hold back. *As for the rest,* I thought, *I'll try to save it. I'll eat it later.*

Someone went past me, brushing my shoulder. It was another boy, a head taller than me, a teenager. He looked back at me and went on. Strange, where did I know him from? He had slitlike blue eyes, the look of a cat. His clothes were dirty and torn, black with soot. He had no boots, only the remains of a pair of old galoshes, tied up with rags. Had I really seen him before? Might I be mistaking him for someone else?

The big loudspeaker came to life. Someone blew into the microphone, and from above came the sound of a loud woman's voice: "Holders of special tickets — I repeat: holders of special tickets — please prepare to board."

Only a few people got up. A train was pulling into the station, a real passenger train, a train for privileged people. I had seen such trains before, but only from the outside. They had real seats, not wooden benches but padded seats. Mama had said you could even buy food on such trains. But they weren't for the likes of us. Only well-connected people could ride them — government officials, people with special passes — not the crowds of people who slept outdoors on bundles of belongings.

I stood looking at it. I hadn't even paid attention to where the train was going; it wasn't for me anyway. The conductors were standing at the entranceways checking tickets. There were even policemen on hand, two of them. Once the few additional passengers were on board the train whistled and got under way. I watched it, fascinated. *Could it be going to Tashkent after all? Why hadn't I asked them to take me along? I could have explained, told them that I was lost, that Mama had gone on without me and that I had to look for her, to find her . . .*

Someone dashed by me, snatching my chocolate bar and running off. The boy! He ran across the platform, jumping over the baggage and around the people, until he reached the end of the train. I stood aghast, not grasping what was happening. The conductors had already moved away from the train and were standing around talking. The boy ran alongside the last car; the train was picking up speed. Suddenly he leaped and caught hold of the iron railing next to the steps. For a second his body flew out behind him, exactly like a flag unfurled in the wind. Then he pulled himself up, put one foot on the steps, then the other, climbed into the open doorway, and disappeared inside the car.

Someone next to me said, "A brave boy!"

"They'll catch him!" said another. "These special trains are crawling with conductors. They'll catch him in no time!"

"So what? What can they do to him? At worst they'll throw him off at the next stop, but meanwhile he'll have gotten somewhere."

"They'll hand him over to the police is what they'll do!"

"Did you ever try to hold water in your hands?" the first one laughed. "Boys like him slip through your fingers like water, like wind. I've seen these godforsaken kids before. They always make out. He's a brave boy, no two ways about it!"

I looked at my hand. It was empty. Now I had nothing, neither the pocketknife nor the chocolate. I was without mother or father, without my knife, without even the chocolate. Alone, without anything.

The two people who had been talking came over and asked, "What happened, boy? Why are you crying?"

I couldn't answer. I couldn't stop crying.

"What's the matter, little fellow? Are you all by yourself? Did you lose your mother?"

I nodded and broke into a wail.

"Never mind," one of them said, patting me on the shoulder. "Come, we'll go to the office and ask them to announce over the loudspeaker that you're lost. Your mother will hear it and come and get you."

He gave me his hand. I couldn't tell him that Mama was far away and wouldn't hear the loudspeaker. I couldn't talk at all. But he gave me his hand, a grown-up hand. I took it, and we went to the office together.

Sixteen

The man explained something, patted me on the shoulder again, and left the room. I had stopped crying. I knew grown-ups were taking care of me and everything would be all right. The station manager stood looking at me. His glasses were fogged up. He took them off, pulled a handkerchief out of his pocket, and began to wipe them. His eyes were red and tired, as if he had not slept for many nights.

"So, you've gotten yourself lost, have you?" he asked, putting his glasses back on.

"Y . . . Yes," I stammered. "I've lost my mama!"

"Where did you get lost? Here in the station? We can make an announcement over the loudspeaker!"

"No!" I replied. "Not here. On the way here, yesterday. There was a bomb. We jumped off and ran. I ran off on my own, and when I came back the train was gone!"

"Where did your mother go?"

"I think to Tashkent. Maybe to Bukhara or Samarkand. She went with Sarele and Feigele. They must have come through here! They must have gotten off here during the stopover to buy some food. Did you see them? Sarele has reddish curls, and she's always holding a doll, the doll Grandma made . . ."

"What do you think?" the man said, interrupting me. "Do you really think I know who comes through here? Hundreds of people pass through every day. They wait in the station, outside. They clutter up the place for days and weeks on end. And you're telling me about a little girl with curls and a doll?"

His words fell on my head like hammer blows. I shrank toward the door.

"Hold on a minute! Don't run away!" the man said. "A Tashkent train went through here yesterday morning. A freight train with passengers on it."

103

I was overjoyed. "Yes!" I cried. "Yes! That was our train!"

"It's gone on," the manager said. "You won't be able to catch up with it."

"But Papa told me if I ever got lost I had to look for them until I found them!"

"Where's your father?"

"In the army!" I answered. "He went to teach the Germans a lesson!"

The man stood stroking his chin for a moment. His hand made a rasping sound like sandpaper on wood in Papa's carpentry shop.

"We'll see," he said at last. "But you can't do it. You'll never find your mother. We've got to take you to an institution."

I didn't understand. "An institution? What institution? I'm going to find Mama, just the way Papa said!"

"Not a chance!" the man said firmly. "I've seen lost children like you. They die like flies, whether it's from the cold or from hunger or from sickness. Some fall under the wheels of trains . . ."

No, it can't be, I thought. *He's just trying to scare me.* But suddenly I started to tremble.

"There's no way you're going to find your mother," the man declared. "I'm going to make a call now and have them come and take you away. You'll stay there, go to school, and make friends, and when the war is over your father will come and get you, and they'll find your mother too."

Now he could see I was afraid.

"Gave you a scare, did I? Well, you've got to understand what kind of a world we're living in. But people will look after you. Here, while I'm waiting for the phone why don't you have some tea?"

He turned to the samovar and drew a glass of hot tea. He paused for a moment.

Will he put in sugar cubes or not? I wondered. There were only a few small ones in the dish.

"Sit down," he said, putting the glass on the table. "Have a drink, warm up a bit, and by that time the phone will be free."

The phone kept ringing. The clerk would answer it, speaking loudly, sometimes even shouting, as if she were trying to project her voice all the way to Moscow. I touched the glass in a gingerly way. It was hot. How good it was to rest my frozen fingers on the hot glass. I touched it again and again, then blew on the tea and took a little sip. Oh, how good it was! It had been a long time since I had drunk hot, sweet tea. It slid down my throat and warmed my insides. I was starting to thaw out. Now I could think clearly.

Take me to a children's institution? Which one did he have in mind? And why to an institution anyway? Mama was not far away, after all; only yesterday she had been right here. She couldn't have gone far. I'd probably find her at the next stop. And we had promised we would look for each other. So what sense did it make to go to an institution until the end of the war?

The man sat behind a big desk leafing through some papers. I had the feeling he had forgotten about me. The telephone rang.

"In three minutes?" the woman asked. "All right, thanks. I'll announce it."

She turned and pushed a button. Outside, on the other side of the door, I heard the familiar sound of the loudspeaker coming to life. Now the woman spoke in two voices at once: a high, clear voice there in the room and a distant, muffled one that came from the loudspeaker outside.

"The next train will be for Tashkent, Kokand, Fergana . . ."

I hesitated for a moment. There was still a little hot, sweet tea at the bottom of the glass. Then I jumped up, opened the door, and ran toward the train. Behind me I heard a chair fall. The man might have jumped up too, to try to catch me. But he was too late. I had already been swallowed up in the throng of people pushing to get on the train, the train to Tashkent.

Seventeen

I had never gotten on a train by myself. Mama had always been with me. Mama would get us through the crowd pushing forward with its baggage. Sarele would hold on tightly to her coat so as not to get lost, and I would follow closely behind with my little pack. But this time I was alone.

I was surrounded by a wall of people, backs in gray coats, endless grown-up backsides crowding together in an effort to get on the train. Something sharp stuck me in the ribs: the corner of a cardboard suitcase. I tried to get away from it, to push my way forward, but I couldn't. They were all so big and strong, just like a wall.

The train blew its whistle. People pushed harder. I almost suffocated between the people and the bags. They pressed, squeezed, and cursed trying to get to the cars.

The woman on the loudspeaker announced above our heads:

"The train for Tashkent will depart in one minute. Please stand clear of the cars . . ."

It was as if no one had heard her. The pushing did not let up. The train whistled again and began to move. The cars glided slowly by, one after another. Many people jammed the steps, trying to climb inside. Those who didn't manage to get hold of the railing fell back. Finally the pressure eased. I broke through and ran to the edge of the platform. Another car went by, and another. I began to walk alongside the train. I looked at the stairway railings. *If I were only bigger, like that boy, I could grab hold of one of them and climb up!* But I was still small, and the railing was so high up!

The cars went by in a long chain. I looked back. Three more, two more. Those who had been on the steps had already climbed up and pushed their way inside. The train to Tashkent, to Mama! Another blast of the whistle, another car. Now this one too was

106

going by! I began to run. I ran alongside the last car and then, suddenly, I jumped and grabbed a railing. I don't know how I did it, but I held on to that iron bar and didn't let go. I felt as if my body were flying behind me, my feet fluttering. It seemed to me as though any minute my arms would be pulled from their sockets — but I didn't let go of the bar. Summoning all my strength, I got a foot onto the steps. Then the other. The train picked up speed. All at once the platform ended and we were in the open, in the fog. Someone gave me a hand and pulled me up. I climbed and pushed my way in, into the semidarkness of the car. I couldn't see a thing, but I heard the wheels clattering faster and faster. They seemed to be singing: "To Mama! To Mama! To Mama!"

Tonight, I thought, *tonight, when I meet up with Mama, I'll tell her everything. I'll tell her how the man had wanted to put me into an institution and I'd run away, how I'd jumped up onto the train. Yes, Mama, really, just like a grown-up! You always said I was stubborn, right? You and Papa used to call me "stubborn mule." Well, you see, it helped me this time. I was stubborn and didn't let go of the railing, and in the end I made it up into the car!*

No doubt Mama would be horrified and say, "You mustn't do such things, Yankele! You must never jump onto a moving train! You could fall off, God forbid!"

"But I had to, Mama!" I would say. "If I hadn't jumped I would never have caught up with you!"

I looked around. I barely managed to find a place to sit on the floor, in the aisle. It was cold in the car, almost as cold as outdoors. A rusty iron stove stood in the middle of the aisle, but instead of radiating heat it just let out smoke and ashes. I could tell right away who had just gotten on and who had been riding for a while: those sitting on the wooden benches were black with soot, while the "newcomers" like me, the "clean ones," were crowded into the aisles. Actually, no one was really clean. Who could keep clean on a trip lasting weeks and months?

There was a foul odor in the car. It was familiar to me: the smell of soot and dirt — and especially of hunger. An odor of hunger arose from the empty stomachs. I thought about the chocolate the boy had snatched from me. Next time I would know what to do: whatever I got hold of I would eat right away! I wouldn't save anything for later. I would eat it all immediately and be done with it. No one could snatch anything from my stomach!

The woman on the bench across from me began undoing the bundle in her lap. She rummaged around in it for a while, then pulled a clenched fist out and brought it to her mouth. She was eating. She had something to eat!

I couldn't take my eyes off her. Mama would have said it was bad manners to stare at someone who was eating, but I couldn't help myself. *Really, Mama, I couldn't!*

I suppose the woman tried to chew quietly, so as not to attract attention, but to me every movement of her teeth seemed audible. I swallowed again and again.

I tried to get a look out the window. I couldn't see anything. It was foggy, fog the color of milk. Every so often a clod of snow would stick to the glass and then immediately slide off. I couldn't restrain myself and stared again at the woman. Her eyes were lowered. She put her hand to her mouth again and took a bite of whatever it was she was concealing in it.

Suddenly she looked up and met my gaze. Her mouth froze for a moment, then she went on chewing. She stopped, then swallowed again. I swallowed too. The woman looked at me. Brown eyes peered out at me from her sooty face. I didn't say anything, but I knew that she understood. Why should she share with me anyway? Only because I was hungry? Everybody was hungry, including those who had some food, so why should she give me anything?

She reached into her bundle again, then pulled out her hand. This time she didn't hide what was in it: she had two biscuits, two dry cookies. She handed me one of them. "Take it, child!" she said, smiling. "Traveling by yourself, are you?"

"Thanks!" I said, nodding. I couldn't say any more. I gobbled down the biscuit right away. I knew no one would grab it from me there on the train, but I ate it immediately. It was sweet and just a little salty, maybe from the tears. I was ashamed: at one time I hardly ever cried, and now the tears came so quickly — even when someone was good to me. Strange!

I closed my eyes. Suddenly I remembered: what if the conductor comes? My eyes opened wide with fright. *I'll explain*, I thought. *I'll tell him I'm looking for my mother. He's a grown-up. He'll understand. Maybe he'll even help me find her!*

The car rocked back and forth, and I became sleepy. What a night I had had there, on the platform with Sergei, and how much had happened since then! I tried to remember everything that had happened to me that morning, but I dozed off. I slept deeply.

Someone shook me.

"Wake up!" a man's voice ordered me. "Wake up, boy, wake up!"

Eighteen

I opened my eyes and looked around. What was this? Where was I? This wasn't Mama's car! Since when did our car have benches? Before it had been light out, and now it was almost dark. Someone tugged my sleeve and pulled me to my feet. Directly in front of me I saw a brass button on an old military coat. Looking up, I saw another button, then another, and above them a chin covered with gray whiskers, a huge mustache, and a pair of eyes. Piercing, angry eyes.

"Have you got a ticket, boy?"

109

It was the conductor! The ticket checker had caught me!

I began to stammer, "N . . . N . . . No . . . but Mama . . ."

"Where's your mother, little boy? Did she buy a ticket?"

"No! She's on another train. I'm l . . . lost!"

"Aha!" said the conductor. "A familiar story!"

I felt hurt: did he think I was just making it up?

"You're getting off with me at the next stop," he went on, "and then it's straight to the police with you!"

"But I've got to get to Tashkent! I've got to find . . ."

"Children like you should be sent to institutions," the man said, interrupting me, "not allowed to just wander around. Stand on the side here until the train stops!"

I stood near the door looking out. Night was falling. The train slowed. Many different tracks ran alongside ours, crisscrossed, and diverged. The engine whistled. A station sign came into view and disappeared. I couldn't make it out. A number of other people crowded around me. The conductor had caught them too.

"It's a dirty business!" someone said standing nearby. "If I had a few rubles to drop into his pocket he'd look the other way without a second thought. They're all the same!"

Next to him a man stood silently, chewing his lower lip.

"They want documents!" the first man went on. "A letter from the committee where you work, a letter from your neighborhood committee, one from the police, everything imaginable. And what if you don't have a job or a place to live?"

The other bit his lip without answering. His face was gaunt and gloomy.

The train pulled into the station. In the light of the blacked-out lamps we could see the police waiting for us. The train stopped. Two policemen took up positions on either side of the exit steps. They looked up into the open doorway like cats lying in wait for their prey.

Now the conductor reappeared. "Off!" he ordered the first

110

man. The man obeyed and climbed down, straight into the waiting arms of the police.

"Documents?" the officer asked without further ado. The man rummaged through his pockets. Meanwhile another man had gotten off and a woman after him. It was my turn. All at once the thin man pushed me aside and jumped straight onto the platform, butting the waiting policeman in the stomach and running for the gate.

I froze. The policeman was writhing on the platform, clutching his stomach, while his buddy took off after the fugitive. Hesitantly, I climbed down the steps. *If he can do it,* I said to myself, *why can't I?*

"Hey, kid, you stay here!" the conductor cried. "Don't you run off!"

His admonition struck me like a whiplash. *Run for it! This is your chance!*

I squeezed through the crowd waiting on the platform. There were many people there, as always, but this time I behaved differently. This time there was nothing I wouldn't do: I squeezed and pushed and elbowed and even butted people, as the man had done. I made my way to the gate, went through it, and was outside in the square, running across it as fast as I could to get away from the station. My side hurt, but I kept on running until I reached an alley, then dashed on through the heavy snow until I had no strength left. I was out of breath. I walked on a few more steps, then sank into a snowdrift in the entrance to one of the houses. My heart was pounding, and I couldn't hear whether I was still being followed or not, but no one came into the alley.

Nineteen

I have no idea how long I lay there. I got chilled. High above the alley, stars were twinkling in a strip of dark sky, but they seemed so far away, so cold. Occasionally someone would go by in the street, but they walked quickly, bundled up in their coats. I did not see their faces: their heads too were wrapped up, protected. They must have been hurrying home, to some warm, cozy place, and they didn't even notice me.

A freezing wind was blowing. I had to get back to the station. Only there could I continue my search for Mama, and only there could I find refuge from the wind. But the police were there too, and so was the conductor. Yet how likely was it that they would recognize me? So many people passed through that station! The station manager himself had said that a lot of children got lost there; so why should they remember me in particular?

The hunger pangs were gnawing at me again. What had I eaten that morning? A few squares of chocolate. And I had drunk a little tea. And, oh yes, I had eaten one biscuit on the train. But that was all. I just had to find something to eat. Maybe at the station? Maybe there, among all the people, I would come across a bite of something. Even a crust of bread would do. Even — even a potato peel. Just a little something to put in my mouth!

But I didn't find a thing at the station. I entered it cautiously, hugging the walls so as not to be noticed, but no one paid attention to me anyway. As always, crowds of people were sleeping there, on the platform. They were waiting for a train.

I had nothing to cover myself with. A freezing cold wind was blowing. I looked for shelter, but the wind was whistling and howling all up and down the platform, so I went around inside the station looking for a vacant spot. Finally I gave up and sat down in the doorway of one of the side offices. There was one step there, recessed into the wall, and then the door, a little bit

112

of protection against the wind and something to lean against. I settled in. Pulling down the sleeves of my coat, I slipped each hand into the opposite sleeve. I had tried to warm my hands by rubbing them together, but they were terribly cold, almost frozen. I curled up, wrapping my arms tightly around my chest and drawing up my knees. But the cold wind kept on blowing, and the hunger kept gnawing away at me. I tried to think about other things, but all I could see in my mind's eye was the tasty dishes Mama would make for me: dumplings filled with cheese and sweet blackberry dumplings, hot cabbage soup with potatoes, and slices of fresh black bread.

I don't know how long I sat there curled up. I must have dozed off. Suddenly I awoke with a start: someone had stumbled over my feet. The light was far off and dim. Maybe he simply hadn't seen me and so tripped and fell. He cursed loudly. He had a childish voice.

I peered around the edge of the wall and froze: it was that boy, the one who had snatched my chocolate and escaped onto the special train. The very one! *Oh God, what will he do to me now?*

The boy stood up, looked me over closely, and said, "Feet like those should be cut off!"

I kept quiet. Leaning back against the door, I prayed it would open and swallow me up.

"But it won't be necessary to cut them off," the boy went on. "They'll be frozen stiff by tomorrow anyway — and so will you!"

I was seized by a deathly chill. I stared at him helplessly.

"What're you hanging around here for?" the boy asked, putting his hands in his pockets. "There's always room at the black hotel!"

"The . . . black hotel?" I stammered. I could hardly get the words out of my mouth. It was as though it too were frozen.

The boy examined my face. "What's with you? Are you new?"

"Yes," I said, "I got lost, just yesterday . . ."

113

Just yesterday? I thought. *It can't be. So many things have happened since then. Only yesterday I was with Mama!*

"Come with me, then!" said the boy, turning to go.

I pulled myself to my feet and started after him. My limbs were stiff as boards. *Maybe he's right,* I thought. *I probably would have frozen during the night.* I had already seen people who, because of the cold, failed to wake up in the morning. I wondered whether he remembered me, remembered grabbing the chocolate from me that morning. No, he didn't seem like the type to remember, or maybe he just didn't care. But I remembered him from somewhere else! Where could it have been?

At the end of the platform the boy turned and jumped down. I stayed close behind him, trying not to lose him in the darkness. He made his way confidently among the somber-colored cars, skipping over the rails as if he were quite at home. At last he came to a stop.

"Here we are!" he said.

I looked around but didn't understand what he meant. A dark mass loomed in front of us like a huge, black hill. A current of warmth stroked my face. I took my hands out of my pockets and reached out. They too felt the warmth.

"What is it?" I asked, still not comprehending.

"Coal," the boy answered, "burned coal. Every station has a pile of it. They take it from the engines when they clean them."

"Then what do they do with it?"

"What do they do with it? Here, see for yourself."

I went over to him and looked: he was digging in the side of the black mound, digging and digging, and then suddenly I saw the live coals: deep in the pile there were hissing, red, burning embers.

"See?" he said. "It's burning! This is where I sleep!"

"Sleep? But there's fire here! You'll get burned!"

"I can see you're new!" the boy said contemptuously. "You don't have to dig very deep. I only did that to show you. Here, look!"

114

He covered up the live coals. It was dark again, but the pile still gave off heat.

"You only need to dig a little," he said, burrowing into the hole he had made. "And if it's really cold, you can cover yourself with it!" he added, brushing some coal over himself. "And now, good night! I'm already half asleep."

I hesitated for a moment. The next day, when I got up and pulled myself out of the coal I would be black like the boy, black and filthy. And what would Mama say? The next day, when I caught up with her, what would she say when she saw me?

The freezing wind was still blowing, blowing without letup. I began digging with my bare hands. I knew that if I stayed outside I would freeze to death. The lumps of coal were light and brittle. I lay down on my side in the hollow in the side of the pile. The lumps crunched against each other near my ear. A pleasant warmth rose from below and spread through my body. Above me it was cold. I got up and made the hollow deeper. Now I could cover myself up too. I brushed the coal over myself and made a pillow with my hands.

He's right, I thought. *Here, at least, I won't freeze, no sir! I'm sure he didn't recognize me. Otherwise he wouldn't have helped me out the way he did. But where do I know him from?*

Suddenly it came to me: from the Crimea! I had seen him in the Crimea! Well, not him actually, but a boy who looked just like him! We had been standing in the marketplace. Papa was listening to the news, and I saw him. He was bigger than me, maybe ten years old, thin, dressed in rags, and barefoot — barefoot, even though the spring was just beginning and it was still cold. He had stared at me like a hungry cat, stared and stared, and when my attention was distracted he had snatched my bag of raisins and run. And Papa — Papa hadn't wanted to run after him. "He must be hungry," he had said to me.

"But he stole from me!" I had protested, showing him my empty hand. "Stealing is forbidden!"

"Right," Papa had answered, "it's forbidden to steal, but when

115

a person is hungry . . . maybe he has no parents, and I'm sure he has nothing to sell, and he is hungry!" No, Papa didn't run after that boy.

Papa smiled at me in my sleep and gave me his hand. "It's all right," he said. "You'll be eating soon."

I held his hand all night.

Twenty

I was awakened by the clatter of wheels. I opened my eyes and didn't know where I was. A trolley car full of spent coal was coming down the track. Where was I? Something crunched under my head. I turned over on my back. Little lumps of something slipped aside beneath me. Soot showered my face. I sat up and remembered: I was in the coal pile! I had slept in the mound of burned coal. It was morning. The coal trolley would be pulling up any minute and dumping its load there!

The trolley came closer and stopped. A big man in a cloak lumbered down, clapped his hands, and called out, "All right, rats, out of your holes!"

A head poked out of the black mound.

"You're a rat, an old, fat one!"

It was the boy! How could I have forgotten the boy who had brought me here?

How did he dare talk that way to a grown-up, cursing and all? Still, he did climb out of the coal. He brushed off his black clothes and hands and turned to me. "Well, how'd you sleep here in our black hotel?"

"Fine!" I replied. "I never knew there was such a thing!"

"I told you. Every station has a coal pile like this. We were

116

lucky it didn't snow. When it snows, the coal gets wet, and it's not so . . ."

The trolley dumped its load on the edge of the pile and moved on.

Suddenly my head began to hurt. I felt weak and sat down.

"What's the matter?" the boy asked, looking me over the way he had the day before.

"I'm hungry," I whispered.

"Hungry? So go get something to eat!"

"But where?" I asked. "Are they giving out food here?"

The boy laughed. "Who's giving out food? Get it yourself, the way everybody else does. Steal it!"

I wanted to tell him it was not allowed to steal, but I knew there was no choice here. Even Papa wouldn't be angry with me if he knew. Besides, I didn't want to remind him that he himself had stolen food from me.

"How do you do it? Where?"

The boy shrugged and walked away. I got up and went after him. I didn't want to stay there by myself. Anything but that.

"Just don't bother me!" he blurted over his shoulder.

"I promise!" I said, trying to catch up. "My name is Yasha."

"Mine's Grisha. Now watch me from a distance and maybe you'll learn something, okay?"

"Okay!"

"Actually, would you like to help?"

"Sure!"

I didn't know what he had in mind, but I didn't want him to get angry with me. I didn't want Grisha to get upset and leave me alone.

We made our way among the people on the platform. Grisha looked around. I could see he was looking for something but evidently not finding it. If you had food in your pack you wouldn't leave it unattended even for a second. We went out to the square. There were some food stands on the far side. We drew closer. There was a stand laden with potatoes and a barrel

117

of salt fish. Next to the barrel was another stand. What was on it? I couldn't see it all, but there was bread there, several loaves cut up in quarters! Alongside it stood a man selling pastries. I recoiled. I remembered the woman who had chased me away the day before.

Grisha stopped and looked at me. "What's the matter?"

I didn't say anything.

"Don't want to play? Then get the hell out of here! If you want to eat you've got to work. Don't hang around me. You're in my way!"

"No!" I shot back. "I'll do whatever you tell me! I promise!"

"Okay, look," he said, "you go to the first street, the one near the food stands. See it?"

"Yes."

"I'll make my getaway through there. If they chase me, run in front of them and trip them up. Got it?"

I nodded.

"Then go! Why are you standing there staring at me like an idiot? Go!"

I went to the first street, stopped, and looked back. From a distance I could see Grisha walking around, not even looking at the food stands, as if they didn't interest him. He put his hands in his pockets. I thought he even whistled, but I couldn't hear. A few people passed by in the street, all bundled up and lost in their thoughts.

I was cold and began stamping my feet to try to warm up. How much longer was he just going to walk around? Suddenly I heard someone shout, "Thief! Thief!"

Grisha darted into the street, right in front of me. I froze.

"Catch him! Thief! He stole my bread!"

He went right by me as if he didn't know me. Someone was running after him. This was my moment! I broke out and ran toward the man, then suddenly pretended to stumble and rolled in the snow. The man ran into me and fell flat on his face.

118

"Damn it!" he shouted, getting up. He started running again, but Grisha was already gone. The street was empty. Two women came out of one of the houses and set out slowly through the snow.

The man came running back. I froze with fear. He picked me up, stood me on my feet, and slapped me, once, then a second time. "Damn you!" he growled. "Thief!"

My eyes filled with tears. I had never been hit by a grown-up before, never!

"But I didn't steal anything! I didn't take a thing!" I said at last, unbuttoning my coat. "See, my pockets are empty! I haven't got anything!"

"Tell it to the police!" said the man, grabbing me by my coat collar. "I know your type! Gangs of thieves are what you are!"

And he gave me two more loud slaps for good measure. I burst out crying.

"What do you want from the poor boy?" one of the women asked, coming over to us.

"These little thieves hang out in gangs. One sets up a commotion, another steals something, and the third trips you!"

"But I didn't . . . I didn't steal a thing . . ."

The woman kept shaking her head. "He's so little, scarcely in second grade, or third at the most, and you beat him like that . . ."

The other woman pointed to the far-off food stands and said, "Now someone can really steal something. How could you leave all that merchandise unguarded?"

The man let go of my collar and looked in the direction of the square. This was my chance. I slipped out of his grasp and began running up the street. I ran and ran. I don't think he followed me. After all, I hadn't taken anything from him, and there was plenty left behind to take. At the end of the street I stopped and looked back. The man was gone. I turned into a side street and went back to the square by a different route.

What a dummy, I thought. *Why didn't I arrange to meet Grisha somewhere? Now he'll probably eat it all himself, the way he polished off my chocolate yesterday.*

Again I felt weak and a little headachy. I entered the square from the side, taking cover in the crowd. I was afraid the vendor would see me and nab me again, but he didn't notice me.

I went into the station. No, Grisha wasn't there either. On the platform I saw a woman walking away from me, carrying a big bundle on her back. Two little girls were clutching her coattails. Suddenly a great wave of joy flooded over me. "Mama!" I called out, running after her. "Mama!"

Mama kept on walking as if she hadn't heard.

"Mama! It's me, Yankele!"

But Mama didn't stop. I ran, caught up with her, and tugged at her coat. "Mama!"

She turned and looked at me. I felt faint. I almost collapsed. It wasn't Mama after all, just another woman.

The children looked at me with big blue eyes, gentile children. The woman smiled sadly and said, "Sorry, sonny, you've made a mistake."

I sank to my knees. Covering my head with my arms, I wept like a baby.

Someone sat down next to me and tapped me on the shoulder. I looked up. It was Grisha!

Twenty-one

"What now, crybaby?"

I looked up at Grisha's sooty face. I tried to restrain my tears.

120

"Mama," I said. "I saw Mama — but it wasn't her."

"Make up your mind. Was it or wasn't it?"

"It wasn't Mama. It was someone else."

"Well, never mind," Grisha said, "you'll find her. I don't even have anyone to look for. I'm on my own!"

"On your own?"

"They're both dead, my parents. Papa was killed in the war, and Mama got sick and died while we were on the run."

I looked at him uncomprehendingly. How could he manage like that, all alone, not looking for anyone, no chance of seeing his father or mother again? And what about Mama? My tears welled up again.

"Don't start that again!" Grisha said to me angrily. "You were doing just fine. Here, you get some of this too."

He gave me a little of the stolen bread.

I pounced on the bread and began gobbling it down. I hardly chewed it. I just swallowed and took another bite. I couldn't restrain myself.

"Take it easy!" said Grisha. "If you eat that way you'll stay hungry!"

I tried to eat more slowly, to chew each bite many times, but it wasn't easy. I was so hungry! Grisha sat down, leaned against the wall, and took the rest of the loaf out of his coat. His share was bigger than mine, but I couldn't complain. He was the one who had taken the bread to begin with. And maybe I was just imagining it; maybe I had already eaten most of my share.

We ate silently. Little by little, I managed to slow down. I didn't want to finish before Grisha. I didn't want to have to watch him eat without having anything left for myself. I almost did it.

"Do you always hang around here, in this station?"

"Fat chance," Grisha snapped, his mouth full. "Do you think I'm crazy?"

I didn't say anything. I really hadn't intended any criticism of him. Did a person have to be crazy to stay in this station?

121

Grisha swallowed some bread, belched, and said, "No one stays in one place for long."

"Why not?"

"Because after a while they get to know you, and then you can't steal anymore."

"What do you do then?"

"Then you move on to the next town. You can always sleep in the coal pile and grab things in the marketplace or the station there. The best 'bargains' are in the station, because there are lots of people there, and when the trains come they always rush off and leave things behind."

"So where do you go from here?"

"South, to Uzbekistan. Everybody's going there."

I almost hugged him with joy. "Really? I'm going there too, to look for Mama! So we can go together?"

"What the hell for? You'll just hang on to me like a little kid!"

I was hurt. Why should I hang on to him? As a matter of fact, I had helped him, just the way he asked me to. I turned away so he wouldn't see. Why did I always have to cry?

Grisha patted my hand. "Okay, okay, don't be offended. You were actually just fine. Only remember: the most important thing is to know how to run fast, understand?"

"I was the fastest runner in my class!"

When was it that I had gone to school? I had finished second grade in the Crimea, but when? It seemed so long ago.

"Why do you have to run fast?" I asked.

"Oh come on, you mean to tell me you got left behind and you still don't know? You need to be speedy so you can get away: from the shopkeepers in the market, from the people you steal from in the stations, from the conductors, from the police who catch you and take you in or bring you to a transit center."

"Transit center? What's that?"

"They gather up the abandoned children and take them to institutions, orphanages; but first they put them in transit centers. It's just a place where you don't do anything except wait until they send you on."

"But if you're by yourself, if . . . if your mother and father are dead, why shouldn't you go to an orphanage? They'd take care of you, you'd have food every day . . ."

Grisha burst out laughing. "Food? You must be dreaming! You hardly get a cup of warm water and a black hunk of stuff they call bread. You can bounce it like a ball, that 'bread' of theirs, or stick it to the wall if you wet it. It's like a jail!" Grisha concluded. "There isn't even anyone to steal from!"

What luck to have met Grisha, I thought. *Such a brave fellow. And he knows so many things!* I'd been learning from him ever since I met him. I wasn't even angry at him anymore for taking my chocolate. Well, maybe just a bit, but even that had taught me something. Mama would save things, giving us some food and keeping the rest for later; but she was a grown-up, and I was little. I couldn't save anything. Not a thing.

On an outlying track a freight train slowly approached. Grisha got up and looked at the cars. "Let's check this out!" he said.

"Check what?"

"Where it's heading. Maybe it's going south."

"But it's a real freight train. It's not for passengers!"

Grisha dismissed my objection with a wave of his hand. "You've still got a lot to learn, kid. Come on, let's find out what's going on!"

Twenty-two

That was the first freight train I had sneaked aboard — I mean a real freight train, with freight on it rather than people. There were many more afterwards. At first I counted them, but then there were too many to keep track.

We took what we could get, whatever train came along. At least with a freight train you didn't have to push to get on. Grisha taught me to wait until no one was looking, then sneak aboard. We would hide among the cartons, the crates, the huge barrels, working our way into cracks like mice, and when the train got under way we would come out of our holes. The noise of the train would silence the grumbling in our stomachs, but I always felt it, felt hungry.

When we were really starving we would get off at stations along the way to steal something to eat. I hadn't managed to carry it off yet; I just couldn't. The whole way I would be thinking and planning how I would sneak up and jump out and snatch some bread or a few apples and how I would run away and disappear down an alley. But when the moment came, I would freeze in my tracks. My feet simply wouldn't budge.

We went on and on, a whole week, maybe two. In the little stations along the way I didn't see a single fat person; everybody was skinny, even the adults. They all looked hungry, as if they too had lost their mothers and had no one to feed them. And in every station there were people sitting and waiting for trains to take them south.

"Why do they all want to go south?" I asked Grisha.

"Dummy!" he answered. "You know they're running away from the Germans, don't you?"

"But why there? There are lots of other places!"

"Because it's warm there!" said Grisha. "They want to get to warm places."

"But isn't it supposed to be warm here, too?" I said. "This is the desert, isn't it?"

Grisha said, "Yeah, it must be the desert. When I was in school I saw a picture of a desert once in a book, and it looked just like this."

Imagine! How did he know that? Well, if I were as big as

124

Grisha I guess I'd know straight off too. He was eleven already. But I knew some things too. Grandma had once told me a story about a man who got lost in the desert. At night, when he was sleeping, a lion came and licked his face. Then the man got up and climbed on the lion's back, and it took him straight home. Maybe I would be lucky and find a lion that would take me to Mama. I didn't say it out loud — Grisha would just have laughed at me again. I said what an older boy would say. "If this is the desert, it should be really hot here, shouldn't it?"

Grisha looked through a crack. A cold wind was blowing in.

"Yup," he said. "I always thought a desert was yellow and hot, but here it's cold as can be!"

I climbed down from my barrel and peered through the same crack. Nothing but sand everywhere, and a river. We were traveling along a river, a big one that wound through the dunes next to the tracks. But I had no idea even which direction it was flowing, because the water was frozen. A desert with ice!

"I'm thirsty!" I said, looking at the ice in the river. "I want to drink something!"

Was it any wonder we were thirsty? We had been lucky that day. We had sneaked onto a freight car loaded with barrels of salt fish! We recognized the smell right away, and my head ached once more from hunger.

I pounced on the barrels and tried to pry off their covers, but they were all sealed tight, fastened with big nails.

"Calm down, kid," said Grisha. "One of them's bound to be open."

"Why should it be?" I asked, tugging at the lid of one of the barrels with all my might.

Grisha inspected the lids one by one. "One of them's got to be open, because the watchmen steal too!"

"The watchmen? You mean the railway watchmen? Aren't they supposed to be the ones who keep people from stealing?"

"Come on!" Grisha sneered. "They're all a bunch of thieves! The watchmen are the first ones to steal!"

125

"Really?"

"Really. Whoever doesn't steal goes hungry. So the grown-ups steal a lot and the kids steal a little. It's just easier to catch us, because we're smaller."

"Do they get caught too?"

"Sometimes, but not too often."

"And what happens to them?"

"They pack them off to jail, and from there they're sent to Siberia!"

I pictured the watchman I'd seen at the last stop. He wore a military coat and carried a rifle, but he looked old enough to be the father of a soldier, no, a grandfather! How would a police-man catch him? By the collar? By the ear? Do they really send them to Siberia, straight off to that terrible cold that everybody is scared to death of? I was embarrassed to ask Grisha. He'd just make fun of me again, the way he always did when I didn't understand something.

Grisha was still examining the barrels. I heard a squeak.

"I found one!" he shouted. "This one's already been opened!"

He pried up the lid. It squeaked again. A strong smell of salt fish spread through the car.

I ran over and began pulling on the lid as hard as I could. Now that both of us were pulling, it slowly gave way. Just a little more — there, it was open at last. I reached into the barrel. I wanted to grab a fish and eat it on the spot, bones and all — but my hand came up empty.

"He took all of them!" I cried. "He didn't leave us a single one!"

"That can't be," Grisha said. "If they don't take the barrel, they usually leave some inside for the weight, so nobody will notice right away."

He put both his arms in. They were longer than mine.

"I've got some!" he said, pulling his arms out of the big belly of the barrel. "Here, have one!"

Now the party could begin. We ate and ate and couldn't stop

126

eating. I had always loved salt fish. Bread with salt fish was the best thing Mama could take along on a trip. These fish were packed in coarse salt. At first I ate them salt and all. I couldn't help myself. Then I began shaking off the salt before I ate the fish. But even without the salt, it tasted salty. Why else would they call it that? I went on eating, but something was missing. Was it bread? Yes, but something else. Of course: water! I was thirsty.

I sat on the next barrel, my feet dangling over the side, and looked at the fish in my hands. I couldn't still be hungry. I had eaten so many fish! Then why couldn't I stop? Hungry or not, I began to be bothered by thirst.

"I'm thirsty!" I said to Grisha.

"Me too," he groaned, his mouth full.

"So we'll get off at the next stop?" I asked.

"What for?"

"To drink! I'm dying of thirst!"

"But if we get off we might not be able to get back on in time. Or we might not be able to . . ." Grisha tossed the tail of a fish back into the barrel. He couldn't eat any more either.

"But I'm dying of thirst!" I said again, feeling like I couldn't stand it anymore. When would we ever get to the next stop?

"It's either food or water," Grisha announced. "How often do we get a chance to eat like this? And if we get off, who knows what we'll get on next? On a passenger train you can't steal food, and on another freight train there might be nothing but crates of machines or God knows what else. I'm staying on!"

I didn't say anything. I saw the river I had swum in in the Crimea, Mama's samovar and tea, the big jars of lemonade with crushed ice floating in them that we had in the summertime. I saw lakes, and I saw a dripping tap I had noticed at the last stop. I even heard the sound of the drops falling, one by one.

I didn't want any more fish now. That is, I did want more, but only once I had had something to drink. So why couldn't I have both? And what if Grisha really did stay on? How would

I manage on my own? How to choose between Grisha and the fish, on the one hand, and water at the next stop, on the other?

That evening the choice was made for us. When the train stopped at the station we heard a clang of bolts, the door opened wide, and someone climbed in and began rolling the barrels toward the opening. We quickly pushed our way through, jumped out of the car, and ran from the station.

It was Grisha who got to the faucet first. He drank and drank, and I was afraid he'd use up all the water. I couldn't contain myself and pushed him aside. He pushed me back and went on drinking.

I begged him, "Just a little! Just a little!"

Grisha let go of the faucet. I thrust my face down and drank and drank. Then we took turns, switching off several times. Even that night, when it got terribly cold, I left the coal pile to take a drink.

Once we got past Kyzyl-Orda the river thawed. Now I could see the current. The Syr-Darya flowed north, in the opposite direction to the one in which we were traveling and just as that know-it-all traveler, Grisha, had said. He must have read a lot of books! He said the river flowed even when it was covered with ice, ending up eventually in the Aral Sea. What a tremendous river! So much water! But now I was no longer thirsty, only hungry, as always.

We had almost no luck stealing in the little stations along the way. I had no idea if anything edible even grew in those parts. Everything looked like sand: the little adobe houses, the roofs, the streets.

The people looked different. They were darker and had narrow, slanting eyes. The men had big mustaches, and the women wore braids under their kerchiefs. Even the old ladies had thin braids, and their dresses looked like colorful robes. They spoke an unfamiliar language. What did they do in their sandy towns anyway?

128

"Do you think Tashkent looks like this too?" I asked Grisha.

He shrugged his shoulders. "How would I know? I hope not. There's not much to these dumpy villages."

But I did want Tashkent to look like this, a little town of one-story houses, because that would make it easier to find Mama. I would run up to her and hug her, and Mama would kiss me and give me something to eat, and I would never again have anything to worry about, not anything. And what stories I would have to tell her! What tales I would tell her and Sarele when I found them.

Maybe tomorrow? Tomorrow we would be in Tashkent!

Twenty-three

But Tashkent was neither a village nor a small town. It was a big city, huge, in fact. And who ever said it was warm there? When we'd jumped from the train and run we hadn't felt the cold, but later, in the street, we were assaulted by a freezing wind. The sky was clear, and blue, like Grisha's eyes, but the wind went right through my coat and cut into me like a knife.

Grisha put his hands in his pockets and started walking. Catching up with him, I asked, "Where are we headed?"

"To the market, of course," Grisha answered. "They must have a big market here, in fact not just one, probably a lot of them. What a city!"

"Wait up a second! Just a second!"

"Why should I wait?"

"I want to go back and look around the station. Mama might have just arrived. She might have gotten held up on the way and only arrived now."

129

Grisha turned and glared at me. "Listen, this isn't going to work."

"What isn't?"

"Kids like us, 'abandoned' kids, street kids, never stay together. It's every man for himself, just like cats in garbage bins. You meet, then go your separate ways. We traveled some together, and now it's time to split up. You look for your mother, and I'll . . ."

He shrugged, the way he always did, turned, and began walking away. I wanted to run after him, but more than anything I wanted to get back to the station and find Mama. I stood gazing after him. He seemed to sense it, even with his back turned.

"So long!" he cried, waving without turning toward me. "Good luck!"

Again I was alone. I had had an older friend, a friend who knew a lot of things, and now he was gone. I felt the tears welling up once more, but I couldn't tell if it was for my sake or his. After all, I would find Mama, today, tomorrow, next week; but Grisha didn't even have anyone to look for!

I swallowed my tears and went back to the station. I looked and looked, but Mama wasn't there. I asked one of the workers when the train from the north had arrived.

"A freight train," I said, "but carrying passengers."

"They come once in a while," the man said. "There was one last week and two the week before."

"Then where are the people?"

"How should I know?" the man said. "Some of them got off and went in all different directions, others went on to Samarkand, Bukhara, maybe Kokand. There's no way of knowing."

Well, if there was no way of knowing, I had to look. I went out into the street and began to wander through the city. I looked at every woman who came by. Once I even ran after one, shouting, "Mama!" But when she turned around I could see that she had a sad, old face, and she said something to me in a language I didn't understand. I don't know how, but I finally got to the

130

market. I always went to the market. I think it was hunger that got me there.

The streets became narrow alleys, with houses up against one another, as in the towns we had seen along the way. The houses were made of bricks and together looked like a long, yellow wall with little windows in it. Suddenly there was a big open space; I was in the market.

There was a great hubbub: buyers, sellers, people just talking to one another in a language I didn't understand, a donkey braying, and a policeman with a big mustache walking about among the stalls, now and then telling people to get out of the way.

I stood there looking around. I didn't see either Mama or Grisha.

"There must be a lot of markets here," Grisha had said before we parted. So why should this be the one?

I suddenly missed Grisha. I was hungry. If Grisha and I had still been together, we could have managed. Grisha would undoubtedly have been able to steal something for us to eat.

A man passed in front of me carrying a heavy sack on his shoulder. Suddenly a teenage boy in rags sneaked out from behind a counter. I could see he was one of the children who slept in coal piles. He came up behind the man and reached into the sack. There was a flash, and before I could make out what it was, the boy ran his hand quickly down the length of the sack, the cloth came apart, and potatoes began rolling out, falling on the ground and scattering in all directions. Then the children appeared, how many I don't know: six, seven, maybe more. They suddenly converged on the potatoes and began snatching them up as fast as they could. They put them in their pockets and in all kinds of containers. No sooner had one filled his container and run away than another would take his place and a third would get ready to pounce. Meanwhile, the man with the sack walked on without noticing a thing. Three potatoes rolled right by me, but I stood there petrified, unable to move.

A woman called out. The man stopped and looked back. I stirred, bent down, and grabbed the potatoes, putting them in my pockets and running. I ran like crazy. I ran and ran until I was out of breath. It seemed to me the whole market was chasing me. At the end of an alley I looked over my shoulder: no one was there. No one was coming after me. Actually, how could anyone chase after so many thieves at once, when each was running in a different direction?

I was in the clear! I had done it! Alone! The potatoes were all mine, and no one had caught me! Now I would be able to manage on my own, like Grisha, like the older boys! And it was so easy, so simple!

I took a potato out of my pocket. Unfortunately, I had only managed to grab two of them, one in each hand. If only it were cooked, even a tiny bit . . . but it was hard as . . . as a potato. I rubbed it on my coat, the way Mama always did to clean an apple, but I don't know which was dirtier, the potato or my coat. All at once I couldn't hold back and bit into it. It had a strange taste, bitter, sort of bland, but I ate it all. I finished it in a twinkling and was hungry again, as much as I had been before. I took out the other one. I wanted to eat it as well, but I hesitated. I wanted it cooked, baked, roasted, anything but the way it was. Suddenly I jumped for joy. Why hadn't I thought of it sooner? The coal, the coal pile! I could bury the potato deep inside among the live coals, and I would have a potato just the way we used to make them, in the Crimea, in a bonfire by the river, a soft, hot potato that melted in your mouth, something great.

I looked around. All I had to do was find my way back to the station, and everything would be all right. I noticed it was nearly nightfall. The alley was dark, and very few people were passing by. As always, they were walking quickly — they must have been hurrying home — and they paid me no mind. When had it gotten cloudy? It started drizzling, just a few drops. I asked someone where the railway station was. He looked at me suspiciously, answered curtly, and hurried off, as if it were dangerous to answer questions in the street, even if they were asked by a small child.

My boots had grown heavy. It's already getting muddy, I thought. I bet it's yellow mud, like the soil here. But it was too dark to see a thing. The street lights were not lit. Should I ask again? A way off I heard a voice. Maybe the person would tell me where the station was? I got closer. Someone was singing, then stopped, cursed, and belched loudly. I recognized the sounds.

A drunk, I thought. *He's completely soused!*

The man lay in the mud near the doorway of one of the houses.

"Hey!" he called in my direction, belching again. "Hey, Marusinka, what are you running away for, girl? Come here, my pretty!"

I drew back.

The man began to wail. "Again you're running away from me, Marusinka. I won't touch you any more, not even with my little finger. I won't hit . . ."

I went around the corner and began to walk quickly. I was afraid. Papa had told me to stay away from drunks. He had said you never knew what they would do, that even a nice drunk was dangerous.

Suddenly I heard him bellowing. "Have pity on me, good people! Don't strip me naked in this cold!"

Someone cursed.

"They're stripping me!" the drunk cried and began wailing. "Look, my little Marusinka, see what they've done to me. I'm down to my drawers; and you've left me, my beloved, and I'll never lay a hand on you, not a finger!" The man moaned, weeping a drunkard's tears.

Two shadows appeared just past the corner. Quickly, I darted into a doorway. The people ran past me with their arms laden. They didn't notice me. I held my breath until they were gone.

Poor guy, I thought, digging my hands deeply into my coat

133

pockets. *So drunk, and so lonely. And by the time his little Marusinka goes looking for him in the morning he'll be frozen to death.*

When I got to the coal pile I felt as though I were coming home. I dug into it until I got to the red-hot coals, then buried the potato there. I waited and waited until I couldn't wait any longer. I was afraid I wouldn't be able to find it again and began shoving the coal aside. Underneath, the live coals glowed red and yellow among the dead lumps of black. Where was my potato? Where was my treasure?

I kicked and scraped with my boot. I began to smell burnt rubber. Damn! That was all I needed, to burn my boot! Again I began digging with my hands. Ow! I got burned, but I had the potato. I found it, my treasure! I ate it whole, charred skin and all. Inside, it was still raw, but I couldn't wait. It was hot, and that in itself was something!

I hollowed out a place for myself in the coal pile and got in. My belly ached as always, but this time it wasn't just from hunger. This time it was something a little different. Maybe it was from that first potato, the one I hadn't cooked?

I curled up and pulled more coal over me. A pleasant warmth came up from below.

Poor guy, I said to myself, not sure whether I was still awake or already dreaming. *He'll never find his Marusinka again, but as for me, I'll find Mama, tomorrow . . .*

Twenty-four

The next morning, stealing still seemed to me simple and easy, all right — until they caught me. Yes, I was careless and failed to lie in wait for just the right moment. I didn't even have time to run away. There was bread there for the taking, big quarter-loaves, and I tried to snatch one. Then — they nabbed me. A tall Uzbek appeared out of nowhere and grabbed me. He didn't slap me or hit me; he just dragged me off to a policeman.

This time I wasn't able to get away, not from the policeman either. Now, for the first time, I found myself in a police station.

The officer sat behind a big desk leafing through some papers. There were two deep, angry furrows between his eyebrows. I was scared. What would they do to me now? Would they put me in jail, or send me off to Siberia like the man Grisha had told me about, or maybe send me to an orphanage? I prayed it would be anything but that! Grisha had said there was nothing to eat in such places and that you couldn't even steal anything, because there was simply nothing to steal.

"Name?" said the officer suddenly, without looking up.

"Ya . . . Yasha. Yasha Kagan."

He glanced at me. His eyes were gray and cold. "Where's your family?"

"Papa's in the army, and Mama's lost. I mean I'm lost . . ."

"And what did you do in the market?"

I didn't say anything. Was it possible he didn't know what I had done? And if he didn't know, why should I tell him?

"You stole something!" the officer suddenly barked. "You stole bread!"

I looked down at my boots. I noticed that the toe of my right boot was charred. It must have happened the night before, in the coal. The next time it rained that boot would get soaked through.

". . . And it's all because you're roaming the streets by yourself. Here in the Soviet Union there are no homeless children, no abandoned children! We have places for kids like you. For the good ones there are splendid Soviet institutions; but thieves like you get sent to a different kind of place" — here he paused for a second — "the reformatory!"

I was dumbstruck. Here was another thing Grisha had never told me about. If you could hardly survive in an orphanage, how could you manage in a place that was even worse?

The officer was about to say something else when the door squeaked open and someone else was shoved in. He tripped and fell in front of the desk. He would have remained lying there on the floor like an empty potato sack, but the policeman who had brought him in took hold of him and tried to get him back up on his feet.

"Put the kid in the lockup," the officer ordered, "and come right back."

I found myself in a small room with wooden benches. All the benches were occupied, as was the floor. The room was crowded like the train stations, only worse and without the baggage.

There was a terrible stench in the air, the smell of people who haven't bathed or changed their clothes for a long time, the familiar smell of empty stomachs, the smells of smokers and belching drunks, and the smell of disinfectant that I had gotten to know in the railway station toilets.

I stood there in the center of the cell not knowing what to do. All eyes were on me. I was taken aback. From every side, weary, indifferent, half-closed eyes stared at me. There was a little space near the barred window. I quickly threaded my way to it among the people crouched on the floor and sat down with my back to the wall.

I sat there for a while with my head down. The people reminded me of a turtle I had once seen in the Crimea, peering out of its shell, turning its head slowly from side to side, and looking out at the world indifferently.

Someone cleared his throat.

"So what did you do?" asked a man on the opposite bench. Apparently a conversation had been interrupted and was now resuming.

"I tried to get a residence permit, but it didn't work."

136

"How do you get a residence permit around here?" asked the man on my left.

"What, you new here?" asked the one on my right.

"Yeah," the first said. "I got here this afternoon."

"And you're in jail already?"

No one said anything. I looked up. To my right, at the end of the bench, I saw the man who had just spoken. There was something strange about him. Everything seemed to hang on him: his clothes, his tattered coat; even the skin on his face seemed slack and worn, as if its owner had once been fat and had shrunk.

"Well," he said, wrapping his buttonless coat around himself with both hands. "It doesn't matter. We've all got our reasons for being here. And as far as the residence permit's concerned, it's like this: you've got to have a residence permit stamped in your ID card, just the way you would anywhere else."

"And how do you get it?"

"You've got to have proof that you've got a job and a permanent residence."

"And how do you get that?"

"You get a residence permit!"

The man on my left looked up, astonished. "I don't get it: to get the residence permit you need proof of employment and permanent residence, and to get such proof you need the residence permit, so where do you begin? How do you break out of the vicious circle?"

"Who says you do? Here, take a look around. We're all in here. At night they go through the streets picking up homeless people."

"Then where do they take you?"

"Where? How should I know? We'll see tomorrow," someone else said, lowering his head between his shoulders. "To labor camps in Siberia, no doubt."

I began to tremble. Labor camp — that sounded worse than

an orphanage and even worse than the reformatory the officer had threatened to send me to. And it must have been far away, so far that I could never run away and find Mama. I curled up tight and struggled to hold back my tears.

"What're you so upset about, kid? They're not going to take you to Siberia." It was the wrinkled one. He looked at me sadly. "I wish I were in your place. They'd take me to some institution, and my troubles would be over: a roof over my head, food every day — what else does a man need in life?"

He must not know anything about orphanages, I thought. *Grisha knows. He was there.*

"So what do you say?" the man asked again, as if talking to himself. "What else do you need in life?"

"I don't want to go to an orphanage!" I said.

"What do you want, then?"

"I want to get out, to be outside."

"And what would you do if you were?"

"I'd look for Mama, and Sarele too."

"Who's Sarele?" asked the man on the left. "I never heard such a name."

"My sister," I said. "She went with Mama. And Feigele too."

"Who's that? Your aunt? Your grandmother?"

"No," I said. "She's a little girl. Srulik's sister."

Suddenly I remembered Srulik. Strange, the whole time I was running around outside I hadn't thought of him once, but now . . . I closed my eyes, and he was standing there, with his black curls, his dark eyes, his laugh. I saw him in the snow, on that sled back in the Urals. I saw him laughing, hugging Vanka, chasing after my little Stanka. I saw him lying on the train, pale as a ghost, his eyes closed, wheezing for air. Now he was underneath the snow, way up north.

My eyes filled with tears. I shut them tight to hold the tears back. I knew everyone was looking at me, like a circle of turtles sticking out their wrinkled necks, silently studying the situation.

"If you want to get out so much, why don't you just go?"

138

Startled, I opened my eyes. The man who had spoken to me had not said anything up to now. He sat in front of me on the floor, thin and ragged like all the others, but his look was different. His eyes were completely alert. I thought, too, that I saw a trace of mockery in them.

What on earth was he talking about? Was he laughing at me?

"I'm asking you, kid, do you want to get out or not?"

"I do!" I shot back, but I kept up my guard. No one was going to get the best of me again!

"So what are you waiting for? Little tykes like you can get out easily," the man said, motioning with his chin at the window above my head. I got up and looked at the window. It was small and high up. If I stood on tiptoe I could just barely look out. Beyond the bars it was already dark. A single star glimmered in the sky. I looked back into the cell. Only now did I notice that night had fallen. On the ceiling a bare bulb burned. A cold wind came in the window, which had no glass, only bars.

What did he have in mind? I looked again at the bars. As a matter of fact, maybe I could squeeze between them! If I could only get my head through, I could make my escape.

The man stood up and came over to me.

"We're sound alseep," he said, looking me straight in the eye. "We're sleeping and we don't see a thing!"

I nodded that I understood. I couldn't say anything. Without further ado the man bent down, took me by the waist, and lifted me up to the window. I stood on the sill, grabbed the bars with both hands, and tried to get my head through. I got my forehead through, but the bars pressed against my ears, and it hurt. Turning my head a bit, I got one ear through. Then I turned it back and got the other through. My head was out! The rest of me wouldn't be any problem at all. One shoulder was already through. In another minute I'd be free!

I pulled the rest of my body through the bars and stood on the outside sill. I didn't even bother looking back. It was dark out. I could hardly see the street at my feet. It was quiet. There

139

were no passers-by. I let go of the bars and jumped. Not bad: the railroad cars were higher. I landed without a scratch.

I ran, but no one ran after me. I stopped to listen. The street was quiet. I took a deep breath. The air was cold, clear, and pure. It had the taste of freedom.

Twenty-five

I discovered *zhmikh* later. They pressed the oil out of sunflower seeds and then ground up the shells and made big, hard boards out of them, boards so hard you could barely break them — *zhmikh* boards. But since there was little flour to be had, these boards could then be ground up again and used to bake pita. Why not? People were so hungry they would scratch the bark off of trees and eat it; so why shouldn't they eat pita made of sunflower-seed shells?

They also made boards from cottonseed shells. These were harder than the sunflower-seed boards and had a bitter taste, so they used to feed them to animals on the collective farms. They were worth less than the others, but they did have some value, worth taking a risk for.

I do remember that, when I first started stealing *zhmikh*, it was with Danila.

I don't remember exactly when I discovered *zhmikh*. It was still winter, but it was already beginning to get a little warmer out. Nor do I remember whether I was still in Tashkent or whether I had gone on. I went around Tashkent looking for Mama for days on end. I looked in the railroad stations, in the lines at the trolley stops, near the factories, in the hospitals. Why the hospitals? Because I remembered that once, in the Crimea, she had worked at a hospital information desk. It was true that she had not known how to speak Uzbek, but she did speak Yiddish and Polish, and she had learned Russian so quickly! That's my mom! By this time she must have known Uzbek too. Why, even I already understood the local people and could speak with them a bit.

Tashkent is a huge city. I looked and looked — but Mama was nowhere to be found. Could she have gone elsewhere? I myself then decided to move on.

The cars were standing on a spur. They were open freight cars, with no roofs, so it was easy to get into them. We only had to watch out that no one saw us.

We lurked some way off, waiting for the right moment to make our move.

"Take a car with a ladder on the side," Danila whispered.

"Why?" I whispered back.

"Because when you've thrown the board out you've got to jump, right? If the train is moving fast and you jump from up on top, you'll get killed for sure. But if you come down a side ladder and jump you've got a better chance."

Danila was right, I thought. I had already seen the remains of children's bodies, and even those of adults, along the tracks. They must have jumped from ladders at the backs of the cars. There are cars like that, and they're the most dangerous: you jump and get hit by the next car, and you're done for.

Again and again I rehearsed in my mind what Danila had explained to me: the train had to be out of the station or the workers would see you throw the *zhmikh* out and take it for themselves; so the train had to be some way out; but if you threw the board out when the train had already picked up speed you didn't stand a chance of landing in one piece yourself.

"Now!" Danila whispered.

We darted out and ran for the cars. Danila quickly climbed up a ladder on one of them and disappeared inside, as if he had ceased to exist. I hurriedly climbed another one and jumped in.

Let's hope nobody saw us, let's hope, I prayed, tingling with fear. Someone called out in the distance, but I don't think it was to us. It was just someone giving orders.

I tried to control my huffing and puffing and calm my furiously pounding heart, as if someone could have heard them. It took some time, but eventually they calmed down, like a pack of wild horses disappearing into the distance. I sat leaning on the side of the car, waiting for the train to get under way. It was a cold, clear day. Danila said the cold wind came from the Siberian snowfields. I think he was right; how else could it be so cold when snow fell only in the mountains, when there was hardly even any rain and the sky was almost always clear and the sun bright?

But I wasn't cold. When you run and climb you don't feel cold, and there, next to the side of the car, I also began to feel the warmth of the sun. It was almost directly overhead. The wind whipped and whistled up above, but inside the car I was protected.

I just had to wait patiently. What was Danila doing in the next car? No doubt he was warming up in the sun. What else was there to do? Suddenly I felt a jerk, then another. Now the train was picking up speed. I looked at the other car. Danila's head popped up for a second. He signaled to me: now!

I tried to pick up the nearest board. It was heavy. How would I get it over the high side-panel? Its narrow end touched the side. If I didn't do it now it would be too late! Then, suddenly, I knew how. I grabbed the other end of the board, pulled it toward me, and lifted it up until it was leaning against the side-panel. Then I took hold of the lower end and pushed the board up over the side. One big push: oof! I heard the board fall to the ground near the track. Now to run for it, fast! I pulled myself up with both hands, grasped the top of the ladder, turned around, and began climbing down the outside as fast as I could. I heard the whistling of the wind. I heard the clatter of the wheels coming closer and closer. I looked down. The track was going by rapidly: ps–ps–ps–ps. Terror!

"Jump!" Danila called out from a distance.

It was now or never.

I climbed down to the bottom rung, took hold of the railing as far down as I could, and flung out my feet. For a second I felt as though my body were flapping in the wind. My arms felt almost torn out of their sockets, but I immediately touched the ground. I ran as fast as I could alongside the train, my hands clinging to the bar.

"Let go!" Danila shouted.

I let go. Running forward with tremendous momentum, I tripped and fell and rolled down the embankment. The great iron wheels roared by above me. Then suddenly it was all over. The train sped away. The clatter receded, and it was quiet. I rolled over on my side, got to my knees, and stood up. I was still in one piece! No harm done!

Then I remembered: the *zhmikh*. I began running along the embankment back in the direction of the station. *As long as no one takes it! As long as no one steals it!* Off in the distance I could see Danila coming toward me, pulling his board after him.

The baker to whom we brought the *zhmikh* under cover of darkness gave each of us a quarter-loaf of bread and a salted fish tail. What a party we had that night!

Twenty-six

I wasn't always so lucky. Once, the station platform seemed to go on forever, and when it ended there were houses too close to the track. I was afraid someone would snatch my *zhmikh* board before I could jump off to retrieve it. So I waited a little longer than usual, then waited some more. Finally, I couldn't wait any longer and threw the board over. Then I climbed over and down the ladder. But by this time the train was already moving quite fast — boy, was it moving! I could see I wouldn't be able to set my legs on the ground and run along with it, so I turned in the direction the train was moving and just jumped.

That's all I remember. I don't know how long I lay there alongside the track. Behind my closed eyes, I saw many things. The last thing I saw was Mama, but she was walking away, farther and farther away. And suddenly Grandma was there, a little old woman wrapped in a big wool scarf. She smiled at me and reached out to give me a sugar cube, but then she too began moving away. It was as if an invisible train were taking her, sugar cube in hand, far away from me. Then my head started to ache. It ached so badly I finally opened my eyes. Strange, I usually knew where I was when I woke up, but this time I didn't recognize anything or understand what had happened. I tried to sit up, but the pain in my head suddenly hit me like a hammer, and I lay back down.

Where was I? The ground under my ears began to rumble, first faintly, then more and more loudly. Then it began to tremble slightly, and I could hear a clattering sound approach. Suddenly there was a great roar: a train! It felt as though it were going right through my head, on and on with no end. I put my fingers in my ears and shut my eyes tight. The iron monster plowed all the way through me, slicing me like a knife, and then, in an instant, it was gone, vanished into thin air.

I opened my eyes. Now I could see that I was stretched out in a ditch at the foot of the railway embankment. I took my fingers out of my ears. Yes, the train was gone. Then I remembered: the board, the board I had thrown from the train before jumping! With a great deal of effort I got up. I had to find the *zhmikh!* But which way to go, right or left? Which way had I come from? I looked to the right. In the distance the houses seemed to blur together in the drifting fog; yet the sky was clear and the sun shining. What was this fog? I looked the other way. Again there was a foggy blur, this time swallowing up larger houses, a crane, a chimney. It must be the station!

I struggled up the side of the embankment and began walking along the top. There was a hammering in my head, but I kept going. I wasn't going to give up. After all, it was I who had given that board the heave. It was mine, all mine!

But there was no board there, or anything else for that matter, not even the chunks of coal the bigger boys would hurl from the trains, those who knew how to jump off when they were already traveling at full speed. I wasn't aware of entering the station or of leaving it. I just wandered the streets. Waves of pain passed from one side of my head to the other, the fog swirled before my eyes, and I walked and walked. As always, my feet carried me to the old town, to the narrow alleys and little stucco houses. Reaching one of the squares, my strength gave out. I sank to the ground up against the wall of one of the houses.

A big house with a dome on top appeared and disappeared in the fog. Its façade was decorated with blue and green tiles. I had seen such buildings before. Danila had told me they were mosques, where people called Muslims used to pray. But this house was not so ornate, and where was the high tower every mosque was supposed to have? There was something familiar about the tiles, a sight I had seen before but didn't recognize. Another wave of pain flooded my head. I closed my eyes.

When I reopened them I thought I was dreaming. A column of princes — no, kings! — was coming out of the house opposite me. Walking calmly, they seemed to float, to float toward me. I heard them speaking to one another in placid, otherworldly tones, just like in Grandma's stories. But they were speaking Uzbek, yes, no doubt about that. And their cloaks were in the Uzbek style, but particularly festive — striped cloaks with silver and gold embroidered hems. These kings weren't wearing crowns but skullcaps, round and square velvet skullcaps embroidered with gold and silver threads, and they all had the same emblem on them — what exactly I don't remember.

Now I could see the queen too. She was tall and stately, and she had gold and silver embroidery, not only on the hems of her cloak but also around her collar and on her hat, which was covered with a thin kerchief. She stood holding the arm of another, older queen, waiting for the kings to finish speaking. *Grandma dear, what a story you've hatched for me this time!*

A little girl stopped near me, a princess in an embroidered dress. Two thin, black braids rested on her shoulders, and there were gold earrings in her ears. She stood looking me over with her dark, curious eyes, toying with a chain she had about her neck. There was an ornament hanging from the chain, like the one I had seen on the tiles and on the skullcaps. Now I recognized it: it was . . . but then it flickered and disappeared in the fog. I waited for it to come back to me.

Then I heard the kings greet one another.

"Sabbath peace!" they said, going their separate ways. "Sabbath peace!"

The emblem once again shone before my eyes. I put my hand out to touch it. "The Star of David!" I said aloud, and sank into the darkness.

Twenty-seven

A gentle hand wiped my forehead, a loving hand.

"Mama," I mumbled. "Mama! At last you're back!"

Someone tucked in my blanket. I felt warm and cozy. My

146

headache was gone. I turned over on my side and drifted off into a deep, dreamless sleep.

I awoke as if in a dream. I was lying in a big room, lined with rugs. A photograph of an old man with a white beard on his face and a lambswool hat on his head stared at me from one of the walls. He looked like one of the kings I had seen. When? Where had they been? Where was the queen and the little princess? Where had they gone?

I turned my head. A bright light, blotched with shadows, streamed from the doorway. I heard voices there, outside. People were talking, laughing, eating. Yes, I was sure they were eating. I heard the clatter of dishes: food!

Again there were the familiar, gnawing hunger pangs. I threw off the blanket and got up. I staggered a little. Was I dreaming? I was wearing a long, cotton gown. I looked at my palms: they were scratched and cut, but clean. My nails had been trimmed; when had I trimmed them? My bare feet were clean too. When was the last time I had washed them?

Again I heard the voices. They were speaking softly. I walked toward the rectangle of light and stood in the doorway.

In the courtyard stood a big table, and there were a lot of people sitting around it. A flowering tree spread its branches over them like a white cloud, like a dream, casting patches of shade as far as the soles of my feet. At the head of the table sat an old man, his beard bushy and white, like the one I had seen in the picture. On his head he wore an embroidered skullcap. Others were there, too: men, women, and children. They sat and ate in silence, not gulping or grabbing. Two women emerged from one of the rooms carrying big bowls. The taller of the two, her face round and full, stopped short in surprise, lifted her bowl, and said aloud, "Look, the boy is up!"

The old man turned and examined me at length. Suddenly he smiled, a network of tiny wrinkles spreading around his eyes.

"Blessed be He who revives the dead!" he said. "Blessed be He who brings the dead to life!"

147

Many pairs of eyes were riveted on me, black, shining eyes. I was startled and drew back. The big woman quickly set down her bowl and came over to me, smiling. A gold tooth gleamed through her smile like a little sun.

"Don't be afraid, child. You're among Jews!"

Jews! These people were Jews! But they looked just like the Uzbeks I had met in the cities, wore the same clothes, had the same dark skin and eyes, spoke the same language. No, it couldn't be. They wore embroidered skullcaps, just like the Uzbeks, but . . . yes, now I noticed it: there were gold and silver Stars of David embroidered on them.

Suddenly my head swam. The woman caught hold of me just in time.

"He's still sick, poor thing," said another woman.

"No, he's probably just hungry!" said the woman with the gold tooth, supporting me under my arms. "Come, sit at the table."

The old man at the head of the table gave a sign, and immediately one of the children jumped up and ran to get a chair. I sat down and didn't dare look up. I sensed they were all looking at me. I think my ears even turned red.

Someone set a big, full plate of steaming hot rice down in front of me. There was no fork. Unable to restrain myself, I picked up some rice with my fingers and put it in my mouth. It was scalding hot. I blew again and again, then gulped the rice down, almost without chewing.

Mama! Oh Mama, I'm burning up! There's a fire in my throat! The rice was spicy, and I coughed and coughed, until someone patted me on the back and gave me a drink of water. I grabbed the glass and drank. The fire was put out, and I wiped away my tears.

A boy on the other side of the table burst out laughing. I hid my face with a plate. Someone reprimanded him, and he stopped abruptly.

148

"Not that way," said the girl next to me. "Here, I'll show you."

She took one of the pitas that had been set in the middle of the table, tore off a piece, scooped up some rice, and put it in her mouth.

I quickly followed her example.

"Right!" said the tall woman, patting my shoulder. "That's the boy!"

Everyone laughed with relief, as if they had been waiting to see whether I would pass the test, and went back to eating. Now I knew what to expect. I knew what spicy food tasted like. I dug into the pita and rice with a passion.

"Take it easy!" the woman said. "Haste makes waste!"

I tried to slow down, to chew properly, but it was hard. The rice tasted different from any I had ever had. It was pink and crisp, and had little pieces of carrot in it as well as red pepper and onion. It was tasty, oh Mama was it tasty, but so spicy!

I glanced over at the big bowl of meat that was sitting in the middle of the table.

"Not today," said the big woman, noticing where I was looking. "Your stomach isn't ready for it, Lord have mercy."

I finished my rice and wiped the plate with the rest of the pita.

"Want more?" asked the girl next to me.

"A little," I said, looking at her for the first time. Then I recognized her. She was the little princess in the story. She had the same black eyes with the long, curly lashes; the same dainty braids, golden earrings, and chain, the chain with the Star of David on it.

Then it all came back to me.

"Is today the Sabbath?" I asked.

"No," answered a fellow sitting next to the old man, "today's Monday. We found you on the Sabbath near the synagogue."

I tried to figure it out: on what day had I jumped from the train after the *zhmikh?* Before that, when I was trying to snatch

149

something in the market, I had heard someone say something about Wednesday. Wednesday or Thursday? Then I had jumped and fallen and lain below the track until I woke up. I had awakened on the Sabbath, hadn't I? If so, I had lain in the ditch for two days, maybe even three. And today was Monday. Was it any wonder I was so hungry? As if I had eaten anything even before that.

Now they served dried fruit: apricots, raisins, even apples. And they brought out tea, strong tea in little glasses.

The old man at the head of the table sipped his tea noisily, as if he were sucking it in. When he finished, he stretched in his chair and looked at me, and I froze. I wanted to go on eating, at least a little, but they were all staring at me. The chair beneath me felt as though it were getting warm, as if I were sitting over a campfire.

"Welcome to the Pinhasovs!" the old man said cheerfully. "What's your name, son?"

I wanted to say "Yasha," but I suddenly remembered.

"Yankele," I said. "Yankele Kagan."

"Ya'akov!" said the old man, smiling warmly at me . "Ya'akov Cohen!"*

I nodded but couldn't speak. Grandpa had once called me that, so long ago I couldn't remember when. What else had there been back then? Grandma in her little room, and Mama and Papa and little Sarele too. I felt strong hands picking me up.

"The boy is still sick," said a woman's voice. "Take him inside. He's got to stay in bed for a while. But he'll be all right, thank God."

*The old man is translating the names back into their original Hebrew forms. Kagan is a Russian form of the Hebrew Cohen.

Twenty-eight

"So you're sure you aren't royalty? Really sure?"

Miriam laughed. "Of course not. My father's a shoemaker. He works in a factory and also at home."

"And your uncles?"

"Uncle Shlomo is a tailor, and so is Asher. And Uncle Moshe works in a textile factory. He's an expert weaver. He's very well thought of in the cooperative."

"On the Sabbath, when you found me, I thought you were all kings and queens!"

"In honor of the Sabbath Queen* we are all kings and queens!" said Miriam's grandmother. She was sitting in the doorway knitting. I hadn't even realized that she was listening to our conversation. Nor would it have occurred to me that she would understand: she looked like someone from another story, an exotic tale.

"If you aren't royalty, where did you get these rugs?" I asked, pointing to the floor. "It's like a palace! Grandma used to tell me about royal palaces!"

"That's from before I was born," Miriam said, getting up. She hopped from rug to rug. I wanted to try it myself, but my head still hurt.

I looked outside. The apple tree in the yard was slowly shedding garlands of blossoms. They drifted down like white butterflies and landed softly on the ground. The bees buzzed incessantly in the spring sunshine.

"It's because of the beautiful rugs, Grandma," said Miriam. "He's saying they only have such rugs in royal palaces."

"Our family dealt in rugs," the old woman said, adjusting her

*In Jewish tradition the Sabbath is personified as a queen who pays a royal visit each week and must be greeted in one's finest clothes.

151

head kerchief. "That was a long time ago, before the war, before the Russians came. But since then, trading is forbidden, so all the boys learned crafts. Not all of them were drafted, thank God, and those who remained behind work in the cooperatives and make a decent living, God be praised. Whatever we have is what is left from before. We try not to sell anything. As long as we have enough to eat, we don't complain."

As long as they have enough to eat . . . It seemed to me they must work pretty hard, because after hours they worked at home too and sold whatever they made in the market. And they certainly had plenty to eat.

In fact, it seemed like forever since I had seen people eat this way: together, peacefully. It was only after I got over the worst of my hunger and learned not to grab and gulp that I began to try eating the way they did. I was used to just stuffing food into my mouth, because I was so hungry. And when the hunger wasn't so pressing I would eat whenever I felt like it, when there was good food to be had. But here it was different. They ate at least one meal a day together, all together: grandmother and grandfather at the head of the table, Miriam's parents, and her brothers and their wives and children. Even Miriam's aunts, whose husbands had gone off to the war like Papa, were not left alone. They too would sit down to the table and eat with their children. I had noticed that there wasn't always so much food on the table — there were something like twenty mouths to feed, or more. But they always ate together, quietly, peacefully, as if to say, "We eat together because we're one big family!"

Family. When I first understood this I felt a lump in my throat and couldn't eat. Now this lump had a name. It was my "aloneness," my "aloneness" as opposed to their "togetherness." At such times I missed everyone terribly: Mama, Papa, Sarele, Grandma, who had stayed behind. I had never missed Grandma so much as I did now. These people were good to me, hospitable, but I was a guest, just a guest. My home was where my mother

152

was. And then that lump in my throat would take on another taste, the taste of leaving this big family dinner table, these people, Miriam.

"Grandma says you almost made it to the next world!" said Miriam, hopping onto her other foot, "but she knew it was just almost. She knows a lot about sickness."

I remembered the hand that had wiped my forehead and tucked in my blanket.

"She told me a story about a famous doctor, too," Miriam went on, "and how he knew who was going to live and who was going to die."

"How?"

I really wanted to know. I wanted to hear stories. My own grandmother used to tell me stories, and they were even better than sugar cubes!

Miriam sat down on the floor next to her grandmother and hugged her knees. "Grandma, tell us the one about the woman who made the Devil's life miserable!"

"But Miriam, you've heard that story so many times you could tell it yourself."

"No, you. It's not the same."

Miriam's grandmother put aside her knitting. She looked toward the sun and closed her eyes. We sat quietly. Only the bees buzzed in the cloud of white blossoms. I waited. I wanted her to start telling the story, but I also wanted this moment — with the sun, the flowers, Miriam and her dark curly eyelashes — to last forever.

Miriam's grandmother opened her eyes and smiled at me like a wrinkled sun — like my own grandmother. She wasn't as small or thin as my grandmother, nor did my grandmother wear a colorful robe like hers or a kerchief over an embroidered skull-cap; all the same, yes, she did look like her.

"I'll tell you about the woman who made the Devil miserable," she began. I drew closer. I didn't want to miss a single word.

"Once upon a time God decided to punish the Devil."

"What was the punishment?" I asked.

"He banished him, sentenced him to fifteen years' exile among human beings."

"Where, in Siberia?"

Grandma smiled. I realized I had said something foolish and decided to keep quiet. From now on I would just listen.

"So the Devil went to live among people, and he got married. Now what sort of woman does the Devil find for himself? A wicked, evil sort of woman, so wicked that no man would want to marry her.

"A year went by, and the woman bore him a son, a beautiful baby boy, smart, unusually talented. The Devil loved his son, but the woman made his life hellish. In this way, fifteen years went by. At last it came time for the Devil to return from exile. He wanted to go back to the real hell, which would have been better than the one his wife had made for him, but he couldn't bring himself to leave his only son.

" 'My dear son,' he said to him, 'how can I leave you to such a mother?' The Devil thought and thought. At last he said, 'I'm going to make a great doctor of you!'

" 'But Father, how can I be a doctor? I haven't studied anything!'

" 'Never mind, son. Just tell people you're a great doctor who can treat the hardest cases. When they take you to examine someone, I'll be there. Only you will see me, son; the others won't even know I'm there. If I stand at the sick person's head, it will mean he's going to get well and there's nothing to worry about. If I stand at his feet, say they called you too late and the person is going to die. In this way you will build up a reputation as a great physician.'

"And that's just what happened. The Devil's son went from city to city, and wherever he went he proclaimed his great skill. In the course of this journey he also made a lot of money. One day he arrived in the realm of a king whose daughter had fallen ill. No one had been able to cure the princess of her ailment.

The king had announced: 'Whoever heals my daughter will receive a great reward, and I will give him her hand in marriage!'

"The Devil's son came and said, 'I can heal the princess!'

"They brought him to her room and there was his father, standing at the foot of her bed.

" 'Father,' he said silently, 'why must you take her soul? They have promised me a great reward as well as her hand in marriage!'

" 'There's nothing to be done, my son,' the Devil said. 'The hour of her death is at hand.'

"The son turned around and said aloud, 'Mother, Mother, Father's here!'

"The Devil got scared and ran for dear life. The princess opened her eyes and stood up, restored to perfect health. The son received his reward and the princess's hand in marriage.

"The wedding celebration lasted seven days and seven nights, and in the whole kingdom there was no happier man than he."

Grandma went back to her knitting. For a long time we didn't say anything. I was sure she too had seen the Devil. She had seen him standing near my head. Grandma knew I would get well!

I got up to stoke the fire in the stove out in the courtyard. Soon, when the oven was hot, Grandma would go and bake some pita. I loved the way she tapped the sides of the stove to see if it was hot enough, I loved the ringing sound it made, and I loved to open it and see how the slabs of dough had been pressed one by one onto the hot oven walls.

"Wait," said Grandma, "soon you'll see how we bake *matza* for Passover in the special oven!"

Twenty-nine

But I didn't stay there until Passover. How could I? The better I felt the more I longed for Mama. These people were a family, and this made me even more lonesome. They never asked me to leave, and I don't think they would have said anything if I had stayed; but one day I thanked them for everything and left. I went back to looking for Mama.

I set out in clean, well-mended clothes. Miriam's father had even repaired my torn boot for me. Only my coat did I leave behind, because that could no longer be mended. It was torn and frayed and consisted mostly of holes. Instead they gave me another one, an old wool-lined workman's coat. It was a big one, reaching down past my knees. Miriam's mother said this would actually be good, because it would keep me warm down to my boots, but she wanted to shorten the sleeves. I asked her not to, because I could always roll them up, and when it was very cold it was good to have sleeves long enough to cover your hands. True, she had also given me woolen gloves, but I knew it wouldn't be long before I would have to trade them for food. Yes, they also gave me provisions for my journey, but how long would they last?

I went to Samarkand to look for Mama. I knew I could go on looking for her in their town indefinitely, but I was ashamed to do so. I thought, *What if Miriam's father saw me stealing in the market? And what if Miriam herself saw me?* Well, I won't tell you how I said goodbye to her, but I will tell you about the coat. What happened wasn't what I had in mind when I asked that the sleeves be left the way they were; it just happened this way . . .

I stood looking around in the market in Samarkand. I was hungry. I had already been wandering around there for a week, and the provisions I had brought with me had long since been used up. I had already traded the gloves for food, and again I was hungry. But I was scared, scared the way I had been at first. At Miriam's I had been protected, and I had gotten used to it. Now once again I felt small and vulnerable and, most of all, hungry.

A few stalls down I saw someone selling seeds. I went closer. I had always hung around seed sellers. They kept a close watch on their merchandise — did they ever! — but a few seeds always fell to the ground, and I could pick them up one at a time. There were several cups next to the pile, full and ready to sell. Customers would empty the cups straight into their pockets, or else the vendor would roll up a sheet of newspaper, making a little package out of it, and pour the seeds inside.

A teenage boy was standing there, a big boy, one of the "abandoned children," and he was dickering with the vendor.

"Too much!" he said, spitting out the shell of a seed he had taken to taste. "They're stale! They're not worth a cent!"

"Scram!" the vendor shouted. "You haven't got a cent to your name anyway! Only real buyers are allowed to taste."

The boy rummaged in his pocket. There was a clink of coins inside.

"You hear? I've got enough here to buy your whole rotten carload!"

I drew closer. These big, fearless boys always fascinated me. I would never learn to talk or behave the way they did, to be cool like them, to treat people in authority — anyone who tells you what to do — with brazen contempt. I leaned unintentionally on the stand, entranced with what was happening there. The boy took another seed and cracked it expertly between his teeth. He spit out the shell with an indifferent air and said, "Ten cents. That's my last offer!"

"Get out!" said the vendor angrily. "If you don't get out of here I'll call the police!"

"You want the police? Here, I'll call them for you," said the boy, pointing past the vendor's shoulder. The man turned

157

around. In a flash the boy grabbed a cup of seeds, put it in his pocket, darted off, and disappeared in the crowd.

"Thief!" cried the vendor. "Stop him! Quick! Thief!"

He shouted and shouted, but he didn't move. No one was going to get the better of him twice.

There arose a great commotion: people shouting and running to and fro, chickens squawking and hurrying fearfully out of the way, and I . . . I, meanwhile, simply froze. Suddenly it occurred to me that one of my hands, hidden in the big sleeve, lay on top of a cup of seeds. I was too frightened to move. I was sure everyone would jump on me at once, pecking at me like birds of prey, hitting me, and dragging me off to the police.

But nothing happened. No one even looked at me. The vendor glanced at me briefly, then went back to waving his arms at the pursuers and cursing the boy. Then I understood why no one suspected me of stealing. When you steal you run away; I was just standing there quietly. Under the cover of the sleeve I took the full cup of seeds. No one saw me put it in my pocket. I put my other hand in my pocket too. After standing there for a moment, I simply turned and walked away. I even whistled something to avert suspicion, whistled and left the market.

It was in this way, completely by chance, that I discovered another use for the sleeves. Perhaps if Miriam's mother had known what I was going to do she would have shortened them. I'm not sure. But I had no doubt about one thing: she would feel bad if she knew how hungry I was. So I made good use of it, this gift of hers. And maybe, just maybe, she had known she was giving me a magic coat.

Thirty

I learned from the long sleeves that everything has more than one use, including things I had never thought of before.

Take bathing, for example. We bathe when we're dirty, right? But couldn't it also be a way of doing laundry? Suppose you decided just for the fun of it to jump in the lake, and for some reason you had all your clothes on. The result would be that you would not only have a good time but you'd get yourself and your clothes clean too!

This happened to me for the first time that spring. The arrival of the blossoms had, as usual, stirred wild thoughts in my head. In the yards of the old houses, the trees were blooming madly. Branches laden with intoxicating colors and smells spilled over the tops of the high walls. There was still a residue of snow up in the mountains, but in the valleys, on the lower slopes, and in the villages along the railroad, a crazy profusion of white, pink, and purple flowers heralded the arrival of spring.

The frozen soil was thawing. This was the time to get out into the country, I thought. At least there I could wander in the fields and vegetable patches and fill my empty stomach without fear. And maybe, just maybe, I would come to a *kolkhoz*, a collective farm, and find Mama working there. She had to be somewhere, didn't she? And she had to work, right? So why not in the country?

But I guess I went too soon. I got off at a little station in a remote mountain town. There were villages round about. I went to the nearest one. The Uzbek houses, which they called *kishlaks,* clung to the hillside, with orchards in full bloom stretched out behind them. The doors were open. Old men in fur hats were warming themselves in the spring sunshine. Clear water flowed rapidly in a ditch alongside the street, and soft grass sprouted around the cottages. In the shade of a flowering almond tree, tied to the trunk with a long rope, stood a kid. It looked at me

159

for a moment with its big eyes and went right back to pulling up the grass at its feet. It was Vanka! Or at least it looked an awful lot like my Vanka back in the Crimea: the same light color, the same long ears. Only its dark little tail was like Stanka's. Where were they now, my Vanka-Stanka?

I came closer. The old man sitting at the doorstep of the cottage smiled at me under his white mustache. I stroked the kid's head. The old man said a few words, and his laugh turned into a long cough. I knelt down and hugged the kid, nestling my head against its soft hair. Vanka! My Vanka! The kid turned its head toward me and licked my face. Like all kids, it loved the salt of tears.

I didn't play with the kid all day. I had to move on, to keep looking. A woman baking pita in the yard gave me a fresh, hot piece. I hadn't even asked for it, only looked at it. I went out to the fields on the mountainside. People were working there among the flowering trees: men with huge mustaches, women in colorful smocks. But there was no sign there of a thin woman with brown, curly hair, a warm gaze, and arms open to greet me. I had realized that morning that I would not find Mama there, not in the Uzbek villages. They were all families in these parts, and she would have been a stranger, an outsider. I had to look in the *kolkhozi,* in the big cotton fields in the lowlands, in the factories and workshops.

There were no fruit or vegetables to eat there either. A lot of fruit trees were in bloom. Miriam's grandmother had taught me how to recognize them: white blossoms meant apples and pears; pinkish white were almonds; and deep pink were cherries. Why couldn't they bear fruit first and then bloom? How long would I have to wait for the flowers to turn to fruit?

As for the vegetables I was dying to eat, they were all still seeds. The people were hoeing the gardens to prepare them for the spring planting. Nothing had come up yet, nothing.

But the sun was warm and the grass fresh, and there were flowers all around, and water was flowing in the irrigation ditches and the little pond in the valley, and people would call

160

to each other from one hillside to another. A woman would sing a lengthy ballad, and another woman would laugh aloud, and when two people came toward one another on a path they would call out from a distance, "Hello there!" And they would greet me too with a smile, even me! When had strangers in the towns ever smiled at me? In fact, who had smiled at me altogether of late, other than Miriam's family? And when they sat down to eat they would motion to me to join them. And a little donkey, following its mother out into the field, suddenly began braying, running and jumping in the green grass.

Again, I couldn't help myself. Something welled up in my throat and then burst out in a shout of joy. I jumped up and ran after the donkey. I rolled in the grass, brayed at the donkey, and waved to everyone. Then I went on climbing up and down the hillsides, up and down and on and on, until a shadow suddenly spread over the opposite slope and moved quickly up to the summit. The sun was setting behind the mountains, a cold wind came up from the valley, and by the time I got back to the village it was night, and the wind was biting at my back. The cottages were closed up tight inside their adobe walls, and from the smell of smoke I knew people were eating dinner and getting warm in their houses. But soon the smoke disappeared, distant voices faded, and dogs fell silent: the village had gone to sleep.

Then I realized I had gone to the mountains too soon. I was colder that night than I had ever been before. There was no coal pile to crawl into, no open storage shed.

I didn't notice the stars disappear or the snow begin to fall. Snow! Down below, in the towns, the ground would freeze in the wintertime, but there was hardly any snow or even very much rain to bother me. But here the wind whipped me with cold lashes. Any shelter at all would have been better than being outside, any shelter!

I spent the night under a pile of straw and horse manure at the edge of a village, near the big watering trough. I dug myself

161

in as best I could at the base of an adobe wall. The wind whistled over my head but didn't get to me. The fermentation of the manure gave off a certain warmth, and I almost didn't mind the smell; but when the snow covering me melted, it slid down my neck, wetting my big coat and soaking me to the skin. Papa used to say that if I was cold it was really cold out, because cold never bothered me the way it did Mama and Sarele. And this time I was really freezing.

The night dragged on so long I began to wonder if it would ever end. Maybe this darkness, the cold and the snow, the wet straw and the manure would go on forever. But I guess I finally fell asleep.

The next morning the sky was clear again. The first rays of sunshine on my face felt like a caress. I lay there under the snow, the straw, and the manure, lay there shaking from the chill. It was wet, so wet and cold! The sun climbed upward into the blue sky, and the snow quickly melted. Water seeped into my clothes. I roused myself and got up. I was soaking wet, and I smelled like a whole stableful of manure.

Then I discovered the pond, or rather I remembered it. I mean, I had seen the pond the day before, in the hollow just above the village, but then it had just seemed like part of the scenery, along with the flower-covered slope, the river, the mountaintop. Now it was everything! Suddenly, it and only it existed.

When I got there the air was already warming up. Taking off my boots, I stepped barefoot into the water, so as to wash off the mud that had gotten inside and the barnyard smell. Oh Mama, was it cold! It was mountain water, from melted snow, and cold as ice — but it was clear. The river in the Crimea where I had learned to swim had not been clear, or cold either. You needed courage to dip into this!

It wasn't as though I had decided to jump into the cold water; I just did it. I tossed my boots up onto the shore and jumped in fully dressed, coat and all. I thrashed about in the water, then swam like crazy, until my body started to warm up. Finally! I

162

flipped over on my back. The clothes weighed me down, but so what! It was great. How good it was to swim in the clear, blue pond!

It was then that I felt true freedom for the first time. For the first time I enjoyed being alone, doing exactly what I wanted to do, with no one calling me, no one telling me I had to come back before I had finished my swim, no one caring whether or not I came back in time. And besides, as I said, I got in a bath and a laundry at the same time. The sun would dry everything out. So what harm was there in it?

I turned back over on my stomach and swam to the other side. It was there that I discovered the fish trap.

Thirty-one

Since then I've found many traps and nets full of fish, but this was the first, and I'll never forget it. It was tied with a rope to a big rock on the shore of the pond, in a spot where the rocks sloped straight down into the deep water. I swam around it. It was a real trap: the fish could get in but not out. I made another swing around it, then climbed up on the bank. The rock was warm. I took off my coat and wrung it out. It wasn't easy. I wrung out one sleeve at a time, then another part of the coat, then the next, until I had wrung out as much as I could. Then I laid it out on the rock to dry. I took my clothes off too, all of them, and wrung them out and spread them out around me. The smell of the manure seemed to be gone. Quite a laundry!

I stretched out on the rock and gazed at the fish trap down below. The flat surface of the rock radiated warmth to my belly, my chest, and my arms and legs. The sun warmed my back. The thin layer of snow on the grass around the pond was melting steadily. Around me were the sound of water, the flow of little rivulets, and the chirping of birds, things I had always loved, and I lay looking at the trap. I was hungry, as usual. I tugged the rope. The trap came up, scraping against the rock. Big fish writhed about inside, trying to escape to freedom. Their silvery scales flashed in the sun. The water streaming out of the trap sent ever-widening ripples out across the calm surface of the pond. I lowered the trap back into the water.

What should I do? I could easily take out a fish, but what would I do with it? Take it to the village and exchange it for some bread? That didn't make sense. Anyone there who wanted fish could come to the pond and catch it. True, in the village they wouldn't know I had stolen it; no one counted the fish in the trap, and another one would surely come along to take its place. The real problem was, they simply wouldn't have any use for my fish! Then what? Would I eat it myself? If only I could. I would have loved to. But how? I remembered the stuffed fish Mama once made, long, long ago when we still had a house and a kitchen and a stove. I got all knotted up inside. No, I couldn't even make a fire. There was so little wood around that the local people stoked their ovens with charcoal and dried animal dung. Besides, even if I did have enough wood to make a fire, how would I light it? I had no matches, or anything else.

The only place I could bake the fish was, of course, in a coal pile, such as I might find at any of the big train stations. Once I even stuffed a porcupine into one, yes, I swear, a real porcupine! As much as I loved animals I was so hungry that I killed one with a stone. One of us had to die. So I wept and killed it and skinned it, and then buried it in the coal. And then I ate it, even before it was fully cooked.

But the nearest train station was a small one. I had noticed when I first got there that it had no pile of spent coal. What then? I'd have to go on to the next place that had a coal pile. Actually, that wouldn't have been so terrible; I didn't plan to spend another night like the previous one. But the freedom and the sunshine and the soft grass and the flowers and the smiling people . . .

Well, I'd wait a bit. Just until my clothes dried. Either my hunger wasn't so bad yet or my weariness got the better of it, because I started to doze off on the rock. A pleasant warmth spread through my whole body, from the rock below and from the sun above. How good it felt.

And again I saw Mama. She stood stringing up stuffed fish on a long line. I reached out to take one, and she rapped me on the hand and said, "No! Not now!" Sarele took some sweet carrot slices from the pot and stuck them on the fish, like orange-colored eyes. Again I reached out to take one, but Mama said, "No!" I grabbed the pot, which was too hot to hold, and it spilled. The carrots rolled out onto my back and burned and burned.

I awoke with a start and sat bolt upright. Where was I? What had happened? Why was my back burning? I looked around and saw the clothes scattered on the rocks, the pond, the trap in the water, the hillsides round about. Again they were dotted with color: the flowering trees, the clothes of the people working in the fields. Then I remembered. But why was my back burned? And the backs of my legs too? And one side of my face? I looked at my hand: it was red! The sun! I had gotten sunburned! And the thirst — why this terrible thirst?

Without giving it much thought I jumped in the water. Oh Mama! I had forgotten how cold it was. I drank and swam and drank and swam again, until my thirst was quenched and I no longer felt cold. Then I was hungry again. The trap was packed with fish. They twisted and turned, trying to get out. What now? The sun was almost directly overhead; soon it would be afternoon. Someone was bound to come. The owner of the trap would come to take out his fish. It was now or never. I climbed out of the water onto the rock and pulled the rope toward me. I chose the biggest fish, pulled it out, and clubbed it on the head with a stone. It's a good thing fish don't make sounds. Then I lowered the trap, with the rest of the fish in it, back into the water. Now I had to hurry. I gathered up my clothes from the rocks all around. They were dry. Only the coat was still damp and heavy. By the time the wool lining was dry it would be dark, and then I would have to deal with the cold and the snow. No, I couldn't stay here. I got dressed, putting on the coat too. My back was hot, so a little dampness on it wouldn't hurt. The coat had big pockets, including two that were sewn to the lining in front. The fish lay on the rock, no longer struggling. I picked it up and put it in one of the inside pockets, with its head down and half its body and its tail sticking out. I buttoned up the coat and looked around: no, the trapper hadn't come yet. The colored spots on the hillsides were far away, and none of them was moving toward me. No one had seen me. But I was missing something. What?

My boots! The boots I had left on the other side of the pond! I set out running around the shore. It wasn't a big pond. In fact, it was quite a small one, a little mountain pond. But I ran like crazy. How could I go without boots? It was beginning to get warm during the day, but at night . . .

Thirty-two

But the boots were there, right where I'd left them. Just my luck!

I stayed three days at the first coal pile I found. At night I lay inside it, and during the day, when they chased me out, I lay near the wall of the station, burning up with fever. Was it any wonder I had gotten sick, what with that cold, damp night and the cold and heat of the pond and the sun the next day? I don't remember very much. My back must have been peeling, but I ignored it, and it took care of itself. I ate the fish the first night — well, at least a little of it, as much as I could. Afterwards, when I became feverish, I hid it again in the coal pile; but when I came back in the evening it was gone. Whenever Mama went looking for something that had disappeared she would say, "It's like looking for a needle in a haystack." But I would say it's like looking for food in a coal pile!

No matter how bad I felt about that missing fish, at least I had had luck with the boots!

Later I learned that it hadn't been just luck. That's the way it is with Uzbeks. The same with the Kirghiz, who are mountain shepherds. In the summer I went back to the mountains. I knew I wouldn't find Mama there, in the villages, but I was attracted to the area, to the cultivated hillsides, the orchards, the vegetable gardens, the ditches flowing with water, and, above all, the smiling people.

It was an old man who explained it to me one day, as we were sitting in the *tche-khana,* the village teahouse. Every village had one. They always had several big tables, like huge, square, wooden beds. These were covered with colorful rugs and cushions, and people would sit on them crosslegged, oriental style, smoking, quietly drinking tea, crunching seeds, and talking softly — as if a world war weren't raging.

"That's how it is with us," the old man explained. "Before the Muscovites came we never even locked our doors. No one would think of stealing anything."

"Muscovites?" I asked. "Who're they?"

"They're people like you who come from Moscow, outsiders."

"But not all of us come from Moscow!" I said. "I, for one, came from the Crimea."

And before that from Poland, I thought, unable to believe all this had really happened to me. *Had I really been born in Lodz? Had I really fled with Mama and Papa and Sarele? Had I really been in the Urals? Had all these things really happened to me? Really and truly?*

The waiter came back with green tea in little glasses. Unfortunately it wasn't sweet, but there was pita, and I was no longer very hungry. I could eat as much as I wanted to, but I was embarrassed to take more. I had already devoured three pieces. Maybe later.

The old man was smoking. I loved the way he sucked on the *kali*. This is a waterpipe made from a dried gourd. The gourd is hollowed out and partly filled with water, and two holes are made in it, into which reeds are inserted. One reed connects the gourd to an earthen vessel with hissing coals in it, where the tobacco is put; the other reed is for drawing smoke into the mouth. The old man sucked on the tip of the reed, and the water in the *kali* gurgled softly.

"All right," he said, "so they're not all from Moscow. But they're all foreigners. When it was just us here we never locked our doors. Anyone who came by could go into a house and eat his fill!"

"Really?"

"As Allah lives!"

"Even if nobody was home?"

"Certainly! There was always a box of pita and fruit standing in the corner, as there is now. You could eat to your heart's content. That's hospitality for you!"

"And what if the visitor helped himself to extra food to take with him?"

"That was forbidden," said the old man, putting down the reed, "forbidden."

"And what if the visitor took it anyway," I asked, "even a little bit?"

"They'd kill him!" said the old man, trying to sit up straight.

"Who, the police?"

"No, we have no need for police here in the villages. Everyone would come after him with pitchforks and shovels. They'd beat him to death."

I started to tremble. I looked outside. A little wagon, drawn

168

by a donkey, went by in the noonday sun. A broad hat shaded the face of the driver. Even the donkey had a hat made of newspaper on its head to shield its face from the sun. Its ears protruded saucily from the hat. It was hot, very hot. It was even hot on the shaded porch of the teahouse, but my hands and feet were still cold long after the trembling stopped.

"That's why we didn't have any thieves here," the old man concluded, "not of our own people, anyway. But that was a long time ago. Now things are different."

He sighed deeply, mumbled something to himself, and went back to puffing on the *kali*.

But I still had lots of questions. "What do you do now?"

"Now? As you've seen, we now lock our doors. Everything's changed. You can't trust anyone anymore."

"And what if someone comes to visit?"

The old man leaned back. Slowly, he straightened his legs, sighed, and crossed them again. "Oh, that's the same as before. You can eat as much as you want, as long as you don't take anything with you."

Well, I already knew that. I had enjoyed hospitality in the mountain villages more than once. But there was still something bothering me.

"And what if, what if someone takes fruit from the trees, or a tomato or a cucumber from the garden?"

The old man looked at me with raised eyebrows. Suddenly he smiled. "Don't worry, little fellow. Birds peck at the fruit, don't they? And we still have enough."

Thirty-three

I'm telling you, I wouldn't have minded staying there! I could have stayed in the mountains and gone from village to village the whole summer long if there had been any chance of finding Mama there — but there wasn't. It was in the towns that I'd have to look for her, there and in the collective farms down in the lowlands. And that's what I did. But from time to time I would go back up to the country villages, not only for the food or to see the people and the animals I loved, but also because of . . . the national pastime!

The national pastime?

Yes, they all did it. It was the second most important thing in their lives, after food, of course. Everyone — the local people, the oldtimers, even the refugees from Poland and the thousands of Russians who had fled from the occupied areas — spent their time, from morning to night, searching for something to eat. The first thing you had to do was fill your stomach, the emptiness there that didn't stop gnawing at you. But then what? Then they all took part in the national pastime.

It was easy. Anyone could do it, even people who could barely move. All you needed was a hand — to scratch yourself with! And if you had two hands and weren't alone, you would go up a notch in the ranks. You could hunt out your own and other people's too. Hunt what? Why, bugs, of course!

Yes, everybody scratched and hunted for bugs. And no wonder. Where could you take a bath?

At the train stations people did it as they sat there with their baggage. In the streets, waiting in line for food rations, in the market — everywhere you would see people scratching. If they scratched their heads you knew it was lice, if their bodies, fleas.

I scratched too — did I ever! It had started when I was still traveling with Mama. She said it spread like wildfire from one person to another. Mama would inspect my head slowly, patiently, almost one hair at a time. When she found a louse, she'd pull it out and squash it between her fingers. And when I could no longer sit still she would work on Sarele's head. Yes, Mama too took part in the national pastime.

But now she was no longer with me, and it was a hot summer. It might have been six months since my last haircut, and a whole zoo was running around in the thicket of my hair.

I don't know why I got off at that particular station, a small station in the hills, one of those that had no coal pile. It was a small town of stucco cottages, or maybe just an overgrown village. It might have been because of the woman who was sitting there. I knew it wasn't my mother, but she looked like her. She was sitting on a bench in the station, checking the hair of a small boy. The boy sat on the floor at her feet, his head bent forward. I stood in front of them watching. She had gentle, patient hands that almost seemed to caress him. Damn! Those tears again! I thought I was finished with them.

"Ow, Mama, stop it! That's enough!" the boy whined, raising his head. He saw me and stuck his tongue out: naaa.

I gave him a finger and turned away. *Idiot!* I thought. *If I were in your shoes . . .*

Then I saw the older boy. One of the "abandoned ones" like me, he was walking along with his hands in his pockets, whistling, and his head was — shaved! Newly shaved, and shiny as can be.

I had seen shaved heads before — many people had them — but I had never thought to ask where they had it done. Probably at a barber shop. Where else? That cost money, so there was no point in my even thinking about it. But here was a freshly shaved pate, smooth and shiny, and it really made me envious. I reached up and scratched my own head. The zoo there was more active at some times than at others.

The boy passed nearby.

"Hey," I blurted, "where'd you have that done?"

He stopped and ran his hand over the gleaming dome. "This? The same place as everybody else, at the blacksmith's."

"The blacksmith's? Really? And how much does he charge?"

"Nothing. It's free."

"Really? Nothing?"

"Not a penny."

My scalp was crawling more than ever, a regular market day in full swing right there on my head.

"So where do I find him?"

"There, on the third street over. Go that way. He just started shoeing a horse; you'll hear the hammering."

I stood watching. I didn't dare come close. The blacksmith was a large man. The horses here were smaller than the ones in the Crimea — I knew, because they had let me ride the ones in the village — and next to the blacksmith this horse almost looked like a colt. But it was actually full grown; it had been shod before.

The blacksmith lifted one of the horse's legs and examined the shoe. He had huge hands. Could this really be the man who shaved people? Wasn't it dangerous? And what did he use? I watched from a distance. There was a hammer there next to the fire and a big box, probably for nails. A lot of iron bars were strewn about, and there was another big hammer too.

That fellow had just been pulling my leg. Seeing how young I was, he had decided to play a prank on me. He hadn't been the first.

I wanted to go, to run away from this big, dark man with his black mustache, his fire, and his enormous hammers, but I was riveted to the spot. I had never seen a horse shod before. The horse stood still. Didn't it hurt? Its Uzbek owner stood next to it and stroked its neck, but it didn't try to escape. The blacksmith hammered away; no, not with the big hammer, but hard. Then he inspected the shoe. At last he straightened up and said:

172

"That's it. We're done."

The horse lifted its head and whinnied, as if it had understood and was glad. The Uzbek laughed and patted its flank.

"He was a good boy, wasn't he?" he said, twirling his mustache proudly. "Didn't make a fuss at all."

"Why should he?" the blacksmith asked. "He knows me, and he knows I treat him well."

The Uzbek pointed to a half-full sack lying in the corner, offering it as payment. The blacksmith picked the sack up effortlessly, as if it were empty, brought it over to the entrance, to the light, and looked inside. I wondered what was in there, potatoes? Corn? Or maybe watermelon or cantaloupe?

Suddenly the blacksmith looked up, straight at me. I froze. He had big, dark eyes, black as coal, and thick, scary eyebrows. Now what? Slowly he straightened up, without taking his eyes off me. I couldn't move. A great commotion arose on my head again, thousands of tiny feet crawling around. I couldn't help myself: I reached up and scratched.

The blacksmith burst out laughing. He had a big, booming voice. He laughed and slapped his thighs. Two rows of white teeth shone in his black face.

"It itches, eh?" he called out to me. "Want to get rid of it?"

I said nothing.

"Come here! We'll do it quick as a wink."

I began walking toward him, as if pushed by an invisible hand.

"What are you afraid of?" the blacksmith laughed. "I won't take anything for my trouble, except of course what you want to get rid of anyway. Come on! Stand over here."

I went where he was pointing. There was a big trough full of water for the horses. Now what? Was he going to throw me in? Now that I was standing next to him he seemed huge, like a giant. Again I froze.

"Bend over!" the giant ordered. "Stick out your neck! Now down!"

I bent my head forward and closed my eyes. I was done for!

I wondered how he was going to do me in. With an iron bar? A big hammer? Or just a blow of his fist?

Wham! A bucketful of water was dashed on my head. I jumped back, stumbling into the box. I almost fell.

"Sit down!" the blacksmith ordered.

I sat down. The water was dripping onto my coat, which I never took off, not even on a hot summer day like this. It was running down my neck and into my clothes. It tickled my back. I looked up. There was something shiny in the blacksmith's hand, a razor, a real razor, sharp and gleaming! I shut my eyes. Oh Mama! Now I was really done for.

The blade touched my forehead at the hairline and began stroking backward toward the nape of my neck. A strip of coolness divided my head in half. Touching my chin, the man lifted my face toward him. I opened my eyes and looked at him, surprised. That big, rough hand of his had touched me with such gentleness, almost like Papa's hand. He smiled at me again and turned back to what he was doing. Sitting up straight, I felt the razor gliding back and forth, strip after strip. With his other hand, the blacksmith held the back of my neck. Shaving one section at a time, he worked his way down to one ear, then at last to the other.

"There we are!" I heard him say. "Finished!"

"Already?" I asked, looking up at him.

"I told you it would be quick as a wink, didn't I?" he said, patting me on the back. I almost fell off the box, his blacksmith's pat was so heavy. I went over to the trough to look at my reflection in the water. What I saw there was a little boy with a shiny, bald head. I couldn't believe it — that was me! I ran my hand over my scalp. It was smooth and cool. Fantastic!

The blacksmith looked down at me, his eyes sparkling. "First time, eh?"

I nodded.

"Well, remember you can always come back," he said, turning back to his work, "whenever it starts to bother you. As you see, there's nothing to it!" With that he disappeared into his shop.

I stood there in the street shaking my head. Strange, the tangle of teeming curls was gone. How easy it had been! I began to skip, to run. I had been relieved of a heavy load. A breeze caressed my scalp. I ran my hand over it again with tremendous pleasure. Sure I would be back — would I ever!

If only the grass grew as fast in those mountains as my hair grew back! I had a brief respite, then one day I felt the crawling again. It happened over and over again, the same way. I would reach up and scratch, then scratch some more, until I was as fully occupied with the national pastime as everyone else. And when I couldn't take it anymore I would go back to the blacksmith, not just that first one but another one in the neighboring village too. They all did it free for us, the "abandoned ones." Another reason to come back to the country.

Thirty-four

Once, I forget exactly where or when, I managed to "lift" a loaf of bread. A whole loaf! Imagine, a ten-pound loaf of bread, and still fresh, too!

Clutching it under my coat, I looked for a place to hide. I didn't take it out until I discovered the tumble-down building near the river. I didn't even look at it. I suppose I looked like a pregnant dwarf. But so what?

The ruin was some distance from the city, and no one lived there. How could anyone live in a place that had only one wall still standing?

I don't know how I had held back until that point, but as

soon as I saw there was nobody around I tore into the bread and began to devour it. What a heavenly taste!

I bit it off and wolfed it down, almost without chewing. More, more. The loaf began to look as though a mouse had gnawed a big hole in it. I went on eating. They must have put ground shells into the flour as always — shells of what, God only knows — but what did I care? I finally had some bread, a whole lot of it, a mountain of it! And as always, I was hungry.

I was small and thin, so thin that I sometimes imagined I was transparent. A quarter of a loaf should have been enough, shouldn't it? I stood leaning against the wall and went on eating. I had already eaten more than a quarter, and I was still hungry.

Even when I had eaten half the loaf I couldn't stop. I felt weighed down by a heaviness in my stomach. I leaned back against the wall and slowly slid down, eating the whole time. I was still hungry.

I sat propped up against the wall and looked at my tummy. It lay big and round between my legs. *I'm like a snake,* I thought, *a snake that's just swallowed a big mouse.*

I was thirsty. I wanted to go take a drink from the river, but I couldn't get up. I wanted to stop eating, to keep some for the next day, but I couldn't. Little by little the bread disappeared inside. My belly swelled and took on the shape of a big loaf of bread, and I was still hungry.

The sun came around the wall, and the shade was gone. I was hot. I wanted to get up, to go to the other side of the wall, but I just couldn't budge. I looked at the bread that was left in my hand: so little. Should I keep it or not?

Even after I had finished off what remained I was still hungry. How long did I lie there unable to move? Hours? Days? I have no idea. What difference does it make anyway? Only one thing bothered me, then and for a long time afterward: does a snake that swallows a big mouse and then lies digesting it, unable to move, stay hungry too?

Thirty-five

There was a whole gang of "abandoned ones" there in Bukhara. I knew only a few of them by name. I had hung around with Anatol, for an example, for a whole week, but the others came and went constantly, arriving, moving on, being caught by the police and sent to institutions. In the summertime everything was easier, even in the towns. The markets were full of vegetables: tomatoes, cucumbers, carrots, beets; and there was fruit too: huge apples, apricots, grapes. These things weren't as satisfying as bread, nor were they so easy to steal — the vendors watched the little merchandise they had like hawks — but compared to the way it was in the wintertime, we could really live it up.

I wandered around on my own, or sometimes with Anatol, and when the gang got together we would rob the watermelon and cantaloupe vendors blind.

That morning we were a big group. Tulik ran the show, as always. No doubt about it, Tulik was our king, a real monarch. He was sixteen and really big. We would gladly have followed him through fire and water. He generally hung out by himself, but when he needed the gang, he had only to put out the call and we would all be there, hanging on his every word. What would I not do to earn Tulik's smile or some sign, however small, that he had noticed me, that he had seen I was carrying out his orders to the letter?

"That one's worthless. Give me the big one!" said Tulik to the vendor, pointing to one of the watermelons.

"Got money to pay?" the vendor said suspiciously.

Tulik took a ruble note from his pocket, waved it in the vendor's face, and stuffed it right back in his pocket. He had used that bill innumerable times. In fact, I'm not even sure it was real. No doubt it was forged; otherwise how could Tulik have held on to it the whole summer?

177

The vendor rolled the watermelon over to Tulik without taking his eyes off the gang of boys around him.

"My treat!" Tulik announced warmly. "It's for everybody!"

"We'll help you pick it out," I said. I was already experienced at this. It wasn't the first time.

Tulik bent down and, putting his ear to the watermelon, gave it a tap.

"Not so great," he said, straightening up. "Haven't you got a better one?"

The vendor rolled him another watermelon.

"Let me have a look," said Anatol. "I'm an expert on watermelons!"

Tulik passed him the watermelon and began to inspect a third one. The gang crowded around.

"Don't touch!" cried the vendor.

"Don't get so excited!" said Tulik. "What do you think you've got here, tomatoes? A watermelon isn't going to be spoiled just by touching. We've got to choose well, don't we? It isn't every day that I treat the whole gang."

"This one's just fine," said the vendor, glancing at the rest of us. "Now take it and be off with you!"

"Are you making us a present, then?" Tulik asked. The gang burst out laughing.

"Who said anything about a present?" the vendor said angrily, sharply eyeing the many hands at work inspecting his merchandise.

"So what's the big hurry?" said Tulik, as he went on examining the third melon.

As always, there was a big commotion, with everyone wanting to inspect the watermelons, to help Tulik, to give advice. I hung back. Suddenly Anatol turned to me and thrust the watermelon he had been looking at into my hands. I immediately spun around and passed it to the boy standing behind me. I turned back to look at the vendor, while the watermelon moved on in the usual way. He hadn't even noticed. I looked under Tulik's arm.

"That one's bigger," I said. "Better check it!"

Someone nudged my shoulder. I turned, and another watermelon was already being pressed against my stomach. It was a big one, gigantic! I could hardly hold it.

"Watch out!" someone whispered to me as he relieved me of the watermelon. It was a different sort of voice. I looked up and saw shining black eyes and hair cut short like all the older boys had, but the shirt that loomed above the watermelon was cut full and round. My God, it was a girl! Before I could even shut my mouth she had already disappeared into the crowd.

It was a banner day: three watermelons to split open at the riverbank. The ruble was still in Tulik's pocket, as always. When the third melon disappeared, Tulik announced contemptuously, "Your watermelons aren't worth beans!" and turned to go.

The vendor yelled and swore. I don't think he grasped what had actually happened. He was simply put out. Tulik waved at him without even turning around and made off for the river. There we were all waiting for him, just as he had said we should.

The watermelons were still untouched, of course. No one would have dared to cut them open. The girl was there too. She sat quietly off to one side.

I cast a sidelong glance in her direction. She had dark skin and black, slanting eyes. No doubt she was one of the local people, an Uzbek. Her lips were dark, dark red, and the corners of her mouth were turned up as if she were always smiling. Near the left side of her mouth, just above it, there was a large beauty mark. Tulik made straight for her.

"We did great, didn't we?" he said, looking into her shining eyes.

"Fantastic!" she replied, smiling. The beauty mark rose, as if it too were smiling. Suddenly my heart stopped. I remembered something, but I didn't know what. It was as though a bell were ringing in the distance. I wanted her to smile again.

Tulik split open the first watermelon on a big rock. It was all red and juicy inside. The black seeds shone in the sun. A beauty.

With his hand he dug out the center, the heart of it, and brought it to the girl.

"Here, Korasatch," he said, "this is for you."

The girl smiled again and sank her teeth into the red fruit. We crowded around like a pack of hungry dogs with saliva dripping from their muzzles.

"Don't push!" Tulik said. "Get out of the way! There's plenty for everybody!"

We moved back. He split the watermelon into small pieces and passed it around. I tore into my piece. Oh Mama, was it sweet! Sweet as can be! I quickly chomped it down to the rind. If only it hadn't gone so fast! I looked at Anatol's piece. It was bigger. Just my luck. I wanted more, wanted a bigger piece, but I wasn't mad at Tulik. He hadn't done it on purpose. How could you expect someone to cut pieces all the same size when he didn't even have a knife?

I had better luck with the second melon: Tulik gave me a big piece. But it too was gone in a flash. And the same thing happened with the third. I gnawed into it like a mouse into a hunk of cheese, without so much as a glance around me.

Tulik burst out laughing. "Look at you!" he said. "Where did you learn how to eat? You're stuffing yourselves like pigs!"

I looked at Anatol. The red juice was all over his cheeks. Even the tip of his nose dripped with it, as if it too had taken part in the eating. Anatol pointed at me and laughed. I wiped my face on my sleeve. Yes, I was covered with the watermelon juice too, but I didn't find it funny. I was still hungry — boy, was I! I gnawed right down into the rind, first the white part, then the green too. I admit it didn't taste so good. In fact it was even a little bitter. But I couldn't help myself.

"Are you going to have a stomachache!" the girl said. I looked at her, surprised. It had been so long since anyone had cared what happened to me.

The girl laughed. "Why are you looking at me like that, as if you'd swallowed a canary?"

180

"Is your name really Korasatch?" I asked.

"Yes. Why shouldn't it be?"

"Because *korasatch* means black eyes in Uzbek, doesn't it?"

"Right. So what? That's my name!"

"I thought maybe it was because of your eyes," I said. "They sure are black!"

"Her hair too!" Tulik said, stroking her close-cropped hair with the back of his hand. His palm was sticky with watermelon juice, just like mine and everybody else's.

I looked at Tulik's hair. It was fair and curly, and his eyes were blue. He was one of the Russians, from far-off Leningrad. Now Leningrad was under siege. He had been taken from there just in time, on the train with the orphans, but he jumped off the train along the way and since then had been wandering on his own. He knew everything, this Tulik did, and he wasn't afraid of anything. If I had been as big and strong as Tulik, if I had had the beginnings of a mustache like his, I wouldn't have been afraid of anyone either!

"Great watermelon!" said Korasatch. "Like honey!"

She looked at the rind in her hand. She too had chewed down to the white part but no further. Maybe she wasn't as hungry as I was. Suddenly she raised her arm and threw the rind way out into the river. The current took hold of it and carried it away like a little green boat. I looked back at Korasatch. All kinds of questions came to mind, but I was tongue-tied.

"Looking at me again, are you?" she said, cocking her head like a bird. "What's the matter with you, little fellow? Haven't you ever seen a girl before?"

"Sure I have," I said, licking my fingers, "but not hanging out with the 'abandoned ones.' "

"Well, I have," said Anatol, "but they were big girls like Korasatch, not little ones our age."

"Why aren't there any little girls like — like me?" I asked. "Don't girls get lost too?"

"Sure they do," said Tulik, "but they don't last out in the

181

open. If they don't die in the street, they're taken away to the orphan homes, to the institutions, and that's where they stay."

"And they hang on there?" I asked. "I hear there's hardly anything to eat in those places. You could die of hunger!"

Tulik shrugged. "How should I know? It's just a fact that none of the 'abandoned ones' are little girls. Maybe they don't run away."

"Well, I did!" said Korasatch. "You can bet your life on it!"

"All right," said Tulik, "you ran away from home. That's different."

I looked at her incredulously. "What, you ran away? Where is your home?"

Korasatch's expression darkened. "In Samarkand," she snapped.

"You mean you've got a home in Samarkand, and a mother and father?"

Korasatch nodded.

"That's not so far. Why don't you go there?"

"I told you, I ran away."

I didn't get it. She had a father and mother, and she hadn't gotten lost; she just got up and ran away from home — not from an institution or an orphanage, from *home!* It didn't seem possible.

"Why did you run away?" I asked.

"They sold me!" said Korasatch. "Papa sold me to an old man."

This was really beyond me. Sold? How could a girl be sold?

"That's the way it is with them, with the Uzbeks," Tulik explained. "They're Muslims. That's their custom."

"What is?"

"To sell teenage girls. They marry them off."

"Without asking them?"

"What do they need to ask them for?" Tulik said, getting up. Angrily, he kicked the little clay mound we were sitting on. "To

182

them, girls are nothing. They don't bother asking women what they want." He kicked the mound again. "The bastard!"

I didn't know whom he meant: Korasatch's father, who had sold her, or the old man who wanted to buy her.

"Was he really old?" I asked.

"Awfully!" Korasatch said, throwing away the second watermelon rind. This time she threw it even farther, probably out of anger. "He was seventy, or maybe even a hundred! He had a million wrinkles on his face and age spots on his hands."

"And what would such an old man want a young girl like you for?"

Tulik burst out laughing. "What for? To marry her!"

"But why marry her? Doesn't he have anyone to cook for him or do his laundry?"

"Cook?" Tulik laughed. "Do laundry? You've got a few things to learn, kid. That's not what people get married for."

I didn't understand. I really didn't know what he was talking about, but I was ashamed to ask. I wondered what someone would pay for a girl like this — probably a whole palace full of silver and gold.

"What did he offer your father?"

"A camel," said Korasatch, "a camel and a sack of potatoes!"

I looked at her, thinking she must be putting me on. The beauty mark seemed to tickle the corner of her mouth. It looked as though she were smiling, but later I learned that was the way she always looked.

"Seriously?"

"Seriously."

"And that's allowed?"

"No. It was once, but since Uzbekistan became a Soviet republic it's forbidden to sell girls. It's not legal to pay a brideprice anymore."

"So how come they don't obey the law?" I asked.

"Is stealing allowed?"

183

"No, it's forbidden!"

"Then why do you steal?"

"Because I'm hungry," I said. "If I didn't steal I'd die of hunger!"

"But in the Soviet Union everybody's supposed to get what he needs to eat, isn't he?" Korasatch asked. "That's what we were taught in the Communist Youth. 'From each according to his ability, to each according to his need.' But what good does the law do you? You can't eat it, can you!"

I didn't have an answer for her, so I asked another question. "And were you in school like all the other girls?"

"Sure. I went to school, and I belonged to the Communist Youth. Imagine," she said, turning to Tulik, "there I am, a member of the Communist Youth, taking part in activities, working as a counselor with little kids like this, explaining to them about Stalin and the war and all kinds of important things, and all of a sudden — bang! They sell me to some old man, in exchange for a camel and a sack of potatoes. Is it any wonder I ran away?"

"She had a braid that hung down to her waist," said Tulik softly, as if he hadn't heard the question. "Even longer! When she sat down she would put the braid in front of her so as not to sit on it."

"How do you know? Did you see her?"

"No, she told me. I wish I had seen her then."

Down at the riverbank two of the members of the gang were fighting, maybe over a watermelon rind, maybe over something else.

"Into the water! Throw them into the water!" Anatol cried.

Tulik roused himself from his reverie. Looking around at all of us, he suddenly began to laugh. "Look at you! You're filthy! Get into the water! Everybody in!"

I wanted to jump into the water the way I always did, clothes and all, but I didn't know what to do with my boots. I stood there on the bank. It was hot, and I was sticky from the water-

184

melon. I wanted ever so badly to jump in. But what to do with those boots?

"What's the problem, kid?" Tulik asked. "What're you afraid of?"

I didn't answer. I was embarrassed.

"Afraid they'll steal your clothes? Not here! Not in this gang! Here nobody steals from anybody else!"

I pulled off my boots and started to undress. Of course, how could I have imagined otherwise? Tulik had said so, and that was good enough for me. In his gang there was no stealing, from one another, that is.

"Are you coming?" Tulik called to Korasatch from the river. He was in up to his waist.

"No," she said, "not today."

She took off her tattered shoes — she had no socks — and dipped her feet in the water.

"Come on! You'll see, the water's great!" said Tulik. He leaned over, scooped up some water with his arm, and splashed her. Korasatch jumped back, screaming with laughter.

"Some other time," she cried. "I'll watch the clothes."

I undressed quickly, but I didn't take everything off. In the Crimea I used to swim nude in the river with all the other kids, but now I was too embarrassed. I jumped in with my underwear on — I still had underwear then — and began to swim.

There was a strong current. Anatol said the current is strongest in the summertime, because then the snow is melting high up in the mountains. It was swift, but I swam like a fish. I began paddling against the stream. Then I let it carry me for a while, and then swam against it once again. The whole time I had my eye on the riverbank. Was Korasatch watching?

But no, she only had eyes for Tulik.

That evening the two of them disappeared, Tulik and Korasatch. I suppose he only needed us to help with the watermelons, and you didn't need a gang to sleep, did you? I sat by the water watching the full moon come up over the distant mountains. It was round and reddish colored, like the big copper tray at Miriam's house. Then it broke loose from the mountains, and as it rose, slowly turned pale.

I lay on my back, a hand under my head. The moon hung above me now like a great silver platter. It smiled down at me, looking me straight in the eye.

Interesting, I thought, once it would have looked to me like Miriam's face. But tonight, tonight it was like the face of Korasatch, exactly like it!

Thirty-six

When you're hungry, the only thing in the world is bread, potatoes, salted fish — in short, food! But when your belly is full you suddenly start to think about other things, things that have been standing there quietly all along, waiting their turn. The mosques in Bukhara, for example: had they been there last fall too, or during that terrible winter?

Korasatch said they're always there. She laughed and said they've been standing that way for centuries, but I didn't understand: how was it I never saw them before?

In the summertime Bukhara smells of dust and urine. The smell is everywhere, even in the abandoned mosques, but it didn't bother me. I was standing with Korasatch in front of the big mosque. What a beautiful building! It had four minarets, each with a gleaming bluish-green dome. Beneath the domes were ornamental blue ceramic tiles, and under them clay bricks down to the ground. The courtyard in front of it was also paved with clay bricks, and dry grass sprouted in the cracks. It must have been green in the springtime, but now everything was dry from the summer's heat.

Korasatch said it wasn't always like this — abandoned and neglected, that is.

"It's because there's no God in the Soviet Union," she explained. "At one time, before the revolution, the Muslims used to pray here, but now it's forbidden. There's no God here."

I was astonished. "What do you mean? God's not here on earth anyway. He's in heaven!"

"No, you don't understand." Korasatch laughed. "In the Soviet Union there's no religion. No one believes here in the God of the Muslims or the God of the Christians. Here they're all unbelievers, and that's why no one prays in the mosques or the churches."

"How do you know?"

"I learned it in school and in the Communist Youth."

How knowledgeable she was, this Korasatch. She had gone to school for eight years. She must know everything! I forgot to ask her about the synagogues — there I had seen people praying — and I had other questions to ask.

Korasatch explained many things to me: for example, why it was hot in summer and cold in winter, and why it was cold at night even in the summer.

"In geography we learned that this is a desert climate," she said, "hot during the day and cold at night. During the winter there are very cold winds from Siberia, and that's why the ground freezes and nothing grows."

"And aren't there any winds from Siberia during the summer?"

"There are," Korasatch said. "That's why there's sometimes frost at night, even in the middle of the summer. But generally the winds aren't so cold in the summertime. They just dry everything up."

"And that's why it's like a desert here," I said.

"Right," said Korasatch.

I turned away so she wouldn't see how proud I was of having understood what she said, but then I turned back to her. I was curious. "What do they call those tall mountains, the ones near Tashkent and Samarkand?"

"Those are the Tien Shan Mountains," Korasatch said. "They're huge, thousands of feet high. Did you know they were part of the Himalayas? They are! They're a continuation of them, the 'Roof of the World.'"

No, I didn't even know what the Himalayas were. And I certainly didn't know that the world had a roof. How could mountains be a roof? The tall mountains could be pillars for the sky to rest on, I supposed, but how could they be a roof?

I didn't say anything. I was afraid that if I asked any more silly questions Korasatch would just up and leave. I wanted her to go on telling me things. She was almost always with Tulik, except when we all got together to steal and then I could be near her. I don't know why she spoke to me after that. Maybe it was because I was small and quick and could usually help her when it came to making off with things. And maybe I reminded her of the little brother she had left behind at home, in Samarkand.

That day we had done especially well. Finally my belly was full. Actually, I could have eaten more, much more, but the hunger was no longer so bad, and that's why I suddenly noticed the mosque. It turned out it had always stood there, on the edge of the great courtyard.

I went in. It was abandoned, like me, but as beautiful as a palace. I closed my eyes, and for a moment I was a prince among pillars of gold and precious stones. Any minute now, trumpets would sound, and my father, the King, would come riding through the great gate on a noble steed.

From the far side of the courtyard came the sound of a donkey braying. It was like a long, bitter cry of longing from the depths of the soul. And just when it seemed to me the creature couldn't possibly have any breath left, it began to make a series of shorter braying sounds, like wailing, until it quieted down and finally fell silent. Again all was still, the stillness of a hot summer afternoon. I opened my eyes.

Korasatch was standing and looking at me, smiling. Was she laughing at me, or was that big beauty mark of hers just tickling her as usual?

"Come," she said, turning toward the entrance, "let's go. Tulik is waiting for me."

She went to her Tulik, and I continued to search for Mama.

Thirty-seven

When I got back to Bukhara, the storks were already circling over the minaret. They soared in a great loop, way, way up. Then they continued on their journey south, to the warm countries. It was fall, and I stood there envying these winged creatures. They could fly far away to a warm place, to the land of the golden apples that Grandma had told me about, while I had to stay here, where winter and frost and terrible hunger were just around the corner.

I lost track of Tulik and Korasatch. They had wandered off somewhere else. Everyone was wandering, even those who weren't looking for their mothers as I was. When they got to know you in the market, you couldn't "lift" things there anymore, and you had to find another market. And when they got to know you in all the markets in town, you had to go to another town. That's how it was. In the fall, everyone came down from the mountain villages and gathered in the warmer cities on the plains. For us "abandoned ones," these were the "warm countries," but the warmth wasn't much to speak of.

I met them again when winter came. One morning at dawn a light rain was falling. I dug myself into the coal pile, trying to burrow even deeper inside, but there were hissing, live coals farther in, and one had to be careful. Then, suddenly, I heard her voice.

"Tulik, let's go over to the station. It's cold there, but at least we won't get wet."

I leaped out of the coal, slid down the side of the pile, and ran around to the other side.

"Korasatch!" I shouted. "Tulik! Don't you remember me?"

They looked at me with sooty faces.

"No," said Tulik, taking Korasatch's hand. "Come on, let's make a run for the station, or we'll really get wet."

"It's me, Yasha!" I cried. "We heisted watermelons together in Bukhara!"

Korasatch turned and looked at me. "Oh, it's the little fellow from Bukhara!"

Tulik pulled her by the hand.

"Come to the station, Yasha," she called over her shoulder. "It's starting to rain harder."

I ran after them. Was it any wonder they didn't recognize me, covered with dirt and soot as I was? Or maybe they had just forgotten me. After all, I was just one of many children who had followed Tulik around, the little kids in the gang. But no, Korasatch couldn't have forgotten me. It was the soot and the darkness. In the daylight she'd certainly have recognized me straight off.

We didn't hang out together that day. The gangs broke up in the winter, and Tulik didn't give me any sign that he wanted me to join them. I wandered around the market, among the stalls, on my own. The rain stopped, but the sky still hung low and gray. A cold wind blew, "the freezing wind from the Siberian steppes" that Korasatch had once told me about. It attacked me from without, while hunger gnawed at me from within. I walked around and around, until the market closed up. Then I went back to the station, where I had some luck. A coal train was standing on the tracks, a freight train with cars full of coal. I knew what to do. No, I didn't try to sneak aboard. There was always a guard around with a rifle, and even if he didn't have one I wasn't going to take any chances. These men acted the hero with little children like me, and I had seen the kind of beating they could give. They were only afraid of the older boys, the ones who sneaked aboard with sticks and knives.

No, I walked on ahead, past the engine, to the end of the station, where I stopped and waited. I stood there a long time. The cold wind got stronger. I tried to find shelter next to a warehouse wall, but the wind blew right in my face. If I had gone around behind the warehouse I would be protected from the wind, but I wouldn't be able to see the engine from there. Then again, what if the train didn't budge that day? Maybe it would only get under way the next day. In that case, why give up the comfort of the coal pile? There, at least, I wouldn't be cold. There I could get some sleep.

I suppose I could have sneaked aboard one of the enclosed freight cars on the train that had just pulled out, and then I would have ridden somewhere — it didn't matter where — and slept all night in a place that was sheltered from the wind and the rain, and the next day I could have hung out again in some other place — it didn't matter what it was called. But this time I didn't feel like traveling, because Korasatch was here. It seemed to me she had gotten thinner, and Tulik as well. It was probably hard for them to steal food now too. If the eagle is hungry, how could a mere sparrow like me expect to find even crumbs to eat?

The wind bore a familiar sound: a squeal, then a clatter of wheels. I looked toward the station. The engine was moving! Without turning on its lights or whistling, it had just started moving toward me in the dim light. I went over to the track. The engine was picking up speed as it came toward me. Now was the time to start running. I ran out of the station in the direction the train was moving. Now I would have to be careful, to get close enough to grab the ladder but not so close as to fall under the wheels. Voom! The engine went by me, moving faster and faster. One car went by. Now or never! I leaped up and caught hold of the ladder. Again my body flapped behind me like a banner in the wind. I pulled with all my might, got a foothold, and climbed up, then jumped on top of the coal. Now I would have to work fast. I started throwing out chunks of coal at a furious clip — more, more, more. "This is it!" I said to myself. "If you don't jump now, you're done for!"

I threw out a few more chunks, pulled myself up over the side of the car, and went down the ladder. The train was moving fast. It was now or . . .

I jumped. My hands on my head, I rolled down the embankment. I lay in the ditch feeling my body. Lucky! I had come out all right this time. Nothing but a bump on my shoulder and a small one on my leg. Not so terrible. Now I had to hurry before anyone beat me to it. It wasn't yet completely dark. Might someone have seen me? Actually, it was a good thing there was still a little light, because otherwise I'd never be able to find the coal. I began to retrace my steps toward the station, picking up the coal I had thrown overboard along the way. I had no sack or bucket to put it in — who had such things? — so I quickly filled my pockets, first the outside ones, then the inside ones. Finally I picked up my coattails and tucked them into my belt, making a pouch in which I could toss more coal. I had done it! This time I had done just fine!

Thirty-eight

The woman who opened the door burst out laughing.

"What happened?" she asked, pointing to my coat. "Are you pregnant?" I looked down. The coat was puffed out like a big, sagging belly.

"Come in, come in," she said, motioning toward the kitchen. "Don't just stand there in the doorway. You're letting in the cold air."

I closed the door behind me and took a deep breath. I was always struck by the mixture of smells there, of food, cigarette smoke, perfume, and other, less familiar things. It was a pleasant place: closed, heated, protected. I didn't see the bedroom — there was a heavy curtain hiding it from the entrance, with a solitary lamp shining on one side — but I seemed to have gotten the woman out of bed. I always seemed to have awakened her.

I went straight to the kitchen. I knew where to unload the coal. It wasn't my first time. I brought her all kinds of things, whatever I could steal that wasn't edible. I'd give it all to her in exchange for food. She was evidently able to barter everything away — how, I have no idea — so that she always had something to give me in return. She had something for me this time too: three whole boiled potatoes, still warm, and some bread. She gave me a cup of tea too, hot tea. She even put in a sugar cube, a whole sugar cube!

Someone coughed inside, coughed and growled in a deep voice, "Hey, Irgashoi, come here! What're you doing out there?"

"Just a minute!" the woman called out, looking for something in the corner. "I'll be right back!"

It must have been her boyfriend. I had never seen him. He was always behind the curtain, in the dark inner room. He must have been sick, her boyfriend, because his voice was always different. Maybe she too was sick, this Irgashoi, although she certainly didn't look it. She was tall and heavyset, with cheeks so rosy you'd think there was no shortage of food. She always had on a partly open robe, as if she had just put it on. Sometimes a pink nightgown was visible underneath, like one I had seen in shops before the war, and sometimes all you could see was her big breasts. She would laugh, cover them up, bring me straight to the kitchen, and take whatever I had brought her, giving me something to eat and sending me on my way. Only sick people go around in robes, right? So maybe her cheeks were red with fever. Poor thing, this Irgashoi! She probably never got a chance to tie her black hair into a long braid and go out. She might not even have known how good it was to wander in the countryside in the summertime, to roll down green slopes in the spring. The disease was keeping her shut in, and she certainly knew nothing of the sweet taste of freedom.

Irgashoi turned back to me. "This is for next time," she said, giving me a sack. "This way you can gather more. And you won't have to get pregnant either," she added with a jolly laugh.

"Irgashoi!" the man called out again. "Come on!"

I sipped the tea hurriedly. I didn't want to miss a drop. I burned myself a little. Well, what's the difference? The main thing was to finish it.

"That's my sack," said Irgashoi as she led me to the doorway. "I added the price of it to our account. Bring it back to me some day and you'll get a quarter-loaf of bread."

Sacks were worth a lot. They had all kinds of uses. You could even sew clothes with them.

If I could, I would have stayed there in that warm, dark place, with the smell of food, tobacco, and perfume trapped inside its heavy curtains, but the woman had showed me the door. She dragged her pink slippers across the clay floor, making a clicking sound with her high heels: click-clack, click-clack.

I tucked the sack into my coat, close to my body, and opened the door. The cold wind hit me all at once. The door closed behind me, and I heard the squeal of a bolt. I was lucky to have the sack. I could wrap myself up in it under my coat. I put my hands in my pockets. Great! The bread in one pocket, the potatoes in the other. I felt the bits of coal that were left there too. The potatoes were still a little warm, at least compared to the wind. What luck!

Thirty-nine

We filled the sack with coal together, Korasatch and I. I didn't know girls could do such things, but Korasatch did everything I did, as if she had grown up on trains. She jumped onto the car in front of me and threw lots of coal overboard, maybe even more than I did. We were lucky. It had snowed that evening, not much, but enough to cover the ground with a thin white blanket, so in the dark we were able to see the chunks of coal we had tossed out. It started out slowly, this particular train, as if it were in no hurry to get anywhere, and we were able to toss a great deal of coal overboard and jump out ourselves without a scratch. Then we gathered up enough to fill the sack. We tried to lift it.

"Watch out!" Korasatch said. "It probably weighs as much as you do!"

"That wouldn't take much," I said. "Its belly is full, and mine isn't."

This time it was I who made her laugh, not that ticklish beauty mark.

"Too bad Tulik isn't here," said Korasatch, patting the full sack. "He could pick it up without any trouble."

I knelt down with my back to the sack, reached over my shoulder and took hold of it with both hands, then slowly rose with the sack on my back, the way porters did in the market.

Her Tulik was busy "lifting" things somewhere else, and I could manage without him.

"Wait, I'll help," said Korasatch. All at once my load became lighter. She must have taken hold of it from below.

It was a good thing Irgashoi lived near the tracks. I'm not sure I would have been such a hero if I had had to walk three more blocks, even with Korasatch's help.

I knocked three times, exactly the way Irgashoi had told me, but no one answered. What could the trouble be? She had always been there at night, no matter when I came. She had always opened the door for me after three knocks.

"Do you think she might have gone out?" Korasatch asked.

"I doubt it," I answered. "She's always here, in bed. I think she's sick. Maybe she's too sick today to get up."

I peered through the keyhole. There was a dim light inside, as always, and the curtain hung in front of the doorway. I put my ear to the door and listened. I heard low voices and Irgashoi's melodious laugh. She was at home. She just hadn't heard.

I knocked again, three times, the way she had said. Finally I heard the clop of the high heels coming closer: click-clack, click-clack. The lock squeaked, and the door opened a crack. The heat and heavy odors of the closed house hit me in the face. Irgashoi squinted down at me.

"Not now!" she whispered. "Scram!"

"But I brought you a whole bag," I whispered back, pointing to it, "a full sack of coal!"

She bent down a little and whispered right in my ear, "The police captain's here, understand? Get going quick!"

We took the sack of coal and sat down by the wall across the street to wait for the guest to leave.

"You still think she's sick?" Korasatch laughed. "She's not sick. She's something else."

I didn't answer. I knew what she meant. I wasn't a little kid anymore, as she thought.

196

"I don't give a hoot for the police captain!" I said. "I don't give a hoot for the whole police force! I've made fools of them a thousand times."

"Have you gotten caught a lot?" asked Korasatch.

"Oh yeah, but I've always escaped. I've even gotten out of a detention cell — easy as pie."

"How?"

"Through the bars!"

"Really?"

"Yeah. It's because I'm small. I can almost always get through."

"And what'll happen when you get bigger?" Korasatch asked.

"I don't think I ever will," I said.

She looked at me quizzically. "What are you talking about?" she said. "All children get bigger. I'm still growing myself, and I'm fifteen already. So an eight-year-old like you . . ."

"See what I mean? I'm actually nine and a half! And — can you imagine? — people used to tell me I was big for my age. I don't think I've grown at all this past year."

"How do you know?"

"I was in Tashkent not long ago. They caught me in the market there and put me in the same detention cell I had been in the year before, my first. At that time I had escaped through the bars — not easily, but I had done it — and now I was able to do it again. I simply hadn't grown, see?" And I added, "There are some advantages to being small!"

"Do you always try to escape, even when it's cold out, or it's raining or snowing?"

"Sure!" I replied, and suddenly I was able to put into words a feeling I had had for some time. "I can't stay locked up. I've got to be free, even when it's raining, even when it's snowing. Anything to be free."

Korasatch put her arm around my shoulders like a big sister. We were sitting close together to keep warm while we waited for the door across the street to open. But evidently the guest felt nice and comfortable in there. Why should he venture out into the cold and dark?

"And what if the bars are too narrow?" Korasatch asked.

"In that case I've got another trick," I said proudly. "Want to hear?"

"Sure!" said Korasatch. "Maybe I'll learn something."

"It works like this: I pretend I've got the runs. You know, it's often true. Everyone's got all kinds of problems like that because of the stuff we eat. I tell the policeman I need to use the toilet. He opens the door, takes me out, closes it behind us, and goes with me to the toilet. Then he goes back to the cell with me and locks me in. A few minutes later I do the same thing again, and then again. If he gets angry and tells me to sit down and shut up, I start shouting that it's coming and I can't wait. Then he feels sorry for me . . ."

"No one could refuse a little tyke like you," laughed Korasatch.

"Finally he gets fed up and tells me to go on my own."

"And then you make a run for it?"

"Not always," I said. "Usually I go one more round to put him off his guard. A lot of the time he's already sound asleep."

"Or pretending to be." Korasatch laughed, patting my shoulder. "He must get good and sick of you. I'm sure he's happy to be rid of you. Well, good for you, Yasha!" she added enthusiastically.

Fortunately it was too dark for her to see me blush. We were quiet for a while. Then suddenly she said softly, "I wish I could be like you."

"Why? What's the matter? Haven't you ever escaped from the police?"

"Yes, many times. But it's different for girls."

"Why?"

"Because they put their hands all over you. They touch you. It's really disgusting. I'm very careful not to get caught."

Isolated snowflakes fluttered slowly down. Suddenly Koras-atch began trembling. "Let's go," she said. "Tulik's waiting for us at the coal pile." She got hold of the sack and looked across at Irgashoi's tightly closed door. "We can come back tomorrow."

Forty

We stood looking in the display window of the restaurant, Tulik, Korasatch, and I. Right in front of us, near the glass, sat the familiar roast chicken, big, fat, and juicy, surrounded by plump, brown potatoes and fruit: red apples, pears, clusters of grapes, and half watermelons. It wasn't these painted plaster imitations that interested us. We'd seen them any number of times in restaurant windows, and they no longer fooled us. No, we were looking past them at the customers inside.

The sack of coal we had brought Irgashoi had been exchanged for food, and the food, as usual, for hunger. We had been snatching tidbits from one place or another for a week now, but it didn't amount to much. We had already gone through the restaurant's garbage bin, but people who ate there apparently didn't leave any leftovers. Was it possible that people who had ration cards were hungry too? They practically licked their plates clean!

Here and there, there was a clearing in the fog that covered the glass from the inside, and with our noses pressed to it we could see in.

"What do you think you're doing here?" a voice growled right into my ear. Someone grabbed me by the collar and yanked me backward. I leaned my head back and looked up. A big man stood there, with a greasy apron covering his huge paunch. Was it the manager of the restaurant? He must have come out of a

199

side door, and, dizzy with the smells and the sights before us, we hadn't noticed him.

With a quick twist I slipped out of his grasp and moved a safe distance away.

"What's your problem?" Tulik said. "Is it a crime to look?"

"Do your looking somewhere else!" the man said. "There's no standing here. It gets in the way!"

"Here in the Soviet Union there's no law against standing in the street," Tulik declared. "Why don't you complain to the police?"

The man stared at him for a moment, then looked Korasatch over. I felt a wave of anger, a kind of loathing and revulsion. He had dirty-gray eyes and a big mouth. His lower lip was limp and swollen, and he had several days' growth of beard. The man looked at her and said, "Hungry, eh?"

Korasatch moved away a few paces. She didn't answer him.

"There's work here," he said to her, wiping his hands on his dirty apron. "Dishwashing. You'll get food, and you can share it with your friends."

Korasatch didn't say anything.

"I'll do it!" Tulik said. "Can I start right away?"

"Not you, buster," the man said, dismissing him with a wave of his hand. "The girl. It's woman's work."

Tulik swallowed. I saw that he was angry. No, he definitely didn't like this man, not at all. If we hadn't been so hungry he would probably have found a way to get back at him.

"I'm stronger," he said. "Give me a chance. In the end you'll have me washing the floor too."

The man turned to go back into the restaurant. "It's the girl or nobody," he said, opening the door.

Korasatch stirred. "I'll go, Tulik," she said softly. "I'll bring you food."

She was paler than usual — either from hunger or something else, I didn't know.

Tulik took her hand. "I'll come to pick you up." Turning to the back of the fat man, he asked, "When does she finish?"

"How should I know?" the man barked. "Eleven, twelve, maybe later. Whenever they finish eating."

We watched Korasatch disappear into the restaurant and went back to our scrounging.

I tailed after Tulik the whole evening without saying a word, like a dog following an angry master: not too close, for fear of an unexpected kick, and not too far to hear a word of affection.

Tulik looked at the station clock for the umpteenth time.

"Nine-thirty already!" he said. "We'll have to get moving pretty soon."

He went on pacing back and forth from one wall to the other like a prisoner in his cell. Suddenly he stopped and said, "Wait a minute, isn't that a government restaurant? They close early, don't they? After all, they don't serve vodka."

I didn't know what to say. What did I know about restaurants? I only went into them in my dreams.

"I'm going to look for her," he said, turning and hurrying off. I ran after him. I hoped we'd see her right away coming toward us down the street, smiling as always, with all kinds of goodies in her coat pockets. But the streets were empty and dark.

It was hard even to see the restaurant. It was dark and empty, like all the shuttered houses nearby. Tulik tried the door. The bolt was fastened with a big padlock on the outside. He cursed and kicked the door.

"Damn!" he said. "She's left. She must have taken a different route."

He broke into a run, as if propelled forward by some inner force. I ran after him through the alleys. The only sound to be heard was the echo of our footsteps among the houses. Suddenly I stopped.

"Tulik!" I cried. "Wait! I heard something!"

He stopped and came back to where I was standing. We stood

201

listening to the wind blowing through the little alley. There was a kind of weeping in it, a muffled moan. Was it Korasatch?

We found her at the end of the alley, lying on the pavement like a satchel, limp and curled up. Korasatch was crying! I would have given my soul to stop her!

Tulik embraced her, stroking her face. "What happened?" he asked. "Did they take your food?"

Her whole body was racked with a bitter weeping. She covered her face with her hands.

"Did someone hurt you?"

She didn't answer. In the darkness I could imagine how tears must be rolling down her cheeks. If she let me, I would wipe them, one at a time.

"It's that bastard, isn't it, the owner of the restaurant?"

Korasatch clutched her body and let out a soft groan. She was being torn apart by some terrible internal pain and humiliation, as though she had been stabbed with a knife. Tulik got up.

"I'll break every bone in his body!" he hissed. "I'll smash his fat face! I'll kill him!"

The next day they left town. That afternoon, when I went by the restaurant, a big crowd had gathered.

"They found him inside," people said. "He must have just opened. The workers hadn't arrived yet. They could hardly identify his body. His head was split completely open. Someone had hit him repeatedly, someone who had gone crazy."

I took the first train out of town myself.

Forty-one

Winter passed, and spring arrived, the second spring. Once again the gardens were filled with pink and white blossoms, petals carpeted the newly thawed ground, and the hillsides turned green. I wandered from place to place, drunk with freedom and wide-open spaces. I had seen the Kyzyl Kum Desert, the "Desert of the Red Sands," as well as its southern cousin, the Kara Kum, the "Desert of the Black Sands." Between Tashkent and Samarkand I had many occasions to cross the "Hungry Steppe," but I was no longer afraid the way I once had been, the first time, that it would open its maw and swallow me up, together with the car, the train, the tracks, and all. I traveled up the Fergana Valley to the end of the line, to the point beyond which no steam engine was strong enough to pull a train, and continued wandering up into the foothills of the high, snow-covered mountains. In the summer I went back there a second time. The river was flowing through the heart of the valley, and the trees were laden with fruit. It was a paradise of streaming canals, abundant produce, and *tche-khana,* the teahouses scattered along the road, with their pita in boxes in the corner, tea served in little glasses, and beckoning gestures.

In the summertime the gangs would reassemble, bands of hungry sparrows gathering up crumbs. With a single stroke of a knife we would slit open sacks of rice being carried through an alley by a donkey, fill up our containers one by one, and disappear. As if by chance, we would bump into someone carrying a tray of pita, or we would choose melons with elaborate care.

In the evenings we would gather somewhere, near a canal or on a riverbank, and rub stones together to light the cigarette butts we had picked up. All you needed was for one tuft of cotton to catch the spark, and there was plenty of cotton around. Double-humped camels plodded through the streets with huge sacks of it hanging down on either side. The wind wafted little balls of cotton in from the fields and the factories, sent them rolling through the alleys, and carried white tufts up into the branches of the trees.

We would puff on our cigarettes, brag about our adventures, and heap abuse on everything and everyone.

"Know what happened to me today?" asked an older boy whose face was strewn with freckles. "We went to swipe watermelons. The guys up front were inspecting them as usual, and finally someone passed one to me. I grabbed it, turned around and gave it to the guy behind me, and wham! It was a policeman!"

"Did he catch you?" I asked, taking a long drag on my cigarette butt.

"Of course not," the freckled one said, laughing. "I rammed the watermelon into his stomach and ran!"

"And did he chase you?"

"Did he ever! He thought he could catch me, that fatso. I was barefoot, and he was this big guy with a uniform and all. I ran to the lake, turned around and did like this" — he held out his hand and raised the middle finger — "then jumped in the water. Let him try to catch me there!"

I laughed. I was the acknowledged champion at such things, but I loved to hear about others' feats too.

"I swam a little farther," the boy went on, "then went back by a roundabout route and heisted two melons, one for me and one for Korasatch."

My heart skipped a beat.

"Did you say Korasatch? Which Korasatch?"

"Why, you know her? Tulik's girlfriend."

"Are Tulik and Korasatch here? Where are they?"

"Everybody knows that! We bring her food whenever we manage to swipe something."

"But why?" I asked. "Can't she do her own stealing?"

I remembered our exploits in the market the previous summer, and how she had climbed onto a moving train and jumped off

204

it, and how she'd helped me fill my sack with coal and pick it up. "What's the matter? Is she sick?"

"She's got a huge belly," another boy said, "like a watermelon. She can hardly move. Do you think she'll eventually split open?"

"Idiot!" the freckled one snapped. "She's got a baby in her belly, and pretty soon she's going to give birth!"

Forty-two

She lay on a half-full sack in the corner of the abandoned hut. This time she recognized me right away.

"Yasha!" she exclaimed, raising herself with difficulty.

"K–K–Korasatch!" I stammered, then fell silent in embarrassment. The same short, black hair, the same dark, almond-shaped eyes. And that beauty mark, the one that had always tickled her upper lip, was still there. But Korasatch was not smiling. Her beautiful, smooth skin was covered with big yellow blotches, and there were little beads of perspiration on her face. It was hot, a late-summer heat wave.

Yes, it was the Korasatch I had known. But then she had been slender, erect, and jovial, and now a heavy belly hung in front of her and her eyes were sad. How could she have changed so much since we'd last seen each other?

"Hi, kid," she said, and then, right away, as if reading my mind, she added, "You haven't changed: still small and quick. You haven't grown at all, it seems to me. Can you still get through the bars?"

"Sure I can," I said and again fell silent, embarrassed.

Suddenly strong hands grabbed me around my waist and lifted me into the air.

205

"Let me go!" I shouted, kicking helplessly and trying to break free. The hands thrust me upward again and again and finally set me down carefully on the floor. I turned around. It was Tulik!

He was taller, tall and thin, and now he had a real mustache. Tulik!

"Good to see you, little fellow! You're still alive and kicking!"

I was flooded with warm feelings. Tulik, the king, the lone wolf — Tulik actually remembered me and was happy to see me.

We sat down on the floor, that is, on the ground. It might once have been a warehouse or something, but now there was only the frame of a hut with a fiery-hot tin roof. At least we had shade. Korasatch lay on her side on the sack, with one hand supporting her head. Tulik, and the other boys too — everybody loved Korasatch — must have gathered up some cotton to fill the sack. As for me, I was embarrassed. I tried not to look at her big belly, as if it weren't hers, as if it had created a distance between us.

"Well," Tulik asked, "hasn't anyone adopted you yet?"

"That's not for me," I answered. "I want to be free! I don't want anybody telling me what to do."

"I'm sure nobody's interested in a little devil like you anyway!"

"Oh yes they are. There was an officer who was. But he was a drunk."

Tulik laughed. "Just your cup of tea. What did he do?"

"It was during the winter," I said, "after you . . . after you disappeared on me."

I started to tell them what had happened. I spoke quickly, so as to keep my thoughts and memories from getting the better of me.

"He bought me dumplings, a lot of them, more and more. I thought he would buy up the whole stand. I ate and ate, and he paid and drank. Afterwards he wept — you know how drunkards weep — wept and hugged me. I must have reminded him of his own son, I don't know. Finally we got on a train together.

206

Why not? As long as he was feeding me I didn't mind being with him. But he stopped buying. We went from car to car, and he staggered back and forth and sang, and when we got to the crew compartment he just stretched out and started to snore. I was afraid I'd get caught there, so I kept my distance."

"Whatever happened to him?" Korasatch asked.

"What happens to all drunks: the next morning, when I went by there as if by chance, I saw that they had robbed him of just about everything. They took his wallet, his boots, his uniform. I got off at the next stop."

"Idiot, why didn't you take the wallet yourself?" Tulik asked.

"I don't know," I said. "He'd been good to me. I couldn't do it."

"What kind of an officer was he, army?"

"No, police."

Tulik burst out laughing. "Serves him right! I bet they threw him off the force. Or at least demoted him. Serves him right, it does."

Again I said nothing, only looked down again. I had a lot of stories to tell them, but there was a question I kept wanting to ask. At last I couldn't help myself. "What're you going to do with the baby? Will you raise it?"

Tulik looked at Korasatch, and Korasatch looked at the floor. I stole a glance at her belly. Something moved under the tightly stretched garment, as if there were someone else there, inside.

"It's kicking," said Korasatch, and put her hand on her belly.

"You'll take care of it, won't you?" I said, suddenly getting excited. "Hey, it'll be our whole gang's baby! We'll all help look after it! I know how to take care of babies, really I do! Babies love me. I know how to feed them and diaper them and even bathe them when need be. Listen, Korasatch, we'll bring you food and we'll raise the baby together. It'll be great!"

They said nothing.

"I'm sure it'll be a beautiful child. After all, it's Korasatch's!"

"And maybe mine too," said Tulik very softly.

I was silent. A light wind came up and rattled the tin plates overhead, sprinkling rusty powder.

"Where will we raise him?" Korasatch asked, looking around. "Here, without walls or a floor? And where will we get diapers from? And besides . . ."

"They'll take the baby away from her immediately," said Tulik, "in the hospital, right after it's born. That's what they always do."

"Then give birth here!" I said. "I know an old woman who knows a lot. I'm sure she'd know what to do."

We were in Syr-Darya. Pesya, the old Jewish woman in the market, always had ideas and could certainly help.

"And they'll put Korasatch in an institution for teenage girls!" Tulik said, his blue eyes darkening.

"Don't worry about that!" said Korasatch. "I'll just run away! The minute I get a chance, I'll run away!"

"So should I speak to the old woman? Should we try to keep the baby?" I asked.

"We'll think about it, little fellow, we'll think about it."

But when the labor pains started they couldn't put it off. Tulik helped Korasatch stand up and slowly walked her to the hospital. I watched them until they disappeared behind the last house. Every so often they would stop. I suppose it was hard for Korasatch to drag such a gigantic belly along, and maybe she had pain. I don't know.

I met Tulik on one other occasion.

"It was a girl!" he said. "They didn't even show it to her."

I never saw them again. No doubt she ran away from the home for teenage girls. You could count on Korasatch. I imagine them always being together, wandering around in the markets, riding the speeding trains: Tulik, the champion organizer, king of the gangs, and Korasatch with him, slender and erect as always, with the beauty mark next to her ever-smiling lips.

208

Forty-three

I can't remember when I snatched the hat: the second winter? Maybe the third? I went crazy over it the minute I saw it: a red hat, fur-lined, with big earflaps that tied under the chin. A terrific hat. With one like that you could forget about frozen ears in the wintertime. With a hat like that you'd be a king, even in Siberia!

I saw it on a boy's head in one of the stations. Not just an ordinary boy, but one standing with his mother, one of those boys who had a mother and a home and someone to make sure they ate when they were hungry. He really didn't deserve such a hat!

Once someone had told me — I no longer remembered who or when — that I was stubborn as a mule, and that when I wanted something I would end up getting it. Maybe. Anyway, there was no way I was going to pass up that hat. Luckily for me, the two of them hadn't taken the first train. Everything was going just as I had planned.

The boy sat next to his mother, devouring a pie — one of those spicy ones filled with onions and peppers, the kind with the crisp crust — a real beauty! But this time it was not for food that I lay in ambush. The hat was untied, so I wouldn't have any problem.

I waited for the train. It didn't matter when it came; I had plenty of time. What was the rush? I put my hands in my pockets, turned around, whistled to myself, and hardly looked at him. Even when the train came I didn't look his way, as if nothing were going on. Then, when the train began to move, when it started to pick up speed — wham! — I grabbed the hat off his head, ran to the nearest car, took hold of the handles, and, as always, pulled myself up. I saw them waving their hands about and shouting, but I could no longer hear anything. I was far

209

away. I could picture that pampered little face, the tears. Let him cry! What did I care? The main thing was, the hat was mine!

From that time on, the hat went with me everywhere. Winter or summer, I never took it off. I swam rivers with it, and lakes. I would just as soon have died of hunger as traded it for anything in the world!

The hat quickly got dingy and soiled, but you could still tell it was something special. A lot of boys wanted it, but I kept a close watch on it. Once I get hold of something I never let go.

But there was to come a time when that wouldn't be so easy, not at all: there was simply nowhere to run. Two of us were sitting on top of a passenger car munching seeds. He was one of the bigger, stronger boys, a full head taller than I was, maybe two.

The big coat I wore was already old and torn, with more holes than lining, but it was still a magic coat. When the fellow had grabbed the full cup of seeds and run, it was into the innocent sleeve of this coat that the other cup had quietly disappeared.

Now just two of us were sitting on top of the car, headed wherever the wind would carry us.

He had a thin, dark face and black eyes. He sat spitting the shells into the wind, never taking his burning eyes off me for a moment. It was a hot, summer day, but I again tied the hat strings. A chill crept down my back, a shiver. I wouldn't want to meet someone like him in a dark alley.

"Give me the hat!" he said suddenly.

"What for?" I answered defiantly.

"If you don't, I'll throw you off!" the boy said, drawing himself up.

"Go ahead!" I said, getting up myself. Why should I give him my hat anyway?

Legs spread, he started toward me, across the roof of the swaying car. I drew back, steering clear of the side. At the edge of the roof, near the lavatory vent-pipe, I stopped. I clasped it tightly, never taking my eyes off him.

"You'd better give it to me, or I'll throw you off!" the boy said, grabbing my arm. I held on to the pipe. The boy began pulling me to and fro, trying to tear my arms free. He was much stronger than I was, a real bruiser. I felt my arms weakening. I tried to embrace the pipe, but the boy was squeezing my wrist. An awful pain passed through me. I let go.

Now he took hold of my other wrist. Again a sharp pain sliced through my body, and I moved away from the pipe. He held my wrists in his powerful hands. I tried to grab the sleeves of his shirt, so as to get hold of him — if he could do it, so could I! — but try as I might, all my hands could get hold of was the air. We lunged about like two wrestlers in a ring. For a moment we stood facing each other, with the vent-pipe between us. He stood with his legs spread wide, glaring down at me with a crazed look in his eyes. Suddenly he gave me a violent tug. I lost my footing; he pulled me sideways. I was done for! *Mama! It's all over!*

Suddenly a huge shadow came up behind me. Bam! Something enormous struck the boy's forehead, and he instantly let go of me. He didn't even cry out; he simply went flying off the roof of the car and disappeared.

I was thrust toward the vent-pipe, and at the last moment I latched on to it. I wrapped myself around it with my arms, my legs, my whole body.

It was several seconds before I opened my eyes again. Giant iron girders were passing over my head one by one. The train was crossing a bridge over the Syr-Darya River. Then the clatter changed: we had crossed the river. Retreating across the roof of the car, I hadn't noticed we were coming to the river, to the bridge. The boy was much taller than I was; the first girder had struck his head and thrown him overboard, while I, small and weak as I was, remained on the roof, alive. Alive!

I glanced down. Far below the bridge flowed the river. It was a mighty stream, hundreds of yards across. This being midsummer, the high-mountain snow was melting at full tilt, and the water gushed brown with silt and mud. If he hadn't been crushed under the wheels he would certainly have been killed by the distance of the fall, by the terrible force of hitting the water, and swept away by the powerful current.

I finally let go of the pipe, but not until long after we had crossed the river. My whole body was trembling. For days, I had cramps in all my muscles, and my arms ached. My wrists were blue for a week or more. But who cares? I still had my hat, mine forever!

Forty-four

Then, one fine day, the war ended. No, it didn't come as a surprise. I knew from the very first day that we would win. They had said then on the radio that we would crush the Nazi enemy, that we'd trample the fascists underfoot and save the fatherland. It was true that years had gone by. So what? Now the time had come. The voice of the announcer came from the big loudspeakers in the public squares.

"The Red Army," he said, "has driven the Nazi enemy from the soil of the fatherland. Our forces are now liberating the soil of Poland."

After that our forces went into Germany. Any child could see that we were going to win in the end. All you had to do was read the posters in the street. I especially liked the one that said, "The Hitlerites are retreating to a point where the shortest front will be along the River Spree, on which Berlin is located!" Looking up I could see a German officer fluttering helplessly, gripped around the waist by a pair of pincers. No kidding! And how ugly he was, with his big, crooked nose and the swastika on his sleeve. They deserved to be pulverized, the bastards! The pincers were held by two strong hands: on the right, a hand in a glove bearing the symbol of the Soviet Union, the hammer and sickle and star; on the left a hand with the American flag on it. I recognized that without any trouble, the flag of our friend on the other side of the ocean.

On May Day they said the Soviet army had entered Berlin — that day of all days, the workers' holiday, which even during the war they made a fuss about. A few more days went by, and then, one day, they announced that the war was over. Strange, nothing changed. It was the same as the day before, and the days that followed were no different. True, people wept and embraced in the streets, embraced and wept, but the next day everything was the same as always: the hunger, the train rides, the gangs that came together and dispersed, the markets, the people trading rags for food, the vendors keeping a sharp eye on their wares, and we, snatching and running, pilfering and getting caught and running again, playing cat-and-mouse with the police.

Nothing had changed. I had hardly grown, and that too was nothing new. I had made up my mind I would stay that way forever, free and light as the wind — until I developed that fever in the police station. No, it wasn't the first time, and I wasn't the only one. They said there were a lot of mosquitoes hatching thereabouts, in the open canals and in the pools of standing water left after the rivers overflowed, and so we all got malaria. Not a big deal. No need to get excited. I had been through worse things.

When the attack began I knew exactly what to expect. It would start with chills, an hour of chills, even if the temperature outside was 105 or 110 degrees in the shade. Then came the fever. I have no idea how high it was, but it must have been high, because my head hurt, and along with the headache came nausea and vomiting. After all this I would sweat. I think the fever went down then, because I would finally fall asleep, soaked in perspiration and exhausted. When I woke up I would know the attack was over — yet another one; I had lost count — and I would get up, still a little wobbly, and go back to normal life. What choice did I have?

Only this time it happened in a police station. What had I been brought in for? The Devil only knows. Stealing? Sneaking onto a train? I can't remember. In short, I was in the detention cell when I began to tremble like a leaf. The chills had begun.

When the attack was over and I felt like myself again, I found myself in a transit center for abandoned children. Well, I'd find a way out of this place too. I'd just wait until I was a little stronger and had gotten the lay of the land. But how could you get stronger on the kind of food they gave you?

We sat in the dining room around wooden tables, a crowd of hungry, insolent, noisy brats. Fights would break out over the least little thing. The counselors walked around among the tables keeping an eye on us.

Finally, those whose turn it was to serve would come out with the big bowls.

"Don't all reach for the soup, now!" said the counselor. "The waiter will hand it out!"

He wasn't very tall, this counselor, but he had huge shoulders. He must have been stronger than ten of us put together. His face was as pimply as a rotten potato. He looked like the type you wouldn't want to start up with. We followed the waiter's movements closely. He took the ladle and emptied its contents into the first plate.

"Soup again," said one of the older boys scornfully. "Again that lukewarm water of theirs. It's disgusting!"

"Got a complaint?" asked the counselor, coming over. "Nobody's forcing you to eat here, you know. You can leave."

"No complaint," said the boy quickly. He leaned over and began spooning up the cloudy liquid. They all ate quickly. The spoons clattered ceaselessly, but now no one spoke.

The bread was no better: black as coal, familiar, and repulsive. The Devil only knows what they made it with. If I had thrown it at the wall it would have stuck like black mud. But I didn't throw a single crumb. I swallowed it, almost without chewing. What rotten luck! How would I ever get better in a place like this? If I had been on the outside I was sure I could have found something, gotten along; but here . . .

Someone at the other end of the room banged two spoons together. In the kitchen door stood a heavyset woman with a big apron around her waist.

"Quiet!" the counselor barked. "There's an announcement!"

The woman stood there calmly, hands on her hips, waiting for silence.

"Now comes the main course," said the boy next to me, winking, "turkey for everybody, plus cake and ice cream with syrup. Paradise!"

The counselor came over to us with a threatening look on his face. The boy stopped speaking and tucked his head between his shoulders as if preparing to get hit.

The woman took a small piece of paper out of her apron pocket and announced in a loud voice, "The following children will stay after the meal to clean the dining room: Levita, Davidoff, Yoffe, Kagan, and Abramov. No one skips out. I'll repeat the names: Levita, Davidoff, Yoffe, Kagan . . ."

Kagan? Did she say Kagan? That was my name! But why me? I had only just gotten out of the miserable bed where I had been sick with malaria. It was my first time in the dining room. So why me?

The boys made a great commotion as they crowded toward the door. They threw their plates and spoons onto the dirty-dish cart and hurried out. What point was there in staying? They had eaten everything in sight, not leaving a single crumb. There was hardly anything to clean.

I looked at the boys who remained behind with me. Why had

they chosen us over all the others? I had a feeling it wasn't accidental, but what did the five of us have in common? Why us?

The last of the boys disappeared through the door under the watchful eye of the woman in the apron. She surveyed the empty room, fished around in her apron pocket, and pulled out a key.

She's going to lock us in! I thought, and suddenly I felt like I was suffocating, felt imprisoned like an animal in a pen.

The key turned noisily in the keyhole — once, then a second time — and all at once I understood. Jews! We all had Jewish names! I was hit by a wave of fear. All my limbs froze. They're going to beat us, us Jews! This had never happened to me here in the Soviet Union, never! And now, just when I was so weak, when I couldn't escape . . . !

The woman turned away from the door and went toward the kitchen. The key! She had left the key in the door! If I moved fast I might have time to make a break for it! But the weakness, this weakness of mine . . . I couldn't move. Why now, of all times?

Forty-five

The kitchen door opened wide. Who was going to come out? Thugs with clubs?

A big, steaming urn emerged, carried by a short, cheery-faced woman. "Come, children," she said, motioning with her head, "come here with your plates and help yourselves."

From the urn came hot vapors, and a savory aroma filled the air. We couldn't resist the temptation. Getting up from the abandoned tables we gathered around the urn. Unbelievable: it was porridge! The woman ladled it into our plates. We didn't ask any questions. We simply dug into it like starving animals.

"Take it easy, my little ducklings, take it easy!" the woman said. "It's hot! Be careful!"

I blew on the porridge and tasted it. It was thick and sweet. When was the last time I had eaten such porridge? I blew and ate, blew and ate. "Ducklings," she had called us, "ducklings." When was the last time someone had called me that, and where?

The kitchen door opened again. This time the woman who had locked the main door came out. She was bringing us meat, meat and potatoes in a big urn! And bread, big, thick slices of real bread. Could I be dreaming?

Dream or not, we polished off the porridge and devoured the meat and potatoes without a word. Meanwhile, all around us the kitchen staff were at work cleaning the tables, lifting the benches onto them, and sweeping the floor. I saw it all. I went on eating, but to be safe I kept glancing around, and when the workers weren't looking I quickly hid two slices of bread in my pocket. Better safe than sorry. A miracle like this happens only once in a lifetime, and in my life the most dependable thing was hunger. The others took bread as well. Before they had finished cleaning the tables we had finished everything. With the leftover bread we wiped our plates clean.

The heavyset woman came over to us, smiling. She put her hands on the heads of two boys sitting opposite me and, looking me straight in the eye, said, "Now don't breathe a word of this to the others. You'll be on cleanup duty until further notice. But not a word of this outside. Is that clear?"

When we got outside we looked at each other without saying a word.

"New here?" one of the older boys asked at last.

"Yes," I said. "What is this place anyway, an orphanage? I was sick when they brought me here."

"No," the boy said, "it's just a transit center. There are no teachers here or any of the nonsense that goes on in an orphanage. I guess all the orphanages are full. They've kept us here an awfully long time."

I thought about the miracle in the dining room.

"Does . . . does this happen every day?" I asked. He understood immediately what I meant.

"Pretty often," he whispered. "All the workers in the kitchen are 'our people.' "

Then I had been right. We were, in fact, all Jews. I was taken aback. Where on earth did they get such food? Maybe . . . My head was spinning. No, it couldn't be!

The boy looked me in the eye. We seemed to have had the very same thought.

"It's the same in all the institutions," he said softly, "even where there are no Jews. The Russians, the Uzbeks, they all take for their own people. They all want to stay alive, don't they?"

I was silent. I knew he was right. I had been in several institutions, and I'd eaten in them before making my getaway — if you could call it eating. What did I care? The main thing was to have a full belly today, and maybe tomorrow too.

We went out into the yard. The teenage boys were standing around in little groups. As usual, there were only boys; there were separate institutions for girls. Two of the boys were already hitting each other in one corner. A big group had gathered around them, shouting catcalls and cheering them on. There wasn't much else to do anyway. This way at least something was happening, something interesting.

"What about the gate?" I said. "What kind of a gate do they have?"

The boy stopped and looked at me, his eyebrows raised. "You thinking of trying to get out? Are you crazy? You've got everything here you could possibly want. Where would you ever get food like this on the outside?"

"This isn't for me," I said, looking around. "It's like a prison."

"Listen," he said, grabbing me by the arm. "I saw you there, in the dormitory. You've got malaria, no doubt about it. You were so confused you didn't know whether you were alive or dead. Now sit still, take what they give you, and later on, when you're all well, if you still want to you can always run away." He went a few steps further and then stopped again. "Aren't you Kagan?" he asked. "Yesterday they called your name after dinner, but you weren't there. I'm Volodya Abramov. At home they called me Velvele," he added in a whisper, as if entrusting to me his most closely guarded secret.

"And I'm . . . Yasha!" I said, swallowing from the sudden excitement. "They called me . . . at home they called me Yankele."

A flood of memories suddenly came over me. One word was enough to lift a mountain out of the depths. Overcome with emotion, I was swept by the flood to the far side of the yard. I couldn't take the pandemonium of quarreling boys. And Volodya accompanied me in silence. Maybe the flood swept him along too.

Forty-six

Suddenly I heard a dreadful growling behind me, like the snarling of a wild beast. I started, then turned around. If it was a dog, at least I didn't want it to attack me from behind. And sometimes I get along well with dogs, even the meanest ones.

But it was no dog. I looked and looked and couldn't believe my eyes. There was a teenage boy there, one of the bigger boys, thin and unkempt, his hair overgrown like an animal's. He was crouched down and staring at us — from inside a cage, a small iron cage! It was a kind of jail. He gripped the bars and growled. He had filthy, spindly fingers, black at the tips, and his nails were very long. He let out another long growl. There was hunger in it, and pain, and a terrible helplessness. I took a step toward the cage.

"What are you doing in there?" I asked. "Why did they put you inside such a thing?"

The boy didn't answer. He stared at me with feverish eyes as if he had not understood my question. Then he let go of the bars, put his hands on his head and crouched down on the iron floor of the cage like a heap of rags, rags that even I wouldn't have picked up.

I turned to Volodya. "That's 'the monster,' " he said. "That's what everybody calls him."

I felt ill at ease. Calling someone a name like that behind his back was bad enough, but right in front of him?

"What are you afraid of?" Volodya said. "We've tried every-thing with him: Russian, Uzbek, Kirghiz. One boy even tried Turkish, but it didn't work."

"Maybe he's deaf."

"No. Once, when he was sleeping we sneaked up on him and made a lot of noise. You should have seen how startled he was! He jumped up and started yelping and pulling at the bars. At that time he was still strong enough to stand up. Now he's not."

"Why? Is he sick?"

"I don't think so. They just don't feed him. The director for-bids it. He's a Russian, the director, from the north. When he says no, it's no."

"But why? What's he done?"

"They say he killed another boy in a fight. Split his head open."

"Really? So why's he here and not in prison?"

"He must be too young to do time."

"So why don't they send him to a reformatory?"

"How should I know?" said Volodya, shrugging his shoulders. "I suppose they're all full. They say he made trouble here, too, so they put him under lock and key, for two months."

I turned to look at the boy again. He was stretched out on

the floor, lifeless and indifferent. It was even worse than hearing him growl.

"How long has he been locked up?"

"I dunno. Three–four weeks, maybe."

"And he hasn't been given any food in all this time?"

"They do feed him sometimes. A little. The director wants to get rid of him. He doesn't want to be bothered. This one kills somebody with a single blow; the other," he whispered, glancing up at the building, "does it slowly. I don't know which is worse."

Toward evening I went back to the cage. It was late, and soon they would be shutting us into the dormitory for the night. I had been waiting for this moment.

The boy looked up and stared at me for several minutes. His face was deeply scratched. With such fingernails it was a wonder he hadn't hurt himself even worse. He was wrapped in a torn army blanket, but it wasn't enough. Even in the hottest part of the summer it got cold at night, and the summer was over.

I looked around to see if anyone was watching. The other boys were playing some distance away, near the illuminated doorways of the building. Even if they had wanted to they couldn't have seen anything in the gathering darkness. I went up to the bars, took a slice of bread from my pocket, and put it in the cage.

"Take it," I said. "It's for you."

The boy grabbed the bread and gobbled it down all at once. I doubt that he chewed it at all. I was ashamed — I had hidden another slice away somewhere. I had to keep it for the next day. After all, miracles didn't happen every day. But the boy was starving.

A sharp whistle came from the entrance. They were summoning us to come in. It was time to close the gates of mercy.

But the miracle did repeat itself the next day. Again I had enough bread to stow away. I followed my friends around. They too

221

were hiding bread, no doubt about it. But where? None of us had a space of his own, neither a cupboard nor a shelf. We even had to share the pitiful mattresses we slept on. Nor were the clothes on our backs considered our own private property. The older boys would go through our pockets looking for "finds." If they found bread there, they would rob us of it and at the same time try to beat out of us the secret of where we had come by this "treasure." Who had given it to us, and why?

I watched Volodya. He went around behind the building and immediately came back out to play with the others. I waited until he was engrossed in a game of tag, until someone tagged him and he was "it." Then I hurried to the back of the building myself. I followed the side of the building all the way around but found nothing. There were the high, narrow windows of the toilets and showers and a back door to the kitchen — locked, of course; I immediately checked — but that was all. Where could he have hidden his "treasure"?

Not far from one corner I spotted the gutter pipe. It ran down the side of the building almost to the ground. I knelt down next to it and put my hand inside. There was a newspaper there. Someone had stuffed up the pipe with a newspaper. I pulled it out, and, sure enough, several slices of bread fell right into my hand. Not a bad idea, as long as no one suspects you have anything to hide.

By evening I had found yet another hideout, Luba's I think. As I came up to the cage, the boy did not take his eyes off me. I walked back and forth in front of the bars, waiting for just the right moment, and the whole time he followed me with his eyes, like a sunflower turning toward the sun. That evening I gave him three slices of bread, three whole slices! As he was devouring them, I noticed the can. It was a can for water no doubt; there was no cup in sight. But it was empty, dry, and rusty. When had it last been filled? I reached in carefully and pulled the can out. I was afraid the boy would jump on me all of a sudden and bite my arm, like a wild animal, but he just glanced at me and began gathering up crumbs. I rinsed out the can with water from the tap in the corner of the yard — luckily everyone was already headed in, or there would have been a long line there — then filled it and went back to the cage. I quietly set it down inside, this time without fear. Why should I be afraid? Even animals can tell the difference between the hand that feeds them and the hand that beats them.

Forty-seven

For a whole month I sneaked him food, a whole month! I found all my friends' hiding places, or most of them anyway. No matter how often they changed them, they couldn't outsmart me. There wasn't much to do during the day, so I had plenty of time, and they had very few places to hide things. It's beyond me how they never figured out that I was the thief, because I suppose that on days when I was sick again and lay in bed with fever or exhaustion their treasures didn't disappear. Or maybe they did then, too. After all, we were a certified pack of thieves, the whole lot of us.

Then one day a rumor went around that "the monster" had been set free. They had let him out of his cage! They were bathing him!

I ran to the showers and squeezed my way in. I couldn't see anything. The older boys pushed me aside. I tried to crawl between their legs, but they kicked me and pushed my head back with their strong hands. I backed out and stood waiting in the corridor.

The boys stood looking in without saying a word. The ones at the back were standing on tiptoe. Evidently it was a fascinating sight. Suddenly the crowd broke apart and made way. I saw them pulling back and looking up. Then he appeared.

I could hardly recognize him. His head was completely shaven, and so was his face, which had begun to sprout a beard and mustache. Washed, dressed in the gray uniform of the institution, and taller than everybody else, he passed through the crowd like a ghost. I looked at his hands. They were clean, and his nails had been trimmed. The other boys kept their distance in silence.

As he came down the corridor he looked down at me. He stopped for a moment. I wasn't afraid. I looked him straight in the eye. I saw a flicker of recognition. I smiled at him, but his face remained frozen. I think he had forgotten how to smile.

Outside there was the usual pandemonium of games and fights. A lot of boys were crowded around the spigot; it was a very hot day, and this was the only spigot we had. There was always a long line there, and for some reason the bigger boys were always in front. Although the thirst drove us crazy, we smaller ones had no choice: even when our "turn" finally came they would prod us to hurry up and make room for them at the source of the coveted refreshment.

The boy stood in the doorway surveying the yard. Everyone looked at him, and the shouting died down. It was quiet. He turned and walked straight to the spigot, moving slowly, erect and sure of himself. Those who were waiting in line stepped back and made way for him, even the biggest, strongest ones. He went up to the spigot like someone who had been waiting for a long time for this moment, leaned down, and began to drink. He drank and drank and drank, while we all looked on silently. Finally he finished, closed the tap, and stood up. Head and shoulders above the others, he looked all around, until his eyes came to rest on me. He beckoned to me. I went straight over to him. The others made way for me and then crowded in behind me. I stood next to him. He didn't say anything but only pointed to the spigot. I understood. From that day on I could drink as much as I wanted whenever I wanted, and no one would stop me.

From then on no one ever laid a finger on me. I was the protégé of "the monster," a nickname no one ever dared use again, even in secret. The boy had never spoken, and even after they let him out of his cage he never said a word. But all it took was a little growl or the sight of him to make everyone move out of his way and retreat to the far side of the yard. As for me, I had it made. I had protection, plenty of food, and a mattress to lie on when I had my malaria attacks, and I was just waiting for them to end, to get stronger again, so that I could make my escape. This was the one thing I lacked: to be free as a bird once more.

But this time freedom came too soon, before its time. Apparently the older boys had planned it all without telling us. One day they broke through the main gate, and we all ran for it. It was too easy, too simple. Maybe they had bribed the guard, or maybe, maybe, the counselors had helped them break out and escape! Why not? This way they had an empty institution and enough food for hundreds of youngsters. Until it filled up again.

One way or the other, I had regained my freedom. Which way would the wind blow me now?

Forty-eight

No one could have predicted what would happen that day. I found myself in Syr-Darya again. I knew the big railway junction there like the back of my hand. Here there was a change in the gauge of the tracks. A different train went from here up into the mountains, and passengers had to switch. People heading south to Tashkent had to switch too.

I went to see Pesya, the old Jewish woman from the market. On the way there, on the train, I had had another malaria attack, and I was in need of a corner to rest in and someone to stroke my forehead.

I had known Pesya for some time. Even in the last year or two, when I had come to enjoy being free and moving from place to place, I would sometimes grow sad. I was overcome with longing — for what? for whom? I no longer even remembered Mama's face or voice — and at such times I would go back to Pesya. I would sit for a few days in the corner of her little room and then be on my way.

Pesya was a little woman, thin and stooped. Her hands trembled, but they had a homey touch. Thick glasses rested on her hooked nose, and in them one could see circles within circles within circles reaching in toward her eyes, which looked tiny and far away. With her round glasses and her sparse white hair, she looked like an old owl, but her eyes were kind and wise.

She would sit in the corner of the market peddling rags. Trading nothing for something, she somehow made a living on the paltry difference between the two. She always seemed to be at peace, like someone who had seen it all and was no longer surprised at anything. But this time it was different: something was bothering her. She shook her head, her face red to the roots of her white hair, and muttered to herself.

"What's the matter, Pesya?" I asked, taking her wrinkled hand. Her eyes cast about for a while in the circles of her glasses until they came to rest on me.

"It's always the same, Yasha," she said, as if we had just seen each other the day before. "He always picks on our people."

"Who?"

"The police captain. He's arrested one of us again."

"For what?"

"For 'speculating,' what else? Once the captain decides some-

226

one is a 'speculator,' there's nothing that person can do. Everybody's a 'speculator' here; how else can you make a living? But for the most part the captain doesn't bother the others, only us."

"Why us?"

"He's out for money, a lot of money."

She put her hand over her mouth and whispered straight into my ear. "The scoundrel knows the Jews won't let one of their own be taken away to prison. Just now some of our people came by collecting money for the ransom. He doesn't arrest gentiles. What do they care if one of 'theirs' is arrested? It's one less competitor in the market."

She fumbled in the big pocket of her faded dress. I knew there couldn't be more than a few pennies in it at the most. She had probably given a penny or two. She had to give something.

"Oh well," she said, as if putting the matter to rest, "as long as I can help I shouldn't complain. And what about you, Yasha?" she asked, looking me over closely. "Where have you been lately?"

"Here and there, as usual."

"You're pale!" she said firmly. "What happened? Have you been sick?"

"It's nothing," I said, sitting down on the pile of rags, "just a touch of malaria, the same as everybody else has."

"I've been waiting for you," Pesya said. She lowered herself slowly onto a little stool. "It must be six months since you've been here. I've been wanting to ask you something."

"What?"

"How old are you, Yasha?"

I laughed. "Is that what you wanted to ask me? Is that what you've been waiting six months for?"

She shook her head, flexing her thin, shriveled neck. "I haven't been waiting for that. I just wanted to know."

How old was I, anyway? I had been eight, maybe a little more, when I first found myself on my own. Yes, that much I remem-

227

bered. It was winter then, and afterwards came a second and a third winter, maybe a fourth — I didn't know for sure. When you live from day to day you don't keep track of such things.

"I have no idea," I said. "Eleven, twelve, maybe even thirteen. I have no way of knowing."

"Were you already in school when the war broke out?"

"I think so," I said, and vague images began to emerge from the fog, still shapeless and unfamiliar. I didn't really remember anything. "I think I went to second grade, but not for long."

"Then you must be twelve or twelve and a half," Pesya said. "It's been six and a half years since then."

She squinted and examined me as if seeing me for the first time.

"And where did you go to first grade? Where did you live?"

"In Poland," I said.

"Do you remember which city?"

Out of the fog came the old house, the street, the whole ghetto. "Lodz. It was Lodz. Now I remember. Why do you ask?"

"And who else was in your family?" Pesya continued, as if she were getting at something.

"Who else? Well, there was Papa, Mama, and my sister."

"And how old would she be now?"

"Now? She's dead now. She's nothing," I said, lying back on the rag pile. I suddenly felt weak again. The things that had come up out of the fog hurt, and I wanted to push them back down. They tasted of tears, and I was tired.

Pesya put her hand on my forehead. "You don't have any fever now," she said. "It's just weakness. Rest a little, and then you'll be back on your feet."

She rummaged in her other pocket for a while. Finally she pulled out a little bundle, a handkerchief tied at the corners. "Take it," she said, letting go of the handkerchief with trembling fingers. "Eat it. I've got a little bread left. But tell me, Yasha, how far apart were you and your sister?" No, she wasn't going to leave me alone.

228

"I don't know. She was two or three years younger, maybe more. Why do you ask?"

"Because I met a woman here with a nine-year-old — maybe nine-and-a-half-year-old — daughter, a lovely girl, redheaded like you. But the woman couldn't stop crying over her son who had gotten lost."

"There are lots of cases like that," I said, closing my eyes. "Do you have any idea how many 'abandoned ones' are wandering around the countryside?"

"But she was from Lodz too. And she said that if her son was still alive he would be twelve and a half."

I didn't say anything.

" 'Yankele,' she would say, she was looking for her Yankele. That must be what you were called back home."

"That doesn't mean anything. Do you know how many Jewish boys were called Yankele?"

"Yes, but I think you should go see her anyway."

I wanted to sleep, to sink into a deep slumber, to escape. "Do you know how hard I looked, how many times I thought I had found Mama — not thought, was sure — and then it turned out to be someone else's mother? Well, I'm finished looking. It's a lost cause!" I said with finality, turning my back to her.

"If I thought there were a chance that a relative of mine might still be alive I would look and look and never give up," Pesya said softly.

I turned and looked at her. She had never spoken to me about her own family. It had never occurred to me things might once have been different. I assumed she had always been this way, old and alone.

"She's at the station now," said Pesya. "You wouldn't have run into her when you arrived because she works at a collective farm in the mornings. But now she's at the station, selling lemonade."

I was silent. I didn't have the strength for yet another disappointment. Pesya stroked my head. "You might as well go. What

229

have you got to lose? Then come back here. In the meantime I'll fix you something to eat. Go for my sake, Yasha, go!"

I went. The station was full, as always. People were going back north, back home — those who had homes to go back to, that is. I walked slowly. There was no reason to hurry. For the umpteenth time I would find another woman there. And even if it were Mama, how would I recognize her, now that my memory was all fogged?

She was standing in the entrance of the station, bathed in the soft light of dusk. She stood with her back to me, selling whatever it was she sold, a small, thin woman with narrow shoulders, her hair gathered in a kerchief. There were a thousand, ten thousand like her. But I suddenly felt a tug inside, like a taut violin string being plucked. I stood staring at her back. I didn't dare get any closer.

Then she turned around. A flash went through me. An invisible finger was plucking at the string. *Mama! My Mama! Mama!*

I couldn't utter a sound or move a muscle. I recognized her immediately. I hadn't forgotten anything. It was the same face, only thinner and sadder.

She stood next to the big beverage jug looking around. Her brown eyes wandered from place to place until they lit on me. They froze for a moment and opened wide, incredulous. She gaped at me without making a sound. Then she opened her arms, and I, I ran and threw myself into her embrace.

I cried, we both cried. I cried as I hadn't cried for years. I had forgotten how good it was to cry in Mama's arms.

Forty-nine

First came the tears, like an inexhaustible spring; then the words — one word, a sentence; then more tears. Where to begin, Mama, where to begin telling each other all that has happened?

She had been there the whole time, at the collective farm near Syr-Darya, doing whatever was necessary to stay close to the big railway junction: picking cotton in the fields, working in the factory, doing whatever jobs they gave her. But after work she would go to the station. In the winter she would sell a few baked things she had made herself, the way Papa had once done, and in the summer she'd sell cold lemonade.

Again and again she kissed my face, my eyes. Again and again she hugged me.

"I've been looking for you the whole time. I couldn't travel from place to place. I had to work, to make a living, to send Sarele to school. Here I could go on looking. I thought: if you're still alive, if you're not in an institution, you must be wandering around like all the rest of them, like all the 'abandoned ones.' Everybody said I was crazy, that there was no point in going on looking, but I kept on hoping, hoping that you were still alive and that one day you would come this way."

"I've been through here many times, Mama, many times!"

"But never at the right time."

We went toward the cabin. Little girls were jumping rope on the neat dirt path: short skirts, bare feet, braids flapping on shoulders. One of them broke away from the group and came over to us. As she got closer, she slowed down, perplexed, and then stopped. She stood staring at me, at Mama, who had her arm around me, and then back at me. She had big chocolate-colored eyes and red hair. I didn't recognize her, but I guessed.

Mama stood behind me, her hands on my shoulders. "Sarele," she said, "this is our Yankele!"

231

My sister gazed at me, her eyes on a level with mine, and cocked her head to one side. With the bare toes of one foot she rubbed the ankle of the other. "Hi," she said and fell silent. Then she suddenly spun around and ran off to her friends.

Mama laughed. "She's shy. She forgot what you look like, and I didn't even have a picture to remind her."

She raised my chin, her face taking on a serious look. "You haven't changed much. You haven't even gotten taller, hardly at all. Only your expression has changed. It's been so many years! Another six months and you'll be *bar-mitzvah!*"

She spoke Russian. I had forgotten my Yiddish altogether, but that phrase from the distant past, *bar-mitzvah,* suddenly brought back memories of a vanished world.

"What about Papa?" I asked. "Where is he? Has he come back from the war? The soldiers are being discharged and sent home, aren't they?"

"He'll never come back," Mama said, turning away. "I got a letter that he was missing in action. I've been getting a war widow's pension for two years now."

I said nothing. What could I say? It was Mama I had been looking for all this time, but I knew that in the end I would find Papa and Sarele too, the whole family. He had told me he would keep looking until he found me. He couldn't have been killed! He must still be looking for me!

We went into the cabin. There were four beds in the little room, trunks instead of a clothes closet, and towels hung on nails. On a trunk near the window lay a doll, an old rag doll without eyes or hair. Someone had kept it nonetheless. As a memento, perhaps.

My head spun. I leaned against the wall and whispered, "Grandma, what about Grandma?"

"Sleep, Yankele, sleep," Mama said, tucking me into one of the beds. "I'm here now. I'm with you. Always."

Fifty

"Did you really take the boat to the other side? Did you really steal the fish and run?"

Sarele stared wide eyed. My little sister: she was taller than me, but what a baby! She had grown up holding on to Mama's apron strings. What did she know about life? My adventures on my own and with the gang, swiping and scrounging at every opportunity, the people I'd traveled with on the trains and slept with in the coal piles . . .

I began to talk the minute I woke up. I spoke endlessly about what I'd been through. I couldn't stop.

"And what about the policeman? How did you outsmart him?"

"We bumped into each other and fell down. He grabbed me by my boots . . ."

"What did you do then?"

"Me? I jumped up and ran, and left him holding the boots. They were way too big on me anyway, just boots I'd swiped somewhere."

"So after that you went barefoot?" Sarele asked.

"Why not? The boots were mostly holes. And besides, it was summer. It's easier to go barefoot, isn't it?"

"Weren't you ever afraid something would happen to you?"

"Me? Never! I always knew I'd make it, that everything would turn out okay."

Mama came back from work — she had to work even on such a happy day — and I went on telling my stories. The other woman in the room, a big, angry Russian, sat and listened too, snapping at her little brat to keep quiet.

The second night I slept on the floor. Why should Sarele have to give me her bed? And anyway, what difference did it make?

Mama was there, and I had a roof over my head; what else did I need?

At daybreak I awoke with a start. Someone had stepped on me. The room was small, and the other woman, getting up early to go to work, had tripped over me. I sat up and looked around. A pale light shone through the crack in the door. Mama turned over in bed, sighed, raised herself on her elbow, and slowly sat up, as if her whole body hurt.

"Going to work?" I whispered.

"Yes," said Mama, standing up. "Go back to sleep."

I tried to fall asleep again, but I couldn't. I got up and followed her into the communal kitchen. Several women were there in work clothes, Mama among them, pale and weary. I wanted to cheer them up.

"Mama, when you come back from work I'll tell you some more stories. I haven't told you even a fourth of them yet! Did I say a fourth? A tenth!"

"After work I go to the station," Mama said.

"But why? I'm here! You don't have to look for me anymore!"

"I still have to sell lemonade. I need the extra income. My salary isn't enough."

"But you also get a pension from the army, don't you? You told me so yourself."

"Yes, Yankele," said Mama, stroking my head the way she used to, "but I don't get all that much, a salary of a hundred rubles a month and another hundred from the pension. You know very well how much things cost. How can I live on that?"

Yes, I knew. It was strange: two pounds of bread cost two hundred rubles on the black market. That was all Mama made in a whole month! When you were working you could buy bread for pennies, a pound for an adult and half a pound for a child. It was all done with coupons. But I wondered who could afford to buy on the black market. There must have been people who did, or the price would have gone down. And to think that at

234

that time a war widow could only buy a pound of bread a month on her pension!

"What will happen now?" I asked. "Are they going to give you an extra portion of bread for me?"

Mama picked up the big kettle and poured two cups of tea.

"Drink something," she said, settling slowly into a chair as if this were the end and not the beginning of her day's work. "Drink, Yankele."

"Mama, will they give you another ration for me?"

"I'm afraid not."

"But why?"

"Why should they believe me? It's already happened at the next farm. They said to a mother, 'How is it that all these years you were alone, and now all of a sudden a child pops up?' It was all she could do to get him into school. Imagine, they wanted to send him to an institution!"

School! Why did I have to go to school? What could they possibly teach me there?

"Of course they have things to teach you," said Sarele, "lots of things!"

"What do you know, anyway?" I said scornfully. "What did they teach you there?"

"To read and write!"

"I read fine! I learned when we were still in the Crimea. Come on, let's see who can read the bulletin board faster."

"They teach arithmetic there too."

"All right, let's go to the market and see whose arithmetic is better!"

"And geography!"

"I know Uzbekistan better than all your books put together! I've been in the mountains and the desert. I know all the big cities: Tashkent, Bukhara, Samarkand. I know the mosques and the churches in Kokand and in all the other towns, big and small. I've been all the way to Alma Ata, while the whole time you sat here in this hole without ever sticking your nose out. Smarty!"

Sarele burst into tears. I tried to placate her, but she ran off to her friends. Had I begun to quarrel with my sister so quickly?

"Summer vacation will be over next week," Mama said. "I've arranged for you to be in Sarele's class, in third grade."

"Me, in third grade? With all those little kids?"

"The principal said there's no choice, because you never finished second grade. He promised me that if you progressed quickly he'd skip you ahead a grade."

The idea of sitting all day long between four walls, and with those pipsqueaks to boot! Not that the kids my age were any better. They were all mama's boys. At first I was king of the roost. They all wanted to hear my stories. Even the girls came. The boys got excited and wanted to plan all kinds of stunts together, but when I suggested we run away to the city and steal watermelons they got scared, and nothing ever came of it.

I went back to hanging out by myself. Again I would swipe things here and there, and I even brought food to Mama. But she got angry and said that now I was with *her*, and she would work harder, and there would be enough for all of us.

Mama was right — I couldn't go on stealing — but for a different reason: soon my thief's face would be known in all the Syr-Darya markets, and I'd have to move on.

I started helping Mama sell lemonade at the station. I liked being with her, even when we weren't talking, and I liked being at the station: the hubbub of travelers, the whistles of approaching trains, the clatter of wheels. The scent of travel, of new adventures, hung in the air there.

I didn't give it a second thought when I picked up a cigarette butt and asked a man smoking nearby for a light. It was second nature. But Mama was aghast.

"Yankele, you smoking?"

"Sure!" I said, blowing her some perfect smoke rings. But

236

Mama didn't see them. She shook her head and said, as though to herself, "If Papa were here, everything would be different."

Fifty-one

The trains were as crowded as they had been at the beginning of the war. As I said, people were on their way home. Here in Syr-Darya they changed trains and continued northward. Mama's lemonade business did well, what with the midsummer heat and travelers having to wait hours, sometimes days on end.

One day, a woman who had bought some lemonade from us looked up from her glass and suddenly said in Yiddish, "Rosa! As I live and breathe, aren't you Rosa Cohen?"

The ladle fell from Mama's hand into the jug.

"Don't you recognize me?" the woman said. "I'm Gittel, your mother's neighbor. From the ghetto, from Lodz. Remember?"

"Gittel!" said Mama, clapping her hands. "Gittel the seamstress! What are you doing here?"

"What am I doing here? That's a long story. Now I'm on my way back."

"Back where?"

"To Lodz."

"Whom are you going back to, Gittel? Is anyone left there?"

A horn sounded in the distance. Then a whistle blew and the loudspeaker announced, "Train for Tashkent now arriving." Passengers began to get up.

"People are going back," said Gittel. "Maybe my family will too, somebody." She took Mama's hand. "And you? When will you go back?"

"I've got nothing to go back to," said Mama, "and no one.

They say Hitler finished everybody off. Whoever didn't get away in time is gone forever."

"And what about your husband?"

Mama withdrew her hand and put it around my shoulders. "He was killed in the war, in the Russian army. I'm staying here with the children."

The train pulled into the station. The crowd began pressing toward the edge of the platform. Gittel started to move away. "Where do you live? Here in Syr-Darya?"

"No," Mama called after her, "nearby. At the Red Star Collective Farm."

Gittel made her way toward the train. She waved goodbye and was swallowed up in the throng.

" 'Bye!" Mama called after her. "See you!" But her voice was lost in the hubbub.

That night I dreamed about trains, not about bread or food, but about trains. The dreams had a nostalgic flavor to them, of freedom and wide-open spaces. The next day I went back to wandering.

I waved goodbye to Mama from the entranceway of the car. "I'll be back soon," I promised.

That morning she had tried to talk me out of it. I think she was worried about me, but she didn't have to be. I was no longer the same little boy who had gotten lost four years before. She should have known that I could look out for myself. So why did she cry when we parted?

Once again I drifted from place to place, but this time I didn't go far, only a hundred miles in one direction or another, not a thousand, as I had before. Each time I would return home, like a sailor to his home port — to Mama's arms, the little comforts of home, and the admiration of the children. For several days afterward they would all listen to my latest tales, and then they would go back to their regular pursuits. Mama kept urging me to go back to school. Not wanting to make her unhappy, I would confine myself to the four walls, but not for long. When I started fighting with my sister, when Mama's fretting started to get on my nerves, when I lost interest in the company of the children, and when I began to hear distant train whistles in my dreams, I knew it was time to fly the coop — until I calmed down enough to come back.

One day, coming back from some time on the road, I saw a woman standing and looking at our cabin. She was a stranger — I had already gotten to know everybody at the farm. She seemed hesitant, taking a step, then stopping and looking at the cabin as if she were drawn toward it but at the same time reluctant to approach it. I went over to her. The woman was tall, a little stooped, and gray.

"Are you looking for someone?" I asked.

She turned and gazed at me with her big, dark eyes. Her mouth hung open in surprise. She put her hand to her heart and whispered, "My God, aren't you Rosa's little Yankele?"

"Yes," I said, trying to remember: did I know her from somewhere?

I had seen any number of faces like that: thin, sad, deeply wrinkled. Her cheeks were sunken, as if she were missing some teeth. Did I know this old woman?

"Yankele, don't you remember me?"

I hesitated. Her voice was familiar, but I couldn't place it. The woman lifted a trembling hand and tried to stroke my cheek. I pulled back, turning toward the cabin and shouting, "Mama!"

Mama came out and held out her arms to greet me, as she always did when I came back. She hugged me and kissed me, but suddenly she let go. I looked up and saw her looking at the stranger. I slipped out of her arms and stood to the side.

They stood there for a moment, just looking at one another, and at last Mama whispered, "Bella?"

The woman nodded.

Mama put her hand to her mouth.

"Where is Feigele?" the woman asked.

"They took her!" said Mama. "The authorities. Someone told them she wasn't mine. They came and took her to an institution!"

"What institution? Where?"

"I have no idea. They refused to say. I begged and cried, but it didn't do any good."

They stood looking at one another. I got out of there. I couldn't take the tears.

How could I have forgotten him — Srulik, my best friend? Bella's Srulik. No wonder I hadn't recognized her; she had always been big and heavyset, an enormous woman. Even after we fled from the Crimea and were starving on the trains she was still fat. Mama had looked so tiny next to her, and Srulik and Feigele were like little chicks. And her hair — it had been black! But then maybe I had forgotten.

I hid in a remote corner of the farm. I didn't want them to see me, neither Mama nor Sarele nor anyone else. My latest stories I put aside. I was flooded with memories. It was like the end of a chain that you find sticking out of the sand. Bella had handed me the first link, and I had pulled and was uncovering one link after another, memory after memory. A whole world came back to me.

I had gone sledding with Srulik in the Urals. Together we had gone running in the green fields with the kids, Vanka and Stanka. We had whispered secrets to each other in the barn, to the sounds of carpentry out in the yard. With the sounds came the smell of freshly sawn wood, Papa's touch, his embrace.

All at once I felt a painful longing for Papa. I gnawed on my wrist and didn't budge until nightfall.

That night they talked in the kitchen in low tones, talked and talked. I had no idea how she'd found us, and I didn't want to hear it. I didn't want to remember Srulik lying in the railway car and then being laid out, dead, in the deep snow. She had searched all through the war, and now she would go on search-

240

ing. She would probably never find her Feigele; she had been too young when they took her away from Mama.

Mama offered Bella her bed and went to sleep on the floor, next to me. In my sleep I heard Bella sighing, but in my dreams I saw Papa.

Fifty-two

This time I stayed with Mama longer than usual. I'm not sure why, maybe because winter had arrived, maybe because I missed Papa. I thought about him a lot. I knew Mama was thinking about him too, but we never spoke about it. It was only on my birthday that Mama said, musing, "If Papa were here we'd celebrate your *bar-mitzvah.*"

Yes, if Papa had been with us everything would have been different. And maybe, just maybe, he would yet come back. After all, what they had told Mama was that he was missing, not killed.

I didn't want to give Mama a hard time, so I went back to school and didn't steal even once in the Syr-Darya market. I helped her sell cookies at the station. When we were hungry, I would go out into the fields and chop leftover carrots out of the frozen ground. I did all her errands around the farm. Everyone knew me by now. Even at the post office they would give me her monthly war-widow's pension check.

Once again a freezing north wind was blowing, the Siberian wind, and I was on my way to the post office to get the check. Mama was coughing away, and I had a coat, a hat, and boots, so why shouldn't I do it for her?

The sky was gray, and even the houses along the way seemed

gray and colorless. There was nothing of interest anywhere, and as I walked along I thought, *Is it better to be a grown-up or a child? A grown-up can do anything he wants. He doesn't have to go to school, and no one bawls him out when he smokes or drinks. As for a child, he's always forgiven, and he never has to take responsibility for anything. If Papa were here, he would take care of everything, and I could go back to being a kid.*

The clerk at the post office shuffled through his papers at great length. Why did he have to do so much rummaging around? Why didn't he just give me the money and let me be on my way? It was suffocating in there. The closed room was filled with cigarette smoke, the smell of the farm workers' dirty clothes, and the odor of a coat that had dried out without benefit of a stove. I was eager to finish and get out into the open air.

"What's the problem?" I asked. "It's the beginning of the month, isn't it? I came at the right time, didn't I?"

The clerk peered at me over the rims of his glasses.

"What's your rush?" he asked. "Where're you running off to? Afraid you'll miss a train or something?"

"No, but . . ."

"There's something else for Rosa Kagan here, a letter. That's odd, it's been lying around here for three weeks already. Just this morning I saw it, and now, of all times, it's gone again!"

A letter? A letter to Mama? Since I had found her she had not gotten a single letter. Who even knew where we were? Who had our address?

The clerk opened his desk drawer and rummaged inside for a while. Damn! What a slowpoke they had working in this place!

"Found it!" he said at last, holding up the letter. "Here, you see, it says 'Rosa Kagan, Red Star Collective Farm.' Go call your mother."

"What for? I can bring it to her!"

"She has to come herself and sign for it."

242

The old geezer was driving me crazy. "You give me the money but not the letter?"

"Your mother gave you a signed note for the money, right? For the letter, she didn't give you anything."

Try arguing with clerks and their stupid rules.

"Can't you at least tell me where the letter's from?" I said.

The clerk glanced at the envelope. "Polish stamps," he said, "nice ones."

"And who sent it? Who's the letter from?"

The clerk turned the envelope over and wrinkled his brow. "Can't make it out. I think, I think it says 'Lodz.' "

I dashed out the door and ran straight to Mama. She wasn't as fast as I was, but she ran. My God! Mama running! Her hand trembled in mine. What was she expecting? Everybody had been killed. What could it be, a letter from the next world?

Mama took the envelope, looked at the back, and sat down on a bench. "Open it!" she said to me, white as a ghost. "Open it and read it aloud!"

I opened the envelope and took out the letter. The words danced in front of my eyes. I read slowly, out loud:

Dearest Rosa, My Beloved,

You're alive! The children are alive! And so am I — all of us are still alive! Don't even ask what I have been through. It was hell. When we see each other I will tell you everything. After the war they sent me from the prisoner-of-war camp straight to Poland, and I went back to Lodz. None of the family was left, except for my brother Avrum and your cousin Rivka. They told me there was no point in my even looking. The bastards had butchered all the Jews when they conquered the Crimea. They said I should put the past behind me and start a new family.

Then Gittel arrived and told me she had seen you and

our little Yankele! And that Sarele was with you too!
Rosa dear, how lucky we are, how very lucky. Write to
me immediately, and send me whatever is necessary so
that I can arrange the appropriate documents for you to
come back here. I don't say "come home." Everything
has been destroyed here, Rosa. There's nothing but ruins.
They need carpenters to rebuild, so there's plenty of
work. All I lack is you. But I don't want to stay here,
Rosa. Not on this soil. A representative has come from
Palestine. Come here, and we'll go there together, all of
us. We'll build a new home for ourselves, and never
budge again. I can't take any more wandering.

How are you, my dear Rosa? I'm dying to hug you and
the children.

Yours, as ever,
And longing for you,

Yitzhak

Epilogue

Yankele is a real person, and this is the story of his childhood.
For many years now he has been living in Israel. After the family
was reunited in Poland, they moved to Israel, where Yankele at
last settled down and finished school.

At age eighteen, he was drafted into the army. When he
showed up at the draft office he was short and thin and looked
like a boy of twelve. The medical committee exempted him from
service.

"Come back in a year's time," they told him. "Eat properly, get stronger, and then we'll see."

They didn't realize with whom they were dealing. Yankele insisted — and they took him. He was inducted and assigned to a desk job. A year later he was supposed to report back to the medical committee.

This time the examination took a whole day. Yankele was called in, sent out, and called in again, checked and questioned and checked again. Finally he asked the head doctor, "Tell me, doc, what's the matter with me? Am I sick or dying or what?"

"No," the doctor replied, "we just want to make sure there hasn't been some mistake."

"Mistake?"

"We want to make sure you're you!"

It seems Yankele himself hadn't noticed that, in that year, he had grown a whole head taller, filled out, and gotten stronger. He was a new man!

T.B.